What People Are

T0015582

Spontaneous Contacts

Spontaneous Contacts with the Deceased describes a groundbreaking international study of After-Death Communications (ADCs), richly illustrated with graphic first-hand testimonies and fleshed out with the data from a 200-item questionnaire on the nature and impact of the ADC. These life-changing experiences include visions, sounds, smells, and touch that seem to come from the deceased, as well as unexplained movements and breaking of objects at the moment of death and the previously-undescribed partial temporary paralysis during the encounter. Some ADCs involve warnings to the experiencer of an immediate danger, and some convey practical knowledge, such as the location of an insurance policy or other document that had been unknown to anyone still alive. In some ADCs, the experiencers were informed of their loved one's death by the deceased individuals themselves before anyone else knew of the death.

This comprehensive book focuses on the lived experiences of people who have them, both the nature of the ADC and its impact on the mourning process. ADCs do not exempt the bereaved from working through their grief, but they can bring comfort, joy, support, and strength to complete that work. *Spontaneous Contacts with the Deceased* fills an important role in documenting how common and how normal ADCs are, which will vastly help not only people who experience them but anyone who is bereft at the loss of a loved one.

> **Bruce Greyson,** MD, Carlson Professor Emeritus, Division of Perceptual Studies, Department of Psychiatry & Neurobehavioral Sciences, University of Virginia Health System, Charlottesville, VA, USA

In this important book Evelyn Elsaesser presents the research findings of the largest international survey ever conducted on After-Death Communications (ADCs). The strength of this book lies in the fact that the evidence obtained from this rigorous scientific study is illustrated by the lived experience of many of the more than 1,000 survey participants. Because of their ADC they are now convinced that our consciousness continues after death. This wonderful book brilliantly explains the nature and beneficial impact of spontaneous contacts with the deceased. Highly recommended.

> **Pim van Lommel,** cardiologist, NDE-researcher, author of *Consciousness Beyond Life*

Of the more than 35 studies of ADCs that have been conducted since the late 1800s, the study described in this book is the most extensive and in-depth. Results confirm, clarify, and greatly expand on previous research. Rich with both data and experiencers' narratives, this book is a must-reading for anyone who wishes to have a thorough grasp of both the head and the heart of ADCs.

> **Janice Miner Holden,** EdD, LPC-S, ACMHP, Professor Emerita of Counseling, University of North Texas, USA, President of International Association for Near-Death Studies, and Editor of *Journal of Near-Death Studies*

Can we communicate with our deceased loved ones? This is one of humankind's most enduring questions. *Spontaneous Contacts with the Deceased* brings a new and exciting perspective to this ancient question. Evelyn Elsaesser is exceptionally qualified to comment on the after-death communication question as she is a highly respected researcher and author. The dramatic personal accounts artfully bring to life the important study findings. Each turn of the page is a treasure trove of insights and inspiration. This outstanding book is expertly written, remarkably easy to read, and enthusiastically recommended.

> **Jeffrey Long,** MD, author of the *New York Times* best-selling *Evidence of the Afterlife: The Science of Near-Death Experiences*, and founder of the After Death Communication Research Foundation, adcrf.org

The research that Evelyn Elsaesser and her colleagues have carried out on After-Death Communications (ADCs) represents a new milestone in the field of studies related to death. Although there had been anecdotal reports of ADCs for some years, the Elsaesser study is the first scientific research to be conducted on a scale never before even attempted. Involving more than 1,000 respondents, it provides overwhelming evidence of the frequency of ADCs and the life-changing effects on their recipients. It is, in short, a monumental contribution to our understanding of this phenomenon and really serves to put ADCs "on the map," blazing trails that grateful researchers will be keen to travel.

> **Kenneth Ring,** PhD, Professor Emeritus, University of Connecticut, USA, author of *Lessons from the Light*

This book is a rich goldmine of heart-moving experiences and insights from people of many countries who have received communications from family members and others who have passed away. I felt my heart expand as I read their expressions of joy in knowing a loved one was still present, and I laughed with them when their beloved made a humorous comment that only they would recognize. A highlight of this book was the author's careful analysis of these remarkable events, suggesting that these experiences are real, and are a precious part of our connection with loved ones on the other side.

> **Marjorie Woollacott,** PhD, Professor, Institute of Neuroscience, University of Oregon, Eugene, OR, USA

A fascinating and comprehensive account of After-Death Communications and their impact on those who experience them. A Must-Read before you go!

> **Peter Fenwick,** MB, BChir, DPM, FRCPsych, Institute of Psychiatry, King's College, London, UK

This book is a beautiful and well-researched testament to the continuation of our consciousness and the importance of communications from those who have passed. Compelling and powerful!

> **J. Kim Penberthy,** PhD, ABPP, Chester F. Carlson Professor of Psychiatry and Neurobehavioral Sciences, Division of Perceptual Studies, University of Virginia School of Medicine, Charlottesville, VA, USA

Evelyn Elsaesser

Spontaneous Contacts with the Deceased

A large-scale international survey reveals the circumstances, lived experience and beneficial impact of After-Death Communications (ADCs)

Evelyn Elsaesser

Preface by Dr. Christophe Fauré

Spontaneous Contacts with the Deceased

A large-scale international survey reveals the circumstances, lived experience and beneficial impact of After-Death Communications (ADCs)

Survey conducted by Evelyn Elsaesser, Prof. Chris A. Roe, Associate Prof. Callum E. Cooper, and David Lorimer

IFF
BOOKS

Winchester, UK
Washington, USA

JOHN HUNT PUBLISHING

First published by iff Books, 2023
iff Books is an imprint of John Hunt Publishing Ltd., No. 3 East Street, Alresford,
Hampshire SO24 9EE, UK
office@jhpbooks.com
www.johnhuntpublishing.com
www.iff-books.com

For distributor details and how to order please visit the 'Ordering' section on our website.

Text copyright: Evelyn Elsaesser 2023

ISBN: 978 1 80341 228 3
978 1 80341 229 0 (ebook)
Library of Congress Control Number: 2022936694

A CIP catalogue record for this book is available from the British Library.

Design: Lapiz Digital Services

Cover image: *Contactos espontáneos con un fallecido — La realidad de las VSCD* by Luis Tinoco,
Ediciones Kepler (Argentina, Chile, Colombia, España, Estados Unidos, México, Perú, Uruguay)

UK: Printed and bound by CPI Group (UK) Ltd, Croydon, CR0 4YY
Printed in North America by CPI GPS partners

We operate a distinctive and ethical publishing philosophy in
all areas of our business, from our global network of authors to
production and worldwide distribution.

Contents

Dedication

"The plural of anecdote is data."
Raymond Edwin Wolfinger, American political scientist and professor at the University of California at Berkeley, Academic Year 1969–70

We dedicate this book to all those who have generously shared their ADC with us.

Foreword by Dr. Christophe Fauré

At first, I didn't believe it.

During my young years as a psychiatrist in the field of palliative care, I accompanied people in mourning after the loss of a loved one. They shared with me their suffering, their pain, their anger, their guilt… and I walked with them on the painful path of mourning. I saw it as the unfolding of a process of which I initially perceived only the psychological dimension.

But, over the years, curious experiences have begun to emerge in my patients' narratives. They were so constant and recurrent that it became impossible for me not to seriously consider them.

They told me about "signs". Signs interpreted by these persons as a manifestation of their deceased loved one, but about which they kept silent, sometimes for years, for fear of being considered "crazy" if they revealed them to those around them! Moreover, many of them, a little embarrassed to talk to a psychiatrist in those terms, said to me, "Doctor, I am a very rational person, but…" and there emerged the narrative of that unsettling "something" that happened after the death of their loved one. "Something" that I later learned to call "ADC".

ADC: After-Death Communication.

After more than 25 years of bereavement counselling, today I systematically ask this question, in a more or less direct way: "Since the death of your loved one, do you feel that you have had any 'signs' or specific perceptions?" I can't count the number of people who, relieved by my question, immediately tell me about one or more ADCs!

There is therefore a real subject here that deserves our full attention, as its implications are considerable, and I am pleased that my own years of observing and listening to patients in my practice find a powerful echo in the contents of this book.

We must be aware of this: publishing such a book is not anodyne and I would like to salute the integrity and genuine courage of these authors, researchers and university professors of international standing who dare to put their professional credibility at stake in order to venture, as true pioneers, into the mysterious territory of the ADCs.

Make no mistake: we are not here in the realm of belief, beliefs that one would cling to, in a desperate move to suppress the fear of death and the anguish of nothingness. No: the approach of these researchers is quite different. It is based on listening, observing, collecting and analyzing data. It is rooted in a scientific methodology that observes and establishes the facts. Thus, even if the subject of ADCs seems to be the opposite, one could not be more Cartesian in this way of approaching them! The authors of this survey rely on tangible information and this is what makes their work so relevant and intelligent.

To the objections that ADCs are hallucinations or mere productions of the mind, my position as a psychiatrist allows me to oppose them with several counterarguments. In my experience, ADCs do not meet the diagnostic criteria for psychotic-type hallucinations, nor for hallucinations induced by psychoactive drugs. Indeed, hallucinations of psychotic origin occur in the precise context of a mental pathology such as, for example, schizophrenia. People with hallucinatory mental illness suffer from painful psychic confinement. Their mind is in torment, whether before, during or after the hallucinatory episode. However, this is not the case for the vast majority of people with ADCs: they do not present any psychotic pathology that could explain their after-death communication.

Moreover, hallucinations of psychotic origin very often have a negative or traumatic tone (experience of persecution, humiliation, threats, etc.). However, as you will see in this book, most people who have had an ADC describe their experience as positive or even very positive. Also, the after-effects of a hallucinatory episode increase the suffering of the psychotic person, whereas, in most cases, people who have experienced an ADC describe an appeasement, an opening of the heart, often with a beneficial impact on their mourning experience. So, no: these are not hallucinations...

"Yes, but," it is sometimes argued, "isn't it the desire to encounter the deceased person that induces these manifestations? Isn't it a purely psychological projection?" One might think so, because many mourners very often express an intense desire to encounter their deceased loved one. Indeed, what parent, spouse or child would not wish to establish contact with their child, spouse or parent beyond their death? Certainly... but if the desire to reunite were the only element, the driving force, which induces an ADC, would it not be logical to think that all mourners would experience an after-death communication? However, we can only note that this is not the case! Thus, it is difficult to affirm that the sole force of the desire to meet one's loved one is at the origin of the occurrence of an ADC. In the same vein, we can also talk about ADCs that happen to some people who did not have such a desire and yet experience it. Moreover, what to say about ADCs experienced by people who, at the time of the experience, were not aware of the death of their loved one? What about, in this case, any desire to be reunited with a loved one after his or her death, when it is not even known that this person has died? So, no: the sole desire to be reunited with the other person is not the driving force behind an ADC...

What is it all about then?

It is all the intelligence and finesse of this book not to answer this question directly. Indeed, *Spontaneous Contacts with the Deceased* describes the phenomenon of ADCs, based on testimonies. However, it does not venture to interpret the data collected. It leaves the reader to his or her own conclusions, simply offering some avenues for reflection: what meaning should be given to these experiences? What do they tell us about existence beyond this life? Would they suggest a continuity of consciousness after death? Here we enter the spiritual dimension of ADCs, which is not the subject of this book.

Nevertheless, these questions are too fascinating to not dwell on for a few moments.

In studying ADCs, I cannot help but make a connection with another field of investigation: that of NDEs (Near-Death-Experiences). NDE accounts come from people who have been declared clinically dead and who have been brought back to life, thanks to resuscitation efforts. They all describe a similar experience during the period when they were declared "dead". In the hospital, in the palliative care unit, or in my practice, I have often heard accounts of such experiences from the very mouths of the people who had lived through them. I invite you to explore the subject further on your own, if you are interested.

What is unsettling about NDEs is that they too suggest a possible continuity of consciousness after physical death. In NDEs, this possibility is approached through the experience of people who "die", whereas in ADCs, we have the point of view of people who "stay". We are thus offered two viewpoints, two extremely different perspectives, but which nevertheless seem to point in the same direction.

Which direction? It is up to you to define it. It is up to you to form your own opinion on the basis of your investigation and reliable reading on these various subjects to which you will give yourself access.

And this is where *Spontaneous Contacts with the Deceased* can really help you.

Whether it reinforces your feelings if you yourself have experienced an ADC, whether you have not experienced an ADC even though you are grieving, or whether it stimulates your curiosity, inviting you to investigate further and explore the meaning and implications of this phenomenon, you hold a precious companion in your hands. It is able to nourish your reflection in depth.

Who knows where it will take you?

I wish you a good and fruitful reading.

Dr. Christophe Fauré, author of *Vivre le deuil au jour le jour*, Editions Albin Michel

A few words of Introduction

In this book, I present the results of the first part of a five-year international research project on the *Phenomenology and impact of spontaneous and direct After-Death Communications (ADCs)*. This survey enabled us to collect more than 1,000 testimonies in the three languages of the project, i.e. English, French, and Spanish. We thus have conducted the most extensive multilingual survey of spontaneous ADCs worldwide. We had designed a questionnaire with almost 200 questions on the nature and impact of these spontaneous contacts, apparently initiated by the deceased towards their family members and friends. The quantitative results presented in this book provide an in-depth understanding of this very common phenomenon, which is nevertheless absent from the media and public discourse. Researchers estimate the prevalence of ADCs to be 50–60% of the population,[1] in particular, but not only, of bereaved people. Given the frequency and nature of these experiences, it is time to move away from calling them *anomalous, unusual, exceptional,* or *paranormal* and to recognize them for what they are — common, normal, natural and healthy human experiences.

In *Spontaneous Contacts with the Deceased,* the floor will be given very largely to the participants in our survey who have so generously shared their experience with us. Many similarities emerged between the different experiences. The numerous testimonies presented are indeed plural, each with its own tone and color because they are embedded in the context of life and often in the sorrow of mourning of the participants, but a common thread nevertheless connects these different experiences.

In the context of our survey, we focused exclusively on the *experience* of people who have had an ADC (the experients). The question of the authenticity — the ontological status — of these contacts is not the subject of this research project, although a series of questions provide information about the experients' *impression of reality* of the ADC.

ADCs manifest themselves in a multitude of forms and situations. The first part of the book is devoted to the phenomenology of ADCs, that is to say to the different types of ADCs identified, and how they occur. The contacts manifesting by four of the five senses, i.e. visual, auditory, olfactory and tactile ADCs, were the subject of a series of questions, as well as the ADCs of sensing a presence. ADCs during sleep, when falling asleep or waking up, represent the type of contact most often experienced by our respondents. However, more than half of them were awakened by the contact and the rest of the experience fell into one of the other categories. ADCs occurring at the time of death were also the subject of a series of questions. They are particularly interesting, even evidential, because experients claim to have been informed of the death of a family member or friend by the deceased themselves. Other forms of expression of ADCs are reviewed and illustrated by a large number of testimonies. In addition, a series of questions made it possible to draw up a "portrait" of the perceived deceased person.

The second part of the book is devoted to the impact of ADCs on the experients' belief systems and their beneficial impact on the mourning process.

These contacts have consequences for the beliefs of the experients. We have asked a series of questions on this subject and the answers collected are striking. First of all, it should be emphasized that ADCs are not religious experiences. Research shows that the fact of being a believer, agnostic or atheist does not in any way influence the nature of the experience, nor the probability of experiencing it. A pre-existing belief in the survival of consciousness after physical death is by no means a prerequisite for experiencing an ADC. Thus, it is not surprising that these experiences only very slightly strengthen religious beliefs. Spirituality, however, is strongly reinforced as a result of the ADC. In addition, the respondents expressed their views on the changes that have taken place in them as a result of the ADC with regard to their conception of death, fear of their own death, the alleged ability of the deceased to contact the living, and beliefs in favor of survival of consciousness after physical death.

ADCs have a strong impact on the mourning process. In the eyes of the experients, the deceased loved one has succeeded in crossing — very exceptionally and very briefly — the line between the two worlds to express his or her support and love. Beyond the perception of the deceased, which in itself is already a remarkable experience, it is the emotions perceived and felt during the contacts that give them their full meaning. After-death communications open up the prospect of a continued and dynamic relational bond between the living and the dead that would materialize in exceptional moments. The many questions put to the participants made it possible to understand to what extent and in what way ADCs impact the mourning process. Moreover, our respondents gave us detailed and multifaceted descriptions of the messages perceived during the contacts, which allowed us to grasp the full emotional significance of ADCs.

I invite you to discover the results of our survey and the numerous testimonies illustrating them.

The phenomenon of ADCs

Have you ever felt the presence of a deceased loved one? Have you heard him?[2] Have you seen him enter your living room and come towards you with a smile on his face? Have you felt his hand grasping yours in a familiar gesture repeated a thousand times during his lifetime? Have you noticed a smell that characterizes him announcing his presence? Have you communicated with him while sleeping, not in an ordinary dream but in a clear and coherent tête-à-tête that seemed perfectly real?

If this is the case, it is likely that you have experienced a spontaneous and direct contact with a deceased person — an ADC.

A spontaneous and direct After-Death Communication (ADC) occurs when a person, generally but not always in mourning, unexpectedly perceives a deceased person through the senses of sight, hearing, smell, or touch. Very commonly, persons who have an ADC (called experients) simply sense the presence of the deceased person or perceive a contact during sleep, or when falling asleep or waking up. The deceased person is perceived in a manner that is interpreted as indicative of the continued survival of that person.

ADCs are:

- **Spontaneous:** allegedly initiated by the deceased, without intention or solicitation on the part of the experient;
- **Direct:** without intervention of other persons (e.g. spirit mediums), use of devices (Ouija,[3] Instrumental TransCommunication, ITC[4]), or an otherwise mediated contact.

Contacts made on the initiative of the bereaved through a spirit medium, which are much better known to the general public than ADCs, are not the subject of the survey presented and will only be discussed in the margins.

A (hidden) major societal phenomenon

ADCs are common. The literature indicates that 50–60%[5] of people, in particular mourners, have experienced one or more spontaneous ADCs. Testimonies collected on all continents and for centuries suggest this phenomenon to be *universal* and *timeless*. This is clearly not a marginal experience but a major societal phenomenon. Every day, a large number of persons live these experiences and do not know how to name them or how to situate them in their conception of reality. Despite the widespread presence of ADCs, a researcher found only 35 studies on the topic between the late 1800s and 2010,* none of which investigated the phenomenon in the depth of the survey described in this book. Likewise, given the massive occurrence of ADCs, it is surprising that the subject did not get any attention in the media and in public discourse. As a result, experients generally have no frame of reference to understand, integrate and reap the full benefit of this experience, which does not seem to correspond to the conception of reality prevailing in Western societies.

* Streit-Horn, J. (2011). A systematic review of research on after-death communication (ADC). Dissertation Abstracts International: Section B: The Sciences and Engineering, University of North Texas, USA. UMI Number: 3506993.

Survey

The time had come to study these experiences, so common and yet so little investigated. We decided to undertake an international research project to better understand the nature and impact of ADCs. From February 2018 to January 2020, we conducted the first part of an ambitious research project entitled *Investigation of the phenomenology and impact of spontaneous and direct After-Death Communications (ADCs)*. The second part of the project has started in July 2021 and will be completed in June 2024.

Project team

The constitution of the project team reflects the international character of the project.

Team
- Evelyn Elsaesser, Team Leader, Chavannes-de-Bogis, Switzerland
- Prof. Chris A. Roe, Principal Investigator, University of Northampton, UK
- Associate Prof. Callum E. Cooper, Team Member, University of Northampton, UK
- David Lorimer, Team Member, Scientific & Medical Network, UK

Scientific Committee
- Prof. J. Kim Penberthy, University of Virginia, USA
- Prof. Emeritus Peter Fenwick, King's College, London, UK
- Prof. Emeritus Kenneth Ring, University of Connecticut, USA

Evelyn Elsaesser   *Chris A. Roe*   *Callum E. Cooper*   *David Lorimer*

Project concept

This international survey, conducted in English, French and Spanish, had three objectives.

1st objective

Description of the circumstances of occurrence and the phenomenology of ADCs

- Who has an ADC?
- Under what circumstances?
- In what form (type of ADC)?
- How do these experiences unfold?
- What are the messages of ADCs?
- Who are the deceased persons having allegedly initiated the contact?
- What was/is their relation with the experients?
- Are there phenomenological differences between countries?

2nd objective

Analysis of the impact of ADCs on experients

- How do people experience ADCs?
- What meaning do they attribute to them?

- What is the immediate and long-term impact on experients?
- How do ADCs influence the grieving process?
- Does the national and social context influence individuals' experiences?

3rd objective
Dissemination of research results to the general public and the scientific community

- With this survey, we aim to contribute to raising public awareness of the ADC phenomenon. By presenting the data collected about how ADCs occur and unfold, and by analyzing their impact on individuals' lives, we make these findings accessible to people facing the death of a loved one and, more generally, to anyone interested in this topic. In addition, we participate in the dissemination of scientific data at the academic level.

In accordance with the professional guidelines set out by the British Psychological Society (BPS), the survey methodology has undergone a rigorous ethical review to ensure the confidentiality and protection of the data generously provided by our participants. The project received ethical approval from the Faculty of Health and Social Sciences at the University of Northampton, Great Britain, in July 2018.[6]

In addition, in line with current standards of research transparency, the survey design and analysis strategy have been pre-registered with the Koestler Unit Study Registry at the University of Edinburgh in Scotland.[7]

Questionnaire

To achieve the objectives of the project, we needed a very detailed questionnaire. We developed **194 questions** (including follow-up questions after affirmative responses) to cover all these aspects, the major part of which is presented in this book.

Participants had the possibility to fill in the questionnaire without giving their name. This is why the testimonies presented in this book are not credited to individuals. Moreover, all proper names and place names have been anonymized (changed). In any case, once the data had been processed by our team, the results of the survey were presented in a completely anonymous manner, excluding any individual identification.

We first invited participants to describe their ADC in their own words in a free text dialogue box. If the participants had experienced several ADCs, we asked them to describe only one contact, choosing the most significant one. The questions were then presented with multiple choice options. Many questions were combined with follow-up questions with a free text dialogue box.

Two to three hours were necessary to complete the questionnaire. Despite this significant time investment, very few participants dropped out along the way. We concluded that our participants appreciated being able to describe their ADC and its impact in a safe, nonjudgmental space, knowing that it is not always easy to share this experience which seems to be contrary to the materialist conception of reality of Western societies. Experients often encounter disbelief or even skepticism when describing their experiences to their entourage. This is painful and frustrating, as they cherish the experience and wish to share their joy at having experienced this unexpected contact.

The questionnaire was presented in English, French, and Spanish on a secure online survey platform. The survey was announced at the team members' public conferences, on social networks, and information on the research project and the link to the questionnaire were posted on my website. All in all, we did little promotion of the survey. The questionnaire was available online in all three languages for a period of six months respectively.

Data collected

The number of completed questionnaires far exceeded our expectations.

1,004 completed questionnaires

English: 416 I French: 440 I Spanish: 148

- **More than 2 million words in response to the questionnaire**
- **The most extensive multilingual survey of spontaneous ADCs worldwide**

Research findings

The research findings presented in this book refer to the totality of the data collected, namely the combination of the answers of the 1,004 questionnaires completed in English, French, and Spanish. The aim of this book is to present the major part of the *quantitative* results of the survey. All the results expressed as a percentage come from the closed multiple choice *Yes, Unsure,* or *No* questions. We, the core team, have summarized the main findings of our investigation in our flagship paper entitled "The Phenomenology and Impact of Hallucinations concerning the Deceased", published in *British Journal of Psychiatry Open (BJPsych Open).*[8]

Unlike quantitative analysis, *qualitative* or thematic analysis is a deeper and richer analysis based on the open-ended questions in our questionnaire, where participants describe their experience in their own words in free text dialogue boxes.

To get the most out of the data collected, we decided to subject it to both quantitative and qualitative analysis. This mixed-methods approach to the analysis of our database is a strategic choice of our team. Our core team and teams associated with our research project are conducting qualitative analyses on specific themes based on our data in universities in France, Great Britain and the United States. These analyses have or will be presented at international conferences. Some papers have already been published in scientific journals, and others are still in the process of being drawn up. All publications resulting from our research project are available on the project website: www.adcrp.org.

The very many ADC accounts included in this book illustrating the quantitative data come from the free text dialogue boxes. The majority of testimonies were taken from the 416 questionnaires in English, supplemented by cases from the 440 French and 148 Spanish questionnaires.

Several types of ADCs can occur simultaneously, for example, an experient can feel the presence of the deceased putting a hand on his shoulder and talking to him while giving off a familiar fragrance. Thus, a number of the accounts cited in the following pages could have appeared simultaneously in several categories of ADCs, forcing me to make an arbitrary choice for their classification. As a result, accounts listed under one type of ADC may contain elements of another type of ADC presented later.

One of the objectives of our research project is to analyze a possible influence of the cultural context on individuals' experiences. With this in mind, some data will be presented both for the 1,004 questionnaires as a whole and also by language groups for comparison. These indications are only a very first step towards an in-depth analysis of the national/linguistic and cultural differences that potentially influenced the experiences of our participants.

Demographic data

I reproduce here some of the demographics of our participants. There is a clear gender difference in participation, with 853 women having completed the questionnaire compared to only 144 men (7 people checked *other, e.g. transgender*). However, the literature indicates that women and men experience ADCs in roughly the same proportions, but women report them more.[9] This significant difference in the gender of the participants may simply mean that women are more comfortable sharing personal and emotional experiences than men.

- **85% of the participants were women, compared to 14% men, and 1% other (e.g. transgender)**

The age of our participants ranged between 18 and 89 years, with a mean age of 51. A spontaneous after-death communication can occur throughout our lives. Children can experience ADCs in the same way as adults. Unfortunately, they are often not taken seriously by their parents and are left to their own devices to give meaning to this experience. This is one of the many reasons why it is so important to make current knowledge about ADCs widely available. The minimum age of 18 for participation was imposed by us as part of the project design (for ethical reasons), but that does not imply that their ADC occurred only in adulthood — participants could describe experiences that had happened to them in their childhood or adolescence.

The level of education of our respondents is rather high:

- University: 48%
- College or equivalent: 18%
- Technical training: 22%
- Secondary school: 12%

The next question concerned the professional status of our participants:

- In professional activity: 58%
- In retirement: 21%
- In search of employment: 4%
- Housewife/husband: 4%
- In school/university: 2%
- On temporary leave: 1%
- In continuing education: 1%
- In the military/community service: 0%
- Other: 9%

We inquired about their civil status:[10]

- Married: 37%
- Living with partner: 14%
- Registered partner: 0%
- Single: 17%
- Separated: 5%
- Divorced: 15%
- Widowed: 13%

These few sets of demographic data indicate that almost half of the respondents (48%) had a university education, more than half (58%) were in professional activity and a minority (21%) were retired. The civil status of the participants does not reveal any particular specificity. The number of participants who are widowed is not very high (13%). The demographic data reproduced here show that, at several levels, the respondents do not differ from the general population. However, it can be observed that people with a high level of education are over-represented among the participants in our survey.

Multiple ADCs

A large majority of our participants had multiple ADCs with one or several deceased persons. This was a surprise to us since the literature does not report such a high number of multiple ADCs.

- **80% have experienced multiple ADCs, 10% were unsure, and 11% have experienced only one ADC**

When asked about the number of contacts perceived, the majority of respondents indicated a figure between two and ten, but for some the occurrence was much higher.

Slightly more than a third perceived the same deceased each time, while more than half experienced contacts with different deceased persons.

- **34% always perceived the same deceased, 7% were unsure, and 59% perceived different deceased persons**

Types of ADCs

Different types of contacts with the deceased have been identified that can be perceived by four of the five sensory organs, namely sight, hearing, touch or smell. In addition, ADCs of sensing a presence and contacts occurring during sleep, when falling asleep or upon waking have been listed. Very often several sensory organs are involved simultaneously. Experients report, for example, that they heard a deceased loved one tell them that she was fine and that they shouldn't worry about her, while smelling the perfume she used to wear.

Sensing a presence
- **34%[11] sensed the presence of the deceased**

Experients sense the familiar presence of the deceased person, but they cannot see or hear him or her, nor can they feel any physical contact or smell any characteristic fragrance of the deceased. **342 of our respondents have experienced such contacts.**

In the table below and in the following tables describing the types of ADCs, the headings *Men* and *Women* refer to the answers of the 1,004 questionnaires completed in English, French and Spanish. The headings *English dataset*, *French dataset* and *Spanish dataset* reflect the percentages of people who have experienced an ADC of sensing a presence by language group.[12]

Sensing a presence

ADC of sensing a presence	Men	Women	English dataset	French dataset	Spanish dataset
Yes	34%	35%	25%	40%	44%
No	66%	65%	75%	60%	56%

Generally, the identity and personality of the deceased clearly emanate from this presence and allow for immediate identification.

The following is a testimony of this type of ADC:

"I learned in February 2016 that an ex-boyfriend had died suddenly of a heart attack when he was only in his early fifties. We had lost touch two or three years before. The news of his death reached me the day after he died. A few days later, when I got home, just as I turned the key in my lock to open the door of my flat, I received the information that John[13] was there at my place. And I was immediately uncomfortable. I went to the living room and felt John's presence sitting on a chair around the dining table. He was waiting for me and wanted to see me after his abrupt passing. I couldn't see him physically but I knew where he was and I could feel his presence very well. I felt so ill at ease with this sensation that I asked him to leave. I felt that he really wanted to see me and insisted on staying, but I told him that I didn't feel ready, that later maybe I might want to. And he left. I didn't feel his presence anymore, the atmosphere was relaxed again. When I was ready one or two weeks later, I asked him to come in a dream and he did. But this is yet another ADC."

As this account illustrates, the presence seems to have a certain density, almost physical though invisible, and the experient often knows exactly where the deceased is located in space.

- **68% could locate the deceased, 14% were unsure, and 18% could not locate the deceased**

"With my father-in-law, I felt the presence on my right. With my boss, it was in front of me."

"I knew where to locate him in the room where I was. I couldn't see him but I knew exactly where he was. Whereas when I think of him, I cannot 'feel' him."

"I knew he was there. I could feel that he was in front of me."

"Lying in bed, I felt my son's presence. At that moment I felt the mattress sag as if someone was sitting next to me. The sensation of an invisible body mass beside me. I knew it was him!"

"On the evening of my father's death, I was sitting in my chair. I was very distressed when all of a sudden, I felt a presence which subsequently soothed me. Then, when I went to bed, I felt this same presence standing to the right of my bed watching me."

"The day my grandmother died, I was standing in front of the fireplace thinking about her, I couldn't cry. I felt a presence in front of me on the right, then she moved behind me and put her hand on my right shoulder. I felt a lot of love."

This ADC of sensing a presence was followed by a brief visual perception:

"Several days after my best friend passed away suddenly, I was alone in the house and in the kitchen cooking, when I felt a strong presence behind me. I hadn't heard anyone come into the room, so I instinctively turned to see who it was. For the briefest of moments, I saw my friend, standing in the doorway. As soon as I registered what I was seeing, she was gone and so was the feeling of a presence."

Not only the presence but the purpose of it was immediately obvious to our participant:

"Grandfather was present in the car with me a short time after his funeral. I was in my late teens or early 20s. Not sure of the date as I write this. His presence was strong. I had no doubt it was him although I didn't 'see' or 'hear' him. He was there to say goodbye."

This event caught our participant by surprise in the middle of her activity, when she was not thinking about the deceased:

"I was heading to the kitchen to do the dishes. I don't know what I was thinking about, but suddenly I just stopped and froze... I felt him, I felt his energy, his presence. I could almost smell him. I started to sob... and told him not to leave. This feeling lasted for several minutes and then slowly was gone. But for those few minutes it was as if he was right there, with me, loving me, letting me know."

The presence of the deceased is typically perceived as clearly as when we realize that a living person has just entered the room, before we turn to look at them:

"The person (my father who died in 1994) came to me in my mind, then I stopped doing what I was doing, the dishes. I turned around as if someone had entered the kitchen and I stood still. I felt warmth and love. My tears began to flow with joy. I felt cradled, as if he had held me in his arms. I had words of comfort in my head. It felt as if it was going on for a long time. I felt incredibly calm and appeased. Then, still feeling so good, I went back to my activities remembering all at once that it was my birthday!"

The following narrative gives the impression of tranquility and peacefulness:

"In the evenings I will be in my room or my children's room putting them to bed and I can sense my older brother in the room also watching. He seems as a quiet presence just checking in to see how everything is, not interfering at all. Just watching."

The following testimony shows that contacts do not take place when anticipated, but instead they occur in an unexpected and unpredictable way:

"My fiancé had died suddenly/unexpectedly. I was 30, he 43. I was naturally distraught and staying with friends who had known him well. We spoke of him a lot. I talked to him all the time, thought about him but had no sort of ADC. Some of my books and records etc. were at his house, so I went to collect them on my own. I not only longed for an ADC from him but 'expected' one. But there was nothing. I wandered round his house, looking at/touching his things but no sense at all of him or his presence, just overwhelming sadness. I left. A couple of days later, I had eaten supper with the family I still stayed with. We had not talked of him; conversation had been of totally different things. The friend asked me to take a bag to the dustbin. This was in a narrow covered way outside the kitchen door. It was windy so I closed the door behind me and took the bag. As I did so, I stopped in absolute shock and amazement... because he, Donald, was there, waiting for me. I didn't see him, hear, smell anything... but beyond any doubt in my mind, he was there. I spoke to him. I felt unbelievably comforted and loved and relieved. And astonished — when I had expected him, in the place where he was somehow likely to have been, he was not there, it was empty of him. Now, he was there, in front of me, close to me. Hard to convey it but anyone who has had the experience will know at once."

ADCs of sensing a presence are unexpected and typically brief perceptions (a few seconds, a few minutes at the most), which often have a clearly identifiable beginning and end.

- **64% knew exactly when the deceased was coming and going, 13% were unsure, and 23% did not know**

"There was a real, and unexpected, sense of her presence besides, and slightly above, me. Suddenly she was there, and, a few minutes later, she was just as suddenly gone again."

In the narrative to follow, the respondent was also clearly able to identify the location of the deceased during these unusually frequent and extended contacts which occurred over several weeks. This account gives the impression of a friendly and peaceful interaction, and of a mutual understanding that needs no words, which is typical for the relationship between adolescents which they were before the passing of the boy:

"When I was 16 a friend died of accidental overdose. We did not know each other well but had fond feelings for each other and a few close friends in common. A few months after his death I felt him near, around me, as if we were in the same room hanging out together. I did not see him or hear him speak and we did not touch, but I felt him very clearly. I could smell his cologne faintly. He would come and hang out like this regularly, off and on through the day, sometimes staying up to an hour or two while I studied. Other times it was brief and he'd return later in the day. This continued daily or close to it for about three weeks. The visits ended suddenly and I've never felt him since. At the time he was visiting I felt his purpose in coming was to let his friends know he was ok. There had not been a public memorial and it was difficult for me and other friends to comprehend his passing. He also seemed to have some sort of question he was trying to pose to me in his shy indirect way (typical of him in life), or maybe some answer he was seeking from me, which I couldn't work out. The first visits startled me a bit, they were unexpected, and I didn't try to interact with him. As I got more comfortable with his presence I would mentally greet him and invite him to come sit, and that seemed to help him feel more comfortable. He never did sit; he stayed off to the side or behind me. I quickly got into the habit of thinking about him during his visits, what I liked about him, going over in detail the times we'd spent together in life, all fond memories. Towards the end of the three weeks I felt him more strongly and I felt this was his way of saying 'thank you and goodbye'. My understanding was he had been staying close to earth and his friends for these months in some sort of interim place by his choice, and now was getting ready to leave permanently and finish crossing over to his permanent place. I didn't say anything about these visits to anyone until a year or so later. I was talking with one of our mutual friends and discovered she had experienced a very similar series of visits from him too, and that she had interpreted it the same way I had."

This experience surprised our respondent, especially since there was no emotional connection to make sense of its occurrence. The meaning of this event remains open to speculation:

"While working as a nurse in the ED, we received a patient from an auto accident. She was a twenty something African American female. It was a bad accident and she didn't survive. I returned to the nurses' station to put in orders for another patient. While I was sitting at the computer, I felt my coworker (a twenty something African American female) standing behind me waiting to ask me a question.

17

I knew who it was (or thought I did) without seeing her. I turned around to see how I could help her. When I turned around, I saw that there was no one in the nurses' station aside from me. I turned back to the computer. Again, I felt her standing behind me waiting to ask a question. I turned around again, but again, there was no one there. I turned back to the computer, and realized she was still there. This time I realized that the person standing behind me was not my coworker, but the young woman who had just passed. In 18 years of nursing and being present at a number of deaths both anticipated and unanticipated, I had never before had the experience and have never since. I do not believe that spirits like to hang around hospitals so I did not anticipate the encounter. This gives it more credibility to me as it was not something I was expecting to happen and also there was no connection between us two."

Some experients perceive the energy of the deceased and speak of physical sensations. Drops in the ambient temperature or a draught sometimes accompany these contacts.

"One day after my son passed, I stood at the kitchen counter where we often visited. I felt like I was stepping into a vortex or energy field. I could step into it or out of it. It was magnetic. I asked my daughter and husband/partner to step inside this perceived circle of energy. They were afraid to. I loved the feeling of this vortex or energy field. I felt 100% sure it was my son's energy."

"I was infused with my dad's energy throughout my whole body. It ended as soon as he stopped. It was real physical energy."

"My whole body felt as if I was in a 'zone' or 'magnetic field'."

"I could feel his presence in my body, like a vibratory energy."

"Throughout my whole body as a strong energy. It was like drinking ten cups of coffee."

"I had the feeling that there was something else occupying the physical space. Like the echo of a sonar."

"The energy of the deceased fills the space and causes shivers."

"An intense presence, a kind of energy independent of me, very different from what I feel when I think of someone."

"I felt a kind of force, an energy flowing very fast around me."

A feeling of love and benevolence typically emanates from this presence.

"A feeling of love comes over us. You feel nothing but love."

In the next account, the respondent makes a clear distinction between an inner feeling, clearly identified as such, and the emotions allegedly transmitted by the deceased:

"When I think of my deceased loved one (almost all day long, as was the case when he was incarnated...), it is about my inner feelings with my thoughts. Yet, my inner feeling is marked by the painful experience of his absence. When my deceased loved one is present, I first feel him outside of me, and it is his state of mind that I feel, and his state of mind is nothing but love and joy."

We asked whether the feeling of the deceased's presence was the same or different from the times when participants thought about them and felt that they were "always by their side" or "in their heart".

- **For 61% the feeling of presence was different from a thought, 16% were unsure, and for 23% not different from a thought**

The following reports exemplify how the feeling of presence was different from a thought:

"I felt and thought about him all the time but I knew those were thoughts and feelings. The only time I knew his presence, it was quite different. A certainty beyond doubt. He was there."

"It was like when they were alive and would come in the room and I would see them, compared to when I just thought of them. Their sense of presence was there."

"It was stronger than just feeling him in my heart. His love invaded me from the outside, it was not my love that went to him, but his that came to me."

"It was real, not a feeling or a wish; it was as if the real person was present, not an image of the real person."

"The thought of the deceased, as a conscious, daytime thought, was a reasoned, controlled thought (which does not exclude feeling, sadness, etc.). The spontaneous presence at night was more 'present', more... alive in a sense, and almost more embodied than an intellectual thought."

"When I think of him, I only 'imagine' that he is connecting to me, I can only 'think' that he is sending me signs that make me think of him. But during an ADC, I know that he is there. It's a feeling of knowing, not imagining or thinking."

The spontaneous and unsolicited nature of these contacts emerges eloquently from the testimonies to follow:

"It was a completely different feeling. If I think about my grandmother it is my decision to do so, but this experience had nothing to do with my personal decision."

"Because I feel that it is not me who decides to communicate, it is him. I can't do anything even if it's my desire or my need."

This participant was not informed about the death of the perceived person. Thus, he perceived information that was previously unknown to him — the death of this person, which classifies this contact as an evidential ADC:

"I wasn't thinking about the deceased at that time because I didn't know she had passed away."

These contacts are much more than just a simple sensing of the presence of the deceased, which in itself is already an unexpected and striking experience. The experients say that they have also grasped the deceased's *intention*, that is to say their wish to inform them that they continue to exist and that they are well, as well as their desire to make them feel the love they have for them and the comfort they wish to bring them. The modality of making contact, namely the type of ADC, is in itself not very important because it is only the medium for the essential element which is the *information transmitted*.

This alleged transfer of information sometimes takes the form of an awareness that is akin to a revelation, as described by a mother who lost her five month and three week old son to cardiac arrest:

> *"I felt my son's presence several times, always behind my left shoulder. It was strong, I knew it was him, precisely in that place, it never lasted very long. I didn't feel the need to turn around to see him or try to touch him, I knew there would be nothing. But I could feel him. It was as if a simple curtain separated us: you know that the other is behind it, you feel him, even without seeing him. That's how I perceive what I call the Elsewhere: simply behind a veil, very close, really very close by."*[14]

Respondents were asked whether the deceased was transmitting a message by his or her sheer presence.

- **74% perceived a communication, 15% were unsure, and only 11% did not perceive a communication**

The perceived messages are specific to the individual life situation of the experient and are based on the common history with the deceased. I give the floor to some of our participants:

> *"'I am here. I know how you are feeling. I am close to you. Everything is all right'."*

"They stopped me from doing something that I doubt they would have approved of."

"He loved me and, even though I was extremely depressed and my heart was shattered, I'd be OK."

"I felt that I was being comforted, that she was telling me that she was OK."

"He was my oldest and just like me. He was my mini me and because of that we didn't always get along. When he passed I went to pieces and being a former Catholic and him committing suicide, I was in hell. His visit was somewhat reassuring but he said he couldn't keep coming like this and I should get over it, but it was my choice."

"It seemed to me that Jenny wanted to convey that she was now very, very well, and that she was relieved and happy to have this difficult life behind her. She probably wanted to tell this to all the mourners present, possibly not just specifically to me."

"One of my sisters was in trouble and he sent a message for her."

"I felt my mother was trying to comfort me, to tell me that although no longer on this plane of reality, she was still alive. I felt her gentleness, a great gentleness in her presence."

"I felt that my grandfather was trying to soothe my pain by communicating his serenity and the fact that he was doing well."

"I think he was surprised himself that he was still 'alive' on the other side and wanted to let us know so as to console his son."

Hearing a voice

- 43% heard the deceased

430 participants experienced an auditory ADC.

Hearing a voice

Auditory ADC	Men	Women	English dataset	French dataset	Spanish dataset
Yes	49%	43%	48%	37%	50%
No	51%	57%	52%	63%	50%

Sadly, this participant's perceptions proved to be accurate:

"I came home from work and my wife and kids were not home yet. My wife was going to take them to the zoo that day and then pick up my son's friend so they could play video games all night (it was a Friday). There was no reason for alarm as my wife is one of those people that will be late for her own funeral! As I walked into the house, our two dogs were barking in their cage and I very distinctly heard my daughter call from upstairs, 'Hello'. I let the dogs out to quiet them down and called to Lory asking why the dogs were in the cage if you are home? The only answer I got was hearing her footsteps upstairs... she had a distinctive walk. I went upstairs to see what she was doing, but she was nowhere to be found. I searched all the rooms, closets and even under beds! I was so sure I heard her. About 25 minutes later the phone rang, it was the hospital to tell me my family had been in an accident and they were 'pretty bumped up'. I said I am on my way, and they asked if I needed a ride. How silly, I thought, if they are just bumped up, it can't be too bad. As I drove to the hospital, I felt my daughter had been in the front seat and was killed. But, no, that couldn't happen because the evening before Lory settled the long running battle with her brother over who got to ride in front. She agreed to take the back seat for the rest of the month and starting the next month she would be in front. They would switch monthly. So, I felt my imagination was running away with itself. Turned out to be 100% correct."

This warning message, which can be understood as a way of giving support and strength, informed our respondent of a difficult ordeal ahead:

"My husband, Tim, had been recently diagnosed with a rare and terminal form of cancer. I was staying at a [...] Inn about two hours from home because I had started a new job about two months prior and we had not yet found a place to stay. Early one weekday morning, I was awakened by what felt like someone sitting down on the corner of my bed. (My mom used to wake me up for school every day by sitting down on the corner of the bed.) I sensed or heard her say, 'This is going to be really hard.' This was in late 2011 and my mom had passed away in April of 1994. Somehow, I knew she was talking about Tim's cancer fight. Even though I received that message, I was afraid to open my eyes. I was afraid that someone would really be sitting on my bed and that it wouldn't be my mom. When I finally did open my eyes, no one was there. She was right. Tim's cancer fight was horrific and losing him just over a year later was even worse. I still miss him terribly at six and a half years out."

A tough question emerging from the past was asked during this contact:

"I was a mother of two young children aged four and five, divorced, my partner being an alcoholic. I had an eardrum transplant before my children were born, and since then I can't move around in the dark without anxiety. However, on a Sunday night 30 years ago I put my two children to bed and to get back to my kitchen I had to walk through a long dark corridor. Usually I always turned on the light. But that night I walked down the hallway in the dark and felt a presence in front of me who asked me, 'If I had changed, would we have stayed together?' and I said, 'Yes.' It wasn't words as we humans express ourselves but like a communication felt deep inside me. I was immediately certain that it was my ex-husband. The next morning at work the phone rang and before I could pick it up I knew it was the police calling to tell me that my ex-husband had died. Indeed, this was the case. They informed me that my ex-husband had died on Sunday late afternoon, that is to say two to three hours before I experienced what you call an ADC. I experienced this event even before I knew of my ex-husband's death."

The following experience was left uncompleted by the participant's decision, leaving him with a number of questions...:

"One of the strongest ADC experiences was with my paternal grandmother, around 1983. My grandmother, Elsa, had passed away in 1980, aged 84. My mother and I had moved into the house in the mid-70's to care for her in her frailer years. The house had been my grandparents' home since it was built in the 1920's. My grandmother was a typical Victorian lady... very brusque and direct/rude at times. Her final years did little to detract from this personality and she was a difficult woman to get to know, although she appeared to like me as a child. I was 17 when she passed away. I was returning from a long trip to college and just knew she had gone. When I got home, my mother confirmed this. In 1983, aged 20, I was in the house, situated in the north of London.

Aside from cats, I was alone as my mother was out to work. I was getting ready to leave the house and had grabbed my coat from the banister. I had one hand on the door knob and the door was partially open when I heard a loud voice from behind me and upwards... the first floor landing. The voice was that of my grandmother's and called my name out very clearly. What equally fascinated and scared me at the precise moment was the tone of the voice... it was 'sing-songy'... like someone singing a nursery rhyme... 'Maaa... rviiiiinnnn.' I admit, although I had been raised in two haunted houses, my blood went cold. I knew that if I turned around at the moment I would see someone with my physical eyes. The sense of electric in the air was phenomenal. Ultimately, I chose not to turn around and legged it out of the door as fast as possible. I often wonder what would have happened if I had turned around and looked upwards towards the landing. That it was a human voice is not in doubt. It sounded very much like my grandmother's, but stronger than in her final years... a very robust voice."

The following testimony is representative of what many experients undergo: they are immediately convinced that they have had a real experience but nevertheless question it because they consider it a totally impossible event, an event that cannot happen, simply because the conception of reality prevailing in our societies leaves no room for the unexpected, the inexplicable, the mysterious, the transcendent. This participant was able to recognize her experience as authentic only once she had obtained information on ADCs:

"About three months after my daughter died, I heard my mom's voice in my head. My mom died in 2007. My daughter died in 2017. I had been horribly sad and grieving since my daughter's death. My husband was working nights, so I was alone in the apartment. It was quiet, just me and my sadness. I was standing in the kitchen when suddenly my mom spoke to me and the words were inside my head, but in her voice, which I can't recreate, so I know it was real. She said, 'Don't be so sad, Toodles, Mary's here with me' (My mom and dad were the only people who called me 'Toodles'). I was shocked, because I was always told that those things don't really happen. I meekly answered, 'OK, Mom,' and then looked around but nobody was there. I didn't tell anyone for a couple of weeks. I was unsure about accepting this even though I knew it was real. Finally, after learning that ADCs really do happen, I realized that my mom was trying to comfort me and my daughter is safe with her and I began to heal."

The following account of an auditory ADC is particularly interesting as the participant perceived information previously unknown to her. The information about the inheritance in particular was confirmed shortly after the contact, classifying this experience as an evidential ADC:

"One night I woke up and saw my biological father. He greeted me and said that he had come to tell me that he was leaving and that he had left me a small legacy. He added that he had met my children and that I had a beautiful family. He bid me a fond farewell and left. I never had any contact with him and I never met him in person. I learned of his existence at the age of nine when I discovered that the father I grew up with and whose surname I have was not my biological father. However, I never sought to meet him, and neither did he. So, we only met personally after his death. Two days after this experience, his family contacted me to inform me of his death and his wish that I receive a legacy he had left me. This confirmed that my experience was real and accurate."

As the testimonies cited in the previous pages have shown, auditory ADCs come in two forms: either the experients hear a voice that seems to come from an external source, in the same way as they would hear a living person (this was the case for 49% of our participants), or they perceive the communication without an external sound (56% of our respondents[15]). In the second case, they speak of a message "deposited in their mind", while specifying that the origin of the communication was outside themselves and that it was not a thought. It would therefore be a telepathic communication. Experients are not always able to specify how they heard the deceased. The communication may be unilateral or bilateral. In both types of contact, the deceased are generally recognized without hesitation by the intonation of the voice and by a certain way of expressing themselves which is characteristic of them.

This respondent was able to identify specifically from which location in the room the voice was coming from:

"I was woken up by my late wife's voice, it was between 2 a.m. and 3 a.m. She called my name like she was trying to wake me up without startling me, the voice came from the end of and to the left of the bed."

A touch of humor is not incompatible with a funeral...

"B. was a close family friend and regarded as my Aunt, thought we had no family connection. At her funeral mass the church was packed. Her family was giving the eulogies and my mind was drifting. The congregation was silent. I heard a distinctive laugh from behind me (B. had a very distinctive laugh) and the words 'fucking hell, Peter, look at all these people'. This would have been perfectly in character for her. I looked behind me immediately, so strong was the impression. The voice came from above me slightly to my right. The voice was normal speaking volume and would have been clearly heard by others. No one showed any signs of having heard it. I asked my mother sitting next to me, 'Did you hear that?' and she replied, 'No.' I had to explain later what I had heard, but the experience was very real and I had struggled to control my laughter for the rest of the service."

Here are some more illustrations of auditory ADCs:

"I strongly sensed my mother telling me she was with my dad and feeling wonderful. I could hear her voice clearly. I didn't see her, but felt her presence."

"As I was getting into bed, I clearly heard my late husband behind me, saying 'I will never leave you.'"

"One morning, just as I was about to really wake up, not quite asleep but not fully awake, I heard the voice of my father-in-law, seen the day before in a more depressed state than ever. He said, 'Don't worry. I'm fine now.' 15 minutes later my phone rang. My in-laws' neighbors told me that the fire brigade and gendarmes were there 'for my father-in-law'. Death by suicide. He 'spoke' to me at the time of his death."

"On 17 July 2018 my niece's son, Nicolas, had an accident with his bicycle and died on 18 July in a university hospital in Switzerland. Nicolas was nine years old. Nicolas and I were always very close. After his death, I lived with my niece's family for a few weeks. The second night after Nicolas' death I couldn't sleep and I was crying. Suddenly I felt a presence filled with well-being, love, serenity. A voice, without being a voice, said to me: 'All is well. Everything is fine.' It was a comforting situation. After maybe half a minute (I don't really know), this feeling disappeared. I wanted to keep it, because it was so beautiful and comforting, but I couldn't. The next day I was talking to my niece about it. I said: 'It was Nicolas or God.' And she had experienced the same thing in the same night, but twice and probably longer. She was sure that it was Nicolas' presence."

Contacts where experients hear the deceased call their name are not unusual, illustrated by the testimonies to follow:

"I was lying on the bed, totally engrossed in a book, when I heard my father's voice loudly say my name — the name that only he ever called me."

"My father clearly calling my name hours after his passing. Unmistakably his voice, but much younger sounding."

"The day after my partner's death, I was in a semi sleep state. I was woken by hearing my name clearly called by my deceased partner to wake me."

"My mother passed in March 2002. A few days afterward, my youngest sister and I were discussing her memorial plans while standing in the kitchen at my house (I live in my maternal grandparents' house). I was in mid-sentence when I loudly and distinctly heard my mother's voice say my name. I stopped talking and my sister and I both just looked at each other with a look of shock on our faces. I asked, 'Did you hear that?' She said, 'Yes, I did.' I said, 'What did you hear?' She said, 'I heard Mom call out your name.' I said, 'Good, that's what I heard too!' I walked into the dining area by my grandmother's old hutch where I heard my mother's voice come from and said, 'Hi Mom. We love you and miss you.' I returned to the kitchen. My sister and I cried a little bit. We knew it was her."

"My father battled cancer for a whole year. It was terrible to see how he suffered and how it consumed him little by little. He and I were always very close, we did everything together. On the day of his operation I knew something was wrong. I got a call at dawn from my mother, crying, and then I knew straight away, he was dead... He died in 2013. Since then, my mother and my little brother often hear his voice or sometimes they say they see him sitting on the sofa or they see a shadow passing by that looks like him. I had never heard or seen anything since he passed away, but one day that same year, I was in his workshop which is set up on the terrace. I was doing some stuff and then I heard his voice say my name... For a moment I thought it was my imagination but I felt him, I felt that I was not alone, that someone else was there with me. I went out for a moment, sat down in the place where he and I always sat, and for a moment it seemed to me that he was alive next to me, looking at the beautiful day. I remained silent, closed my eyes and felt as if a hand was touching mine. In a low voice I said 'I love you, Daddy.' Then I opened my eyes and I didn't feel anything anymore. I know it was some kind of goodbye or a way of telling me that he was taking care of my family and me."

These contacts, which took place in an ancient family property with a history, were perceived simultaneously by our participant and her partner. Seemingly, the intended recipient of these auditory ADCs was not our participant but her grandmother, who had died years ago:

"I live in an old plantation home that has been in my family for several generations. I inherited the home after my grandmother's death; her name was Victoria. When my significant other and I moved into the home ten years ago, I started hearing a man's voice calling: 'Victoria. Victoria.' I thought my mate was playing games on me, but he promised he wasn't. The clincher was when my mate and I were sitting in the parlor together and we heard the disembodied voice calling for Victoria! This went on for a few months, then stopped. I believe the voice was from my deceased grandfather whom I never knew."

During this rather disconcerting auditory contact, the participant also heard her name called out:

"The voice of my father (a total non-believer in after-life and skeptic) calling my name over and over. The voice was telepathic, like someone had set a radio off in my mind. It was very alarming."

Some experients do not hear words but other sounds which they attribute to the deceased. It was a song which our respondent heard:

"My father passed away on 22 November 2018. I don't live in France and came home on 23 November. When I went into my father's house and closed the door behind me, I heard him humming a song as he used to do when he was healthy. I didn't imagine him singing, I heard him."

Footsteps seem to be another medium of auditory ADCs:

"Some days (~10) after my father died I was at his house. I was in the kitchen and the house was quiet (late afternoon). I heard him come through the door and do a walk through the house. It was his gait, his movement up the steps. I heard the footsteps through the house, room by room. It was immediately obvious to me that he was doing a final walk through his house. After a couple of minutes, he exited the front door. It was clear that there was a shift in energy, a release. The experience was audio. It did not frighten me because the pace and movement of the sound was so like him."

This significant sound was heard by all present:

"After Mom passed away, myself and kids went over to eat dinner with my dad and we heard my mom's chair hitting the wall several times as she would hit the wall getting up or moving, like we would hear when she was living and no one was present in this room, and we all knew it was her."

It looks like our participant had received a friendly collegial advice from the deceased in the form of a noise…:

"I was working in a dark room of a photographer that had been killed. This was at a university and I was the person who had replaced her job after her death. It was my first project to print photographs of the crime scene of her car accident. As I was printing the photographs I heard rattling every time I went to lift a photograph from the developing liquid. After I turned the lights on, I realised the rattling was coming from the pair of tongs on the wall hanging where I had not seen them. I was using my hands to lift the photographs out instead of tongs, as I was new to the darkroom and didn't know where everything was."

The perception of a characteristic cough is the subject of the following testimony:

"I heard my grandfather cough. He had died the day before. It was a very distinct raspy cough! I just knew it was him. I was home alone at the time. No neighbours nearby, flat next door was empty."

It was a heartbeat that was perceived during this contact, combined with a sensation of energy:

"A few days ago, I lay down in my bed to sleep when I felt a strong heat near my back and I perfectly heard a heartbeat... I felt a strong energy behind me."

How can one imagine a communication without an external sound? I present some of the comments from our respondents:

"More than hearing the voice, it's like a transmitted sensation."

"An unmodulated voice. It was more of a thought that I perceived."

"It would be more like telepathy, we hear but no sound is audible, we just know for sure that the deceased has spoken to us."

"It wasn't really a voice, but a feeling that made itself understood. I saw the image and understood."

"It is a very strange thing to 'hear' inside your head, with the same words and tone of voice as the deceased had. It is a unique experience, I think, as it seems that the deceased was in my head but as an individual separate from myself, with the ability to converse and answer questions."

To those who had heard a voice, we asked if it was the same or different from the one the deceased had had during his or her lifetime. For the majority of respondents, the voice was the same.

- **For 68% the voice was the same, 17% were unsure, and for 15% the voice was different**

The following testimonies illustrate a change in the perceived voice:

"It was the same as when he was healthy before the stroke — he had aphasia after the stroke, and so that was not the version of him I interacted with."

"More robust, as if younger... stronger."

"She sounded as if she was talking under water."

"I heard the voice in my head, but with a slight distortion, like a resonance."

"His tone of voice was the same, but slower, calm and loving."

"Different because I heard him say my name as if his mouth was covered with a handkerchief. It was not very clear but perfectly audible."

"His voice was deeper... like a voice in slow motion on a tape recorder."

"The voice was slower, as if blown by the wind."

"Two months after my 16 year old daughter committed suicide, I heard a voice at night in a half sleep that just said, 'Papaaaaaa...' It was like a regret and a loving goodbye at the same time. It was her voice, but a little metallic."

How to differentiate between a perceived communication without an external sound and a thought? For a large majority of our participants, there was no doubt that the communication was different from a thought and that they had not generated it themselves.

- For 87% the communication was different from a thought, 6% were unsure, and for only 7% the communication was not different from a thought

Feeling a physical contact
- 48% felt a physical contact

472 of those surveyed experienced a tactile ADC.

Feeling a physical contact

Tactile ADC	Men	Women	English dataset	French dataset	Spanish dataset
Yes	41%	49%	46%	51%	47%
No	59%	51%	54%	49%	53%

During this type of ADC, the experients feel a contact on a part of their body, for example a brushing, a pressure, a caress, a hand on the shoulder or a real hug. The contact is comforting and the experients often immediately recognize their deceased loved one by the familiarity of his or her characteristic gesture. Some report that the contact was accompanied by an "electrical flow" or "energy wave".

How can one picture such a physical contact? Here are some testimonies:

"I was in the car one day. I felt desperate, I had no courage left. Then I felt the presence of my partner (father of my child). I had the feeling that he was holding me in his arms, putting himself on my back. I could almost feel his warmth. I heard him talking to me too, and we had a few minutes of conversation. It did me a lot of good and calmed me down. It was as if I could feel his love through that moment. That gave me the strength to go."

"Shortly after my husband's death I sat talking to my sons. We laughed and then I felt an energy next to me. I then felt a hand on the top of my leg. The hand patted my leg. My sense told me that this was my husband reassuring me."

"After my daughter passed and we went home, I was in her bedroom laying on her bed crying and very distressed. I felt someone rubbing my arms trying to comfort me. I turned on the light to see if I had a bug or something on my arms. Nothing was there and the stroking on my arms continued until I quieted. I know it was my daughter."

"It was a few days after the funeral of my husband. I was very sad and suddenly I felt his hand on my shoulder and I could smell him. I was sure he was in the room with me, trying to comfort me. I had the feeling that I was not allowed to turn around, otherwise he would be gone. I felt his strength and he gave me power to live."

"My mother passed on 26/11/03 and was buried on 5/12/03. This ADC happened before dawn in January 2004. I was asleep, my partner likewise and at the other side of the bed. I felt a warm hand caress my chin and shot upright in bed, waking Jane, my partner. I asked her if she had touched me and she denied having done so. I suppose she could have done it in her sleep, but she was well away, turned away from me and with her face in her pillow. Furthermore, in sixteen years together I've never known her caress my chin. I'm pretty sure it was not her."

The physical contact is often characteristic for the deceased and immediately assigned to him or her:

"While watching a movie on television there was a scene in which an older male character reminded me of my late father. It affected me to the point that I leaned forward in my chair with my head down and began to cry from missing him. I then felt the palm of a hand tentatively and somewhat awkwardly pat my back twice on my right shoulder blade. I knew instantly it was my dad. He was not a physically demonstrative man and the somewhat awkward touch was just like he would have done in life."

"About a month after the sudden death of my mother, I was alone in the house in my bedroom. I was sitting on the side of the bed, extremely distressed, howling with the pain of my loss and raging at the God I had put my faith in because he hadn't come to my help in my hours of need and darkness. I just couldn't stop crying, and had never felt more alone. I then 'felt' my Mother sit next to me and wrap her arms around me. I know it was my Mum in the same way that you can feel someone you know well physically near you — I could even smell her. As she hugged me, I was aware of being totally enveloped by her love, and, as she soothed me, I felt an intense warmness and a calmness I hadn't felt since she died. I felt her stroking my hair, and I recognised the feeling of being comforted by my Mum. I am 100% sure that my Mum came to comfort me — I recognised her essence and energy. Although I shed many more tears in the months following her passing, I never again experienced the despair that I felt that morning. The experience, along with many others that followed, caused me to completely reconsider my traditional religious beliefs, and explore my own spirituality. I believe that I am more at ease with myself as a result of her contact that day."

The following rather disconcerting experience suggests that a car accident was narrowly avoided purportedly thanks to the intervention of the deceased friend:

"A few weeks after the death of a friend, he appeared sitting on my sofa. He looked completely normal, but as I looked at him he disappeared. A few days later a different friend went to visit a psychic and was told someone had seen the deceased person. The psychic described in detail my lounge and what had happened. I hadn't said a word about my experience to anyone. Discounting the experience, I got in the car and I was driving down the motorway in the fast lane when I felt someone sit underneath me. I felt their arms encircling me and their hands over mine on the steering wheel. The car stereo turned on at full volume and I banged my head on the steering wheel in shock and realized I had been falling asleep at the wheel. The song playing was one of the songs from my friend's funeral."

For this participant, the gesture felt was characteristic of her late husband, bringing her back to the carefree time when they shared their daily lives:

"I felt my husband touch my foot and press it down on the bed, dipping the mattress and waking me up. I thought it may have been my dogs trying to jump up on the bed, but they were not in the room. They were in their kennels downstairs. It was a habit of my husband's to do that when he was walking around to his side of the bed. He would always grab my toes or just touch my foot when he was getting into bed or during the night if he got up for any reason."

This description gives an impression of distress and sadness, presumably linked to the causes and the tragic circumstances of this demise:

"I was in my family room, in the basement, listening to a radio program. My phone alarm goes off at five a.m. and I am usually awake 30 to 40 minutes prior to the alarm. The room was dark and I was halfway sitting on the couch, kind of leaning on my right side. I felt what I thought was one of my dogs climb onto the couch and up towards my waist as if they were trying to hug me. My dogs are about 40-45lbs each and they will usually come up and cuddle. This was different; this was more of a hug, which startled me. When I turned to look, it was my youngest son, Sam, he seemed way younger and he was crying. Thinking back on it the room was dark, but I saw as if the lights were on. The speaker to my Bluetooth crackled which distracted me briefly, I turned and he was gone. I stopped for a second to gather my thoughts on what just happened. Sam had passed a week before from a drug overdose. My mind was trying to come to grips with the situation when I felt what felt like somebody's razor stubble brush my left arm. When I turned it was him again. I got composed and said to him, 'You can't be here, we just went to your funeral,' with that, he made an odd facial expression. The alarm on my phone went off and distracted me which was enough time for him to vanish, for lack of a better word. Both times he seemed somehow illuminated, and I only saw his upper torso. Looking back, I didn't realize when he appeared was a week to the day of his passing and around the time they say he died. Several weeks later, a friend of his posted some pictures of him to her Facebook account, one of them was him making that same face."

This contact occurred in that particular state between sleep and wakefulness that seems to be particularly conducive to the occurrence of ADCs:

"About three months after my wife departed, I was lying in bed one morning, barely awake, enough to be aware of birds outside, but not of thoughts or feelings. Then I felt her kiss me on the lips and I heard (telepathically, not with my ears), 'Sorry it's been so long, they've been keeping us really busy.' Unfortunately, I was startled by these events, jolted to fully awake, and lost that receptive state."

As is often the case, many years passed before this participant was ready to share this uplifting contact with others:

"In 1999, my wife died of ovarian cancer at the age of 56. A few days after the funeral, the children having left, I am in the bedroom. It's early afternoon and I stand and fold one of her cardigans. It's navy blue, still impregnated with her scent, which I know will be gone in a few days, and it's so sad. My mind is totally empty. Suddenly, instantly, my wife is there, standing in front of me, dressed normally. In a spontaneous gesture that I can't explain, I hug her, with a real physical contact. I feel her hugging me too. Realizing what I am doing, I take her by the shoulders (with real contact), pull her away from me and say, looking into her eyes, 'But you are dead!', and she answers, 'Yes, I am dead.' This exchange is mental, from thought to thought, and immediately everything disappears, I find myself with the cardigan in my hands. That was the only manifestation I had. I was sad, but not desperate.

It took me 15 years to talk about this, first to our two children. She had come to say goodbye to me, thus showing me that she continues to exist in another form. I am convinced of this, having now an unfailing serenity and no fear at all of what we commonly call 'death'. I would like to point out that I am a practicing health professional, at the service of my fellow human beings, that I will only quit when 'He/She/They' call me and that to date, at 77 years of age, I am in good physical and mental health."

The next contact appears to have avoided a tragedy, so deep was this mother's despair:

"Exactly four weeks after the passing of my son and my first day back to work, after coming home from work, I cried for hours on end and was feeling very suicidal. At the time, I was alone in my home. I had spoken to my sister previously on the phone telling her that I just couldn't do this. I hung up, went outside to get the mail, came back in, while leaning over the table I felt a hand go across my whole entire back. I jumped and turned around and there was nobody in the room with me and I got on my knees and cried out to my son that I felt him touch me. And I knew at that moment my son was telling me 'no mom, I'm right here, no mom, don't kill yourself, I'm right here mom'. I called my sister back a second time crying and she was scared that something was wrong when I told her that I had felt my son touch me. She started crying and saying 'thank you God'. She had been sitting praying since the first call I made to her. She was asking God to allow Bill to please be able to show me a sign because she was worried I would hurt myself."

The next case describes the immediate, and apparently lasting, impact of these powerful experiences on grief resolution:

"About six months after my wife's death, I had a particularly bad day, suffering profound grief. That night I lay in bed sobbing till I fell asleep. When I awoke in the morning, I was still in a funk and just lay there, sort of numb, listening to the birds outside, and rolled on to my side. Then I felt my wife's energy snuggle up against my back. This is something we often did before going to sleep or upon waking. And suddenly the grief dissipated. I felt calm and comforted, and fell back to sleep. When I awoke, the grief was completely gone and I was ready to get on with my life again."

This experience brought back childhood memories:

"Six months after my father died, I was awakened in the middle of the night by the sensation of someone lifting my foot and gently tugging it. At first, I thought my wife might have pushed her leg against my foot, but she was on the other side of the bed. I then became aware of the strong aroma of pipe tobacco. My dad smoked a pipe. I wanted to be sure I was wide awake so I got out of bed and walked around the room. The tobacco aroma was strong and persistent. I then left the bedroom but the aroma ceased suddenly. When I returned to the bedroom the aroma had gone. There was no subtle after-scent, the aroma had completely gone. When I awoke the next morning, I described what happened to my wife. She asked me why I might have felt the sensation of someone tugging on my foot. When I was a boy and asleep, my father had the habit of coming into my room and tugging on my foot, he would say 'Wake up! Time to get up!' One final piece to this experience was when my wife asked me, 'Do you know what day this is?' I replied, 'Sunday.' She replied back, 'It's Father's Day!'"

The range of tactile ADCs reported is wide:

"The one that was so vivid was when I was in a hypnagogic state right before dozing off on the couch. I felt my deceased son wrap his arms around me from behind. I was able to kiss his left hand and then his right arm. I could feel the hair on his arms and told him that I loved him. Then he left."

"Shortly after losing a dear friend and soulmate two years ago I was in bed crying one night. Suddenly I realized he was there, laying behind me, holding my hand with one of his and with his other arm around me in a hug."

"While I was resting, on my own, I suddenly felt the pressure of my father's hand on my shoulder. At the same time, I felt the gentleness of this gesture."

"The day after or two days after my son's suicide, early in the morning (around 6 a.m.), I was at my daughter's house, still in bed, lying in the fetal position, when I had the sensation of a presence behind my back, arms gently wrapping around me, a thumb in my hand. This lasted for a few moments. Then the sensation became lighter, until it disappeared."

"I was lying in our bed a few days after my spouse had died. I was trying to fall asleep with my eyes closed when I felt an enveloping embrace from my torso to my thighs, even lifting my legs slightly. I opened my eyes in panic, but the softness of the sensation quickly soothed me and then disappeared."

"I had a tactile contact with my dad who died suddenly in hospital. I didn't get a chance to say goodbye and I was very sad. He came between my sleep and my awakening to caress my forehead as one might do to a baby. I knew it was him right away."

"Six months after my husband died, my grandson was born. In the evening I was angry to have to experience this birth on my own. In the night I woke up feeling a strong embrace. I tried to make it last as long as possible, I knew it was my husband and my anger left."

"Less than a month after my daughter's death, I was in the kitchen, preparing dinner, and I 'heard' her coming down the stairs from her room. I felt her presence behind me and she hugged me. It was amazing and very sweet to experience. As real as if she was 'alive' next to me."

The following report suggests an unsuccessful attempt to make contact:

"I have experienced several contacts, mostly physical. The most significant was when a colleague of mine lost her son, whom I knew relatively well. I knew, I felt he was by her side and once I had a feeling that my shirt sleeve was being pulled and then someone was pushing me in the ribs, I'm sure it was him trying to tell me something."

This experience occurred in a stressful circumstance:

"I was on the phone for four hours trying to stop a friend from committing suicide. When I hung up, I felt someone hug me to comfort me. And by the smell, I knew it was my father who had died a few weeks earlier."

This contact was made meaningful by the accompanying auditory message:

"My father ended his life in September 2012 and in the days that followed, while I was at home and walking down the hallway, I felt a presence pushing me forward, giving me a real push. Very strange. When I arrived in the bathroom, while I was stunned and sad, a phrase came: 'you have to move on and enjoy life!'"

The grief of bereavement was relieved immediately, though perhaps not permanently, by this contact:

"The evening of my mother's death, after two months in hospital, I was plunged into a downward spiral of sadness, anguish, loss… which stopped instantly. I heard, or rather felt, a soothing whisper, then a reassuring warmth accompanied by the sensation that someone was sticking to my back and holding me. I fell asleep still held, comforted."

This ADC was the prelude to other manifestations that were to occur over a long period of time:

"My grandmother passed away in hospital during the night of 12–13 December 2013. I went to identify her on the morning of Friday the 13th because I had been called to work. I walked into a tiled room, she was on a stretcher covered with a white sheet. I sat next to her crying and talking to her, asking her why she had left so suddenly. I stayed with her for a long time until I had to leave and, to say goodbye, I stroked her cheek. I returned to my car and as I started it, I felt a softness envelop me. It was so nice, I felt protected, comforted and all of a sudden, I felt a soft caress on my cheek. I understood that my grandmother was thanking and comforting me. I remember this tender interlude in the chaos. A few days later she appeared in her room and several times over a year."

The following account describes a shared ADC, that is to say a contact that was perceived simultaneously by two people gathered in the same place:

"48 hours after my daughter's death, I was in my room with a friend in the late evening. We were discussing other matters. Suddenly my daughter came and hugged us both at the same time. She put a hand on the back of each of us. We both jumped up and exclaimed: 'Marianne!'"

In order to better understand tactile ADCs, we asked in which part of their body the participants felt the contact and how it occurred:

"His hand was in mine, I felt his fingers, the pressure of his hand."

"I felt a kiss upon my forehead, which was her custom before going to bed."

"Felt his arms around me in a hug and his lips on mine in a kiss."

"I was in my father's room, looking at his belongings on his bedside table, when I felt a caress on my cheek."

"I felt his hand touch mine, as if to tell me that he was there with me."

"A caress in my hair and on my face."

"I felt the embrace, he was next to me and he put his arms around me."

"Around my wrist in the middle of the night. I knew it was him because he had a very distinctive palm from third degree burns. My wrist was vibrating slightly."

For a short majority of our collection of testimonies, the contact was familiar because it was typical for the deceased.

- **For 55% the contact was familiar, 11% were unsure, and for 34% the contact was not familiar**

How did the respondents experience this contact in terms of sensations?

"Like a physical contact, only different."

"Like an unknown sensory experience."

"I feel that this contact has brought me a lot of energy."

"All over my body with strong vibrations that kept me awake."

"A powerful energy that I had never known flowed through my whole body."

"I had chills, it was very strong."

"Very intensely in terms of vibrations."

"The body on which my head and neck weighed was soft, 'elastic', but I felt no warmth. The 'warmth' was given to me by his hands on me, but I felt strongly the intimacy of his presence."

"A shiver and a great cold afterwards."

"Sensation of touch on the shoulder and a strong shiver running through my body."

"Totally real, like touching another living person."

"It was so intense that it almost felt physical."

We asked if the participants had tried to touch the deceased. Few had taken this initiative.

- **26% tried to touch the deceased, 2% were unsure, and 72% did not try**

Of those who had sought physical contact, a little less than half could seize the deceased and feel matter.

- **43% could seize the deceased and felt resistance/matter, 15% were unsure, and 42% could not seize the deceased**

Following are a few illustrations of the nature of this perceived matter:

"Subtle, like trying to get your hand through a mixture of persistent steam or highly volatile material."

"It was like kissing water, I could feel it but it was limp..."

"It was totally physical, with the same properties as a living person and I also felt his clothes."

"It wasn't the matter of a physical body, it was like two magnets joined together, energy... That's what I felt during the embrace and the feeling of love connected me even more to him."

"I was able to take my mother in my arms and we held each other tightly: so there was a resistance/matter, I didn't feel like I was holding wind. But it was very, very brief."

Some tried to touch the deceased but were unable to do so:

> "I wanted to touch him, but I couldn't, it was as if there was an invisible barrier, a veil that prevented me from touching him."

And one of our respondents had the impression that this physical contact was not meant to take place:

> "The deceased evaporated when I tried to approach him, as if to make me understand that I had no right to touch him."

Did the participants feel that this contact conveyed a message?

- **For 80% the physical contact transmitted a message, 10% were unsure, and for only 10% no message was perceived**

Here are some examples of messages conveyed through the physical contact. Frequently, they serve to communicate that the perceived deceased is alive and well.

> "I am near you, I am alive."

> "Yes, it's really me. See, it feels like it always did when we hugged."

> "He was letting me know that he was there and I was not imagining it."

> "I'm here, and you know it. I love you. Don't grieve because I am alive, just not in my body."

> "The message was that she wanted me to know that she was still very near, even though I could not see her."

Many messages are essentially expressions of love and support:

"This is how you are loved, without limit, without condition."

"He wanted to be reassuring, loving and soothing, even if it stressed me out, especially at the beginning... or simply because he wanted to, to tell me he was there with me."

Other messages express a plea for support for those close to the deceased:

"That we should take care of my father."

"Definite goodbye to me and my family with an urge to look after his widow."

And sometimes information about the passing is perceived:

"He repeated that he did not wish to die."

Seeing the deceased

- **46% saw the deceased**

460 of our participants experienced a visual ADC.

Seeing the deceased

Visual ADC	Men	Women	English dataset	French dataset	Spanish dataset
Yes	51%	46%	47%	42%	61%
No	49%	54%	53%	58%	39%

These experiences come in a variety of forms. Apparitions can take place indoors, for example at night in the bedroom, or outdoors, even in a car, a plane, etc. Sometimes the experients report that they have perceived an apparition that they did not recognize. Later, based on a photo, they identified it as an ancestor or deceased distant relative. However, some apparitions are completely unknown to the experients.

It may happen that apparitions are perceived in conjunction with a drop in room temperature, sometimes combined with draughts.

I first present a description of a particularly complete ADC:

"The most significant was June 12th 2012. I was awakened around 6 a.m. in the morning. I saw someone walking on my front porch through my bedroom window. I thought, 'Who would be here this early?' I got dressed and went to the front door. I opened the door and saw a woman with her back to me on my left, crying. I asked if she was OK. She turned around and it was my grandmother from my father's side of the family. I was in shock to see her. She spoke and asked me for forgiveness and apologized for no longer talking to me after my father had passed away. I told her it was OK and I forgave her. She walked towards me and we hugged. I felt her frail body hug me and I hugged her back. I felt her clothes, her smell and she thanked me as we hugged. I felt this most intense feeling of love. I started to cry. She then started to turn into this bright white light. I had to close my eyes due to it being so bright. I could see the light fading away through my eyelids. The feeling of her started to slowly leave. I opened my eyes and she was gone. I was standing there with my arms still looking like I was hugging someone. I was in shock. I went back into the house and lay on my bed and my wife woke up. I told her what happened. [...] My grandmother had been dead for about 7 years I and was so in shock from the experience."

It is obvious from this testimony that several sensory organs can be solicited during one and the same ADC. Our participant saw his deceased grandmother, he conversed with her, he perceived her smell, they hugged and he "felt her frail body". It is also evident that, beyond the simple perception of his grandmother, the essence of this contact was the **information** perceived — she asked him for forgiveness — and the **emotions** perceived and felt — "I felt this most intense feeling of love." The completely unexpected and unsolicited nature of ADCs also stands out clearly in this account.

The following experience occurred when the participant was concentrated on a specific activity and was probably not thinking about his deceased daughter. He saw her engaged in an everyday task, as he had no doubt seen her do often during her lifetime:

"I was in the middle of gathering things in preparation for a road trip, loading up my van, out the back door to the shed, carrying things, so I was busy and focused on what I was doing. I walked in the back door of my house with a box in my hands, came around the corner and saw my daughter in the kitchen appearing to cook something on the stove. She was wearing a long, black, flowy type outfit unlike anything she'd worn in life. She was 22 when she passed the previous summer."

The following contact has liberated our participant from the sense of guilt that is so destructive:

"My grandfather appeared to me after his unexpected passing. He had gone into hospital for a simple operation, and I had decided I would visit him after he had gone home as I didn't like hospitals. He died the day he was supposed to go home from an embolism. I had felt guilty for weeks after for not going to the hospital, and I was sitting in my flat during the day. I got up to go to the kitchen and I saw a full apparition of him in the hallway. He looked at me and smiled and then faded away. I took it as his way of saying it's ok and not to feel guilty."

This testimony recounts the perception of a young child:

"Arriving home from the funeral of Mum we just stepped in the hall and started to take our jackets and shoes off, when my at the time three years old son looked up the stairs behind him and asked me, 'Why is the big lady going upstairs?' (Mum was overweight.) I was shocked by the question and didn't want to scare my son, so said I don't know. After a few minutes I went upstairs to the loo with my son and I asked him where the lady was and he said in mummy's and daddy's room. We left it at this. My son never before or after mentioned anything about this or other things, although we speak about lost ones often — this is why we think he really has seen someone that day."

ADCs may occur at important moments in the life of the experients, when the absence of the loved one is particularly painful. The following testimony is a good illustration of this:

"My deceased sister materialized for me only once, at her daughter's wedding. She was my closest sister, emotionally. Her daughter is like a daughter to me. During the vows portion of the wedding, my sister appeared in the front, facing the couple for only a second or two. She was very clear to me. I can describe what she was wearing, even. Once

I realized what was happening, she disappeared. I was very emotionally moved. I only told a few family members about it. Nobody else mentioned seeing her. This was about four years after her death."

I give the floor to our respondents for further descriptions of visual ADCs:

"At age 14, days after my grandmother died, while sitting on the front steps, I watched my grandmother walk past the house and turn and nod to me."

"My brother died by suicide on 3 July 2011. He was 32 years old and struggled for 15 years with depression. He was my little brother, we were five years apart. I always felt he was fragile and I always felt the need to protect him. But I always knew he would die young, so much so that as a child I would look at his lifeline in his hand to reassure myself. The month after he died, I was home alone and watching TV in the living room. I was watching a programme I was passionate about and I wasn't thinking about my brother at that moment. I went quickly to my room to get something. I was in a hurry because I didn't want to miss the continuation of the TV programme. When I entered my room, I saw my brother lying on my bed. He was lying full length in his favourite position, with his arms crossed behind his head and his legs crossed, looking relaxed and serene as he did when he was a child. It was so real, or rather so unreal, that I was scared and turned my head away. I wondered for an instant if I was hallucinating. When I looked back at the bed, he was gone. Seven years later, I am sure it was not a hallucination. This image brings back a memory of him when he was five years old, lying in the same position and whistling happily."

"I was walking by a window in my house when I glanced out and saw my mother who had been dead about a dozen years or so. I was in my mid-fifties at the time. She was radiantly happy, and appeared to be in her early thirties. She died in her middle eighties. She was dressed in 1930's style clothing, and looked prettier than she had even when she was in her thirties, but it was unmistakably her. But the most interesting thing was her huge smile and radiant happiness and joy. She was standing, or perhaps floating, in a gently rolling landscape filled with flowers in the most incredible colours — brilliant colours that we don't have here. She communicated to me without words, but I'll never forget what she 'said' to me: 'There is only forgiveness.' I had a good relationship with my mother, so I don't think she was referring to anything specific, but it was a wonderful message for me personally and also to share in my ministry. I was a Christian minister at the time. I am now an interfaith chaplain, ordained through a metaphysical organization. 'How' I saw her is difficult to say — it wasn't really with my physical eyes, but on the other hand it kind of was — what I saw out the window was not the land that is there physically, the apparition seemed to completely replace the actual landscape. It's hard to explain, but it was a very vivid experience."

Visual ADCs, like any type of ADC, can occur at any time and in any place, as illustrated by this experience that occurred in an aircraft:

"My mother was in the hospital in Pennsylvania after having had surgery. She had been on a ventilator for a week and could not breathe on her own, and so my father decided to take her off the machine. I was on an airplane, on my way to Pennsylvania to be with my family. At about 10:50 p.m. that night, while on the plane, I began to weep a little, and must have gone into a light meditative state during this time. While in this state of mind, and in my mind's eye, I saw my mother. She was wearing a pale blue nightgown, and was walking across a theatre stage from left to right. The theatre had thick velvet curtains and there were clouds of smoke around her ankles. Suddenly, the words 'Now I can rest' popped into my mind. I felt a kiss on my forehead. An incredible sense of peace filled me, and I felt as if I no longer needed to fear death. I remember coming out of this state of mind, wiping my tears away, and looking at my watch. It was 11:10 p.m. — twenty minutes had passed. When I arrived at the hospital and told my family about what happened, they told me that they had gathered around my mother's hospital bed, telling her it was all right to 'go' and for her to 'go find' me (Kaylee) and my sister, Kimberly, who was in Oklahoma City and could not come to Pennsylvania. My younger sister told me that as Mom took her last breath that she had looked at my father's watch to note the time. It was about 11:08 p.m., meaning that Mom 'found' me within minutes of her physical passing."

The purpose of this contact was clearly not to comfort our participant but to answer a concrete question that seemed to preoccupy the deceased:

"The most dramatic one was the evening a friend fell and was in the hospital when he appeared in front of my desk where I was working. I looked up and saw Colin. I spoke first and said, 'Colin?' He responded: 'Do you know what happened to me?' I explained that he had fallen and hurt his head and was in the hospital. Then I said, 'Colin, if you are here talking to me, you must have died.' He said, 'I just wanted to know what happened to me,' and he disappeared."

The following visual ADC has initiated a personal search for spiritual meaning:

"My son Enrique died in an accident on 28 December 2012. He was a very special, much loved boy. Needless to say, we were devastated, lost in time and space... I was not a religious person, and I neither found nor lost my faith. A few days before this event, I continuously felt a presence behind me, even the family cat chased me. He was meowing and behaving strangely, but I didn't care about all that. Since Enrique's death, my house had been in chaos, full of people coming to keep us company for fear that something might happen to us. My husband, my daughter and I had not returned to work. After a month, my husband and daughter went back to work, and I was lying on my bed all day.

The first day I stayed home alone, I woke up around 8 a.m. and saw Enrique standing at the bedroom door looking at me, wearing a T-shirt and a hat he always wore and which were in his wardrobe. I sat up and rubbed my eyes to see if I was hallucinating or dreaming. When I tried to get closer, the figure that was like in a fog started to fade, like it was smoke or something like it. I think I saw him from the waist up. When he disappeared, I turned around and went back to sleep as if nothing had happened, I still don't understand my attitude.

Since that day I have not stopped reading, documenting myself and researching everything related to life after death. It has kept me going and continues to keep me on my feet. The most striking thing is that all those close to him, including his friends, have changed their way of thinking and many are following a spiritual path. I think Enrique wanted to show us the way."

A deferred farewell is the subject of the following testimony:

"I was 13 years old. I used to walk the same way every day. As a 'good deed of the day', I used to go and greet a very old neighbour in his wheelchair. I hadn't seen him for a while. It was winter. One spring afternoon I was very happy to see him and to greet him. I greeted him and he answered. When I got home, I told my mother about it. She asked me, surprised, who I was talking about. I told her I was talking about the old man, the one with the wheelchair, the plaid blanket over his legs and the beret. My mother said, 'That man died in winter.'"

During this ADC, surprise quickly gave way to joy:

"My husband, who had died a week before, appeared to me very clearly in the morning when I woke up. I opened my eyes and saw him sitting on the edge of the bed beside me, looking radiant. Surprised but not at all frightened, I said to him a little stupidly 'but then you are not dead?'... and he disappeared at once. I was stunned but with a feeling of great happiness. It's been two years now and the memory of his 'real' (3D) image is intact."

The ADC described in the next account occurred 18 years after the death of the perceived deceased. This is rather unusual. Approximately half of experiences occur within a year of death, with a high concentration in the first 24 hours and up to seven days after the passing. Other contacts occur with decreasing frequency from two to five years after death. Contacts that happen later, sometimes even decades after death, are rarer and often serve to warn experients of impending danger. These experiences are referred to as "ADC for protection".

"ADC 18 years after my father's passing: it's 6 a.m. on a Saturday, I have to get up early to go to a week-end training course. As I get out of bed I instinctively look in front of me and see my father. I know that this is not a figment of my imagination, nor is it linked to any particular emotion (18 years since his death). I also feel his presence very strongly in addition to this vision. He is dressed in a garment that, by the way, I did not like when he was alive, and he smiles at me with a smile I have never seen on him when he was alive: a joyful and peaceful radiance at the same time. This vision is like the vision of a hologram, if you will, that is to say in 3D and not like an image or a photo. It is also in transparency. Following this vision, I will get scared. I will get up from the bed while telling my father to leave. His presence will still be there, but his vision in front of the window will be gone. I experienced it as a way of telling me that he was there, but also and above all as another 'farewell' from him before going to other planes of consciousness where it is more difficult to have contact with a deceased person (even through a medium). That's the feeling I got from it."

The next experience occurred upon awakening, in that particular state between sleep and wakefulness:

"Shortly after my partner's death, I fell asleep on the sofa. When I opened my eyes, there she was sitting next to me. She was looking at me with a smile, maybe for a second, but I was sure that she had been there longer, that she was watching over me, her presence was almost physical."

The following account, written with a touch of humor, illustrates the naturalness with which our respondent welcomed her perception, which did not fit at all with her belief system:

"My grandmother appeared in my car (I was alone), while I was driving. I sensed her and 'saw' her. I knew that it was not a material body and that I could not touch her because she was like transparent. However (I am a down to earth person!), I took my handbag off the seat (I put my hand through 'her body', apologizing, just in case...) so she could sit comfortably! While I was driving, I was glancing at her from time to time, grandmother was looking at the road. She was wearing a dress and a black coat, her glasses, and a handbag was on her lap. At the traffic lights I got a long look at her. She turned her head to look at me too, without smiling. I was not afraid, despite the situation... It's strange, but I thought it was normal that she was there with me. I was wondering about 'why are you here' and not at all about 'how are you here'. And yet I am a scientist by training and an atheist to boot. The light turned green, I restarted and my grandmother left a hundred metres further on. I thought to myself, 'Gosh, I didn't talk to her' ... I thought she had come to tell me something grave, or to fetch someone close, but everything went on normally after that event."

The deceased can be perceived either partially (head and bust) or in their entirety, with a scale of sharpness.
A majority of our participants perceived the deceased in their entirety.

- Whole body: 60%
- Only upper part of body: 25%
- Only lower part of body: 1%
- Unsure: 2%
- Other: 12%

Following are a few illustrations on this subject:

"My Uncle who had passed over a number of years before appeared at the bottom of my bed. I could only see him from his waist up. He appeared younger than when he died and he told me, as far as I could remember, not to worry and that everything would work out."

"He appeared whole, but I could not really tell because I was sitting at my desk and could not see all of him below the level of the desk."

"I saw his image almost completely... up to his knees. From the knees to the feet, the image faded."

"As a whole, but without seeing the face."

"Just his head surrounded by smoke."

"Bust with a kind of mist in place of the legs."

The most unexpected places can be the setting for an ADC:

"My best friend from high school had suddenly died one day. (We were now about ten years out of high school.) He suddenly died one day while I happened to be on vacation. I had received phone calls and learned of his death. I felt terrible that I couldn't travel the 6,000 or so miles home and attend his funeral, but my husband and I were celebrating his one year being cancer free on a vacation in Florida. This best friend of mine by the way had told me several years before how much he loved me and always had... but I didn't feel the same and we always remained great friends. At the time of his death, I hadn't seen him in about three or four years. So, while on vacation, I think maybe two or three days after I learned of his death, my husband and I were golfing. I was at the first tee and I kept on swinging and missing. This happened about five times. I am not a golfer! I was very embarrassed because I am sure I looked like an idiot. I wound up to swing one more time and, as I did, I looked to my right and I could literally see with my eyes my best friend, just the upper half of his body. I believe he was standing maybe about 20–30 feet from me watching me swing and miss the golf ball. He was just laughing hysterically at me, in a sweet and friendly way. I knew it was him without a doubt. It was comforting. It was fleeting and he just disappeared. It wasn't scary or eerie. Just, I knew it was him, he was with me, he was there, and then he wasn't. I hadn't been thinking of him at the moment. I wasn't sad or worried at the moment. My focus had been entirely on the golf ball."

Descriptions range from the vision of a vaporous, semi-transparent silhouette that reveals the objects behind it to the perception of a perfectly solid body, and all the stages in between. Sometimes there is a dynamic evolution in perception: a foggy form is perceived first, which solidifies as it passes through the silhouette stage and finally takes the form of a solid person who appears to be alive.

What was the consistency of the deceased as perceived by our participants? A surprisingly high number perceived the deceased as a living person:

- Solid like a living being: 62%
- Semi-transparent: 13%
- Foggy silhouette: 11%
- Unsure: 15%

The narratives to follow describe the different stages of materialization of the perceived deceased. I present a range of accounts as our participants had quite varied perceptions, starting with cases where the deceased was perceived to be fairly solid:

"Normal, I saw him as if he were alive."

"He was solid, but airy, as if he was very light, and he also seemed a little smaller and thinner."

"I don't think he appeared solid, but he was very close to that because when I looked up, he looked just like he always did."

"She looked human but not solid like a living being."

"I saw him in its entirety very precisely, he was not transparent but did not give off a feeling of solidity."

"Shortly after my father's death I was gardening near the large central lawn. I clearly saw and recognized my father. He was standing on the lawn, looking as young as he did in my childhood. He was about two or three meters away from me. He was pale grey, a bit like smoke, but perfectly recognizable. This apparition lasted a fraction of a second, the time it took to see him and not to see him anymore."

"I know it was him! He was behind me while I was working... he moved forward, he had the figure of a man, but his body had no details, he was like milky, milky white and dense with some dark parts."

"Semi-transparent... misty... in the form of a hologram... or of a liquid that tries to materialize."

"Bust with a kind of mist in place of the legs. I saw a figure, but her head was turned away, as if I was not to identify her."

"A shadow but perfectly recognizable."

"It was a spectral figure... without consistency."

This short description of the consistency of the perceived deceased is interesting, as the participant differentiates between her inner feeling (what she perceived in her mind) and her visual perception (what she saw with her eyes), which are not identical:

"In my mind she was clear, but just a shadow with my eyes."

This is another good example of the different degrees of materialization described by experients, who typically instantly identify the object of their perception:

"It was the night before my sister's funeral in 2000. I was walking into my en suite and looking at my reflection in the mirror which faced the door. Directly behind me, I CLEARLY saw a column of what I can only describe as crushed tissue paper, in dark greys, mid greys and white. Now I think about it, it was something about light refracting off this energy which gave it the perceived shades or colour. I wasn't at all afraid, but when I spun around to get a good look at it, it stayed in front of me in my room for a good few seconds. Long enough for me to see that it was so tall it appeared to disappear through the ceiling. I knew instantly that this was my sister, or her energy, and it had a sad feeling (she had left behind a 15-year-old son and a 16-year-old daughter). From this moment I knew that all other instances, voices, dreams and visions I'd had throughout my life were real and life doesn't end here, but goes on. Even though I was sad to lose my sister, this event changed my life and gave me immeasurable peace."

The next testimony is noteworthy for several reasons. Firstly, the participant perceived two deceased simultaneously, which is rather rare. In addition, she "knew" that the unknown deceased accompanying her late father was the father of her companion, without having known him while he was alive. In fact, it appears from many testimonies that the identification of the deceased seems to be immediate, without any possible doubt, as if this identification was more in the range of *knowing* rather than of perceiving.

"My father's vision was semi-transparent. He was accompanied by the deceased father of my then new companion. His dad had died 30 years earlier. I didn't know him. I knew it was him, though, and was able to verify it on [a] photo later."

The testimony to follow is interesting because the visual perception of the deceased was preceded by specific and rather unusual physical sensations:

"Spontaneous-direct experience. 9-7-2009, 9 p.m. approx. I was in the house of my friend and neighbour Emilia. We grew up together since we were three years old. On 9th July at 6 p.m., her mother, Laura, had passed away after being bedridden for months with a broken hip. While Laura was alive, we had a very close relationship. Just as Emilia spent a lot of time at my home, I was often at their house. But from 2007 until the date of her death, we had a closer relationship. Laura was a missionary of the *Virgen de Schoenstatt* and because of my more spiritually committed activity, our faith led us to share moments of prayer. On that July 9th, at Emilia's house, one of her cousins and I stayed with her. It was about 9 p.m. when I decided to go home. From the moment I got up... my legs became numb, and a kind of magnetic current prevented me from moving and forced me to sit down again. I started to feel hot, the heat got in my face and I had to take off the jumper I was wearing. Emilia and her cousin looked at me for a moment and continued their conversation. Suddenly, my gaze went to a corner of the dining room where we were, and I saw a kind of mist in which appeared the figure of Laura with a smiling face. The image in color, although somewhat blurred, showed Laura in her usual attire. At that moment, Emilia and her cousin were crying. At that very instant, in a mixture of voice and thoughts, Laura's words came to my mind: 'I'm fine... they should stop crying... I'm fine... thanks for everything... I'm fine.' After the few seconds that this message lasted, first the image of Laura disappeared, then the mist. The heat in me went down and my legs relaxed. I noticed that Emilia and her cousin were looking at me, it was as if time had stopped. They asked me if I was okay and I told them what had happened."

This account describes a semi-transparent but nonetheless clearly recognizable apparition:

"After going to the cemetery with my mother to visit my grandfather's grave, I visited the grave of a girl my age who had recently died. After that, I went home as usual, still accompanied by my mother. In the evening, around 10 p.m., I went to bed as I do every night. Except that when I wanted to turn over to sleep, I saw this deceased girl, all white, lying next to me. She was almost transparent, but her facial features were clear and precise. She was like a reflection, a kind of veil."

One of our respondents felt that she was going through the apparition of her deceased husband:

"Eight days after my husband drowned, he appeared to me in our bedroom (I should point out that I was not sleeping). He held out his arms to me, I felt a force and I did the same. I then felt as if I was being 'propelled' towards him and I was passing through his body as ghosts are represented as passing through walls. I felt at that moment an extreme gentleness, no word in the dictionary to express this gentleness, it was fabulous, and I also felt Unconditional Love. I remember feeling like I was falling back onto the bed. I realised then that he had come to say goodbye. It was the most extraordinary experience of my life."

This respondent reports a similar experience:

"I felt him pass through me, within me and around me. I had to hold on to a wall and he let me know it was him. It was love, comfort and peace as he left this world and moved through me on his way. It was his goodbye and he wrapped me in his love and left this within me as the last thing he did for me."

Were the participants' eyes closed during the visual ADC? Were they in a state of relaxation or daydreaming that could have facilitated the emergence of mental images?

It turns out that the majority had their eyes open when they saw the apparition.

- **60% had their eyes open, 9% were unsure, and 31% had their eyes closed**

Respondents were asked about the position of the apparition in relation to them:

- In the center of my vision (in front of me): 74%
- In the periphery of my vision (at my side): 22%
- Unsure: 4%

This report describes an apparition perceived at the periphery of vision:

"I lost my mother when I was 21 years old. It was a real suffering for me. I never accepted this sudden departure, even though I had given her permission to leave and not to suffer anymore (intensive care). I then lost a little girl at birth, the twin of my youngest and that was also a very heart-breaking event, she was mentally handicapped. One afternoon, while I was doing the dishes, I was alone with my last one, who was only a few months old and sleeping upstairs. There was no particular noise. I was relaxed, busy doing the dishes, and then, I don't know, out of the corner of my eye, I saw a shape, felt that I was being watched and turned around. It was my mum holding my little one in her arms, as if she was telling me that everything was fine, that she was looking after her, that I shouldn't worry. It lasted for a second... I went back to doing the dishes, a bit disoriented."

Our respondent described the nature of this peripheral vision he had of his deceased grandmother:

"I only saw her out of the corner of my eye, too elusive to define it clearly, as if it were a distortion in the visual field, like when you watch the layers of warm air rise and the image is distorted in that area, but I never saw her directly, never."

At what distance was the apparition? For the majority of respondents, the apparition was close to them.

- Within reaching distance: 62%
- Several meters away: 33%
- In the distance: 3%
- Unsure: 3%

Was the apparition moving or static?

- Completely motionless: 19%
- Quite static: 29%
- Moving about the environment: 30%
- Quite animated (gesticulating): 16%
- Unsure: 6%

Apparitions in motion are depicted in these reports:

"He simply walked from one side to the other, until he disappeared behind a door where I could no longer see him."

"He simply left by walking through a door."

"He disappeared when he went through the wall..."

"Six years ago, when I woke up from a nap (I don't know what woke me up), I looked at the door of my room and saw my deceased father enter the room. I saw his whole body, not just part of it. He was standing and he was moving. I saw him take a step into the room and look inside. He had exactly the same attitude as when he was alive. He was holding his hands behind his back and you could see in his eyes that he was discovering the place (he had never been there in his lifetime). He was not hesitant, just there. He was wearing clothes that belonged to him. The action, the vision, was slow like a freeze frame and yet I know it was very brief (three seconds maximum). The time to realize that it was him and then nothing. He made no noise, there was no particular smell."

The following accounts describe in more detail how the apparitions moved:

"Shortly after being widowed, probably a month or two after her transition in 2002, I sat at home one evening thinking about her when she materialised in front of me in the form of her figure from head to shins (the lower portion with her feet wasn't visible). The form looked like it was made out of glass filled with smoke and she moved through the living room into the back room where we used to spend time together. She moved as though on roller skates and 'glided' through furniture going into the back room. I had recently re-arranged the furniture layout and it appeared she was using the path around the old furniture layout present when she was here. She appeared twice within several minutes, then disappeared. I kept calling out her name but she didn't turn around or stop but kept moving into the back room."

"When I was a child (about ten years old), I saw a deceased person walking as if floating and crossing a wall. His appearance was normal even though I could not perceive his face in detail. What amazed me was the way he moved and disappeared through this wall. It was somewhat disturbing, although I felt that he was not trying to scare me."

According to the experients, the apparitions are sometimes surrounded by light. We asked our respondents if the deceased seemed brighter than their surroundings, in other words, if a light surrounded them or emanated from them. This was the case for just over a third of our case collection.

- **For 35% the apparition was surrounded by light, 11% were unsure, and for 54% the apparition was not surrounded by light**

Here are some examples of such apparitions:

"He looked quite solid but he was very pale and mainly iridescent. There was a slight luminescence all around his figure."

"The deceased was haloed by a very white light."

"A dark figure because the light came from behind him."

"Like a living person but with an aura of light around him."

"It was a luminous form."

"His face, arms and hands were very clear, but his shoulders, torso and pelvis were blurred by the white light."

"He seemed solid, surrounded by light."

"I saw my deceased husband at the foot of my bed. It was a luminous form, just the illuminated upper body, and I felt a lot of joy."

This contact, reinforced by the experience of two acquaintances, took place under anesthesia during an operation, when — according to all logic — the respondent should not have been able to perceive anything:

"I received a visit from my deceased wife, in July 2013, ten months after her passing in October 2012, while unconscious under anaesthetic on the operating table for a gall bladder removal in 2012, a year after her passing. At the age of her passing she was 71 years of age. In her visit she appeared younger in age, serene, composed, beautiful, youthful, happy, smiling, full of love and compassion. She was bathed in a gold and white light. The vision was magnificent in its clarity. She assured me with a loving smile that she was 'alright' and that 'things were wonderful on this side' and that 'I would be alright too and had no need to worry'. The experience was timeless, beautifully intense, deep, blissful, full of love. I have no idea how long it lasted. One second, one minute, five minutes — seems irrelevant. When I woke up, or recovered consciousness, I felt incredibly relaxed and had full recollection of the experience. I felt that I had experienced heaven. This intensely relaxed state stayed with me for several days during which time I initially assumed that the wonderful experience might be drug induced (the anaesthetic). In the months that followed, the magnificence and intensity of the experience remained, but I researched as much as possible with medical people, hypnotherapists and the like to try to determine if there was a drug induced explanation which caused the experience. I could find no such explanation. Around the same time as my experience, my dentist (who had treated my wife shortly before her passing) and a very close lady friend of my wife independently advised me, both in a somewhat 'shaken' (for want of a better word) state, that they had been 'visited by my deceased wife' asking that 'they would look after Matt' (that's me) and she told them that she was alright. This happened around the same time that I had my deceased wife's 'visit'. This information came independently from me and was instigated by my dentist and my wife's friend and was not a response to any question I had asked. Now, some five years later, I feel blessed that I have had this very real experience. I have only to recall it to go into an immediate relaxed and peaceful state. It has been a life changer and I have no doubt that I have experienced an after-death communication from my beloved wife and had glimpsed at the other side that I can only describe as heaven."

The perception of this ball of light occurred at a significant moment in the life of our respondent:

"It was May 2015, about a month before my second marriage; my mom had died two years prior. I was crying and spoke to her aloud to say how much I missed her. Then I saw a bright ball of light all around my room, and was able to capture photos with my cell phone. I tested afterward to see if it was some kind of environmental anomaly, but when I tried taking photos after, the ball of light was gone it was not there again. Never happened since then. I strongly feel it was my mother."

This testimony also describes a light, but one that has turned into a recognizable face as the experience unfolded:

"I was awake, lying in bed, thinking about the activities awaiting me that day. Suddenly, with my eyes closed, I noticed a pinpoint of yellow light toward the upper right of my vision field. I thought, 'What's that? Is something wrong with my eyes?' As I calmly and inquisitively watched, the tiny point of light seemed to be coming right at me, slowly getting bigger as it came closer. As it increased in size, I realized that there was something inside the ever-increasing ball of yellow light. I couldn't make out what it was but as it grew larger, I realized it looked to be a face, head, but it was too small to see clearly. It continued to get closer to me and bigger, until I could make out the face inside. 'Mom!' I said out loud as I recognized the face of my deceased mother. And in that second of recognition, it abruptly disappeared."

Additional questions allowed us to deepen the knowledge of visual ADCs.

Did the deceased appear to be the same age as when he/she died?

- Same age: 52%
- Younger: 32%
- Older: 1%
- Unsure: 16%

The deceased are sometimes seen in the prime of life and in excellent health, regardless of the age they were on the day of their death and the illness that may have marked their faces. They may choose to show themselves as they were at a happy and carefree time in their life, far from the old age and illness that would arise later in life. They would have this freedom if it were assumed that they would manifest themselves to the living by creating an image of their choice.

In many cases, the loved one was last seen at the time of death if family and friends were present, or later at the funeral. It is a sad image to keep in one's heart. Visual ADCs can sometimes replace this last distressing memory with a new, beautiful and soothing image.

The data we collected support this hypothesis. Slightly more than half of the respondents said that the deceased significant other looked different from the way he or she looked at the time of death.

- Different appearance: 55%
- Same appearance: 18%
- Unsure: 7%
- Other: 20%

Our participants shared their perceptions, starting with cases where the deceased were perceived to be younger than they were at the time of their demise:

"Although she died at age 82, in the vision I saw her as I had known her in her 30's, radiantly healthy."

"It was lunch-time, I was in the kitchen talking to my daughter. Suddenly I saw through the window in the garden my husband who had died seven months ago from cancer. He looked younger than at the time of his death, which did not correspond to a memory as I had known him only since he was 50. In this appearance, it looks like he only wanted to show the best part of him. He was very thin and he still had hair (which he had lost due to his illness). It was very quick and I did not really see his face, all I noticed was he was quite static. I was extremely shocked and my heart was beating very fast."

"Three weeks after my husband passed, I woke up early one morning to find him sitting on the bed looking 30 years younger than he did when he passed. He was solid, smiling and happy. Before he passed, we had an agreement that whoever passed first would let the other know that there was an afterlife."

"I saw my deceased husband exactly one week after he passed away. He was standing in the doorway of our bedroom wearing a dark blue sweatshirt and dark blue sweatpants. His hair was black like it was when he was younger. He didn't say anything and was gone within a minute."

"The night my grandfather died, I was lying on my bed ready to go to sleep, when he appeared above me, parallel to me. He was in either a shroud or a pristine white light. What surprised me most subsequently was his face. He was young, he looked to be about forty years old. He was very handsome and looked deeply into my eyes. I could hear in my mind that I should not be sad because he was very happy. I felt like he was in heaven."

This ADC reminded our participant of a bygone era:

"He passed in Viet Nam, but he and his friends were dressed in a suit and what struck me 25 years later was that he was wearing the skinny ties the guys wore in the '60s. He passed in 1966. I had forgotten that piece of fashion until I saw him."

Injuries and physical handicaps are erased in these materializations:

"His face was the same as the one he had just before he was murdered (he was shot in the head)."

"I knew him as a lame man after an accident, and after his death I saw him walking normally."

How do the experients manage to identify the apparition? One could imagine that the deceased materialize in such a way that their family and friends can recognize them more easily, for example by wearing their favorite clothes and behaving in a habitual manner. This was indeed the case for a majority of the participants:

- **For 76% the deceased was immediately familiar to them, 7% were unsure, and for 17% they were not immediately familiar**

The following testimony illustrates this point perfectly:

"A few months after my husband's death, as I was leaving the jewellery store where I worked, I recognized my husband at the end of the street. He was walking towards me, with his quiet step, I recognized his long, slim figure (1.93m). At that moment already, I was sure it was him, we were married for 35 years. Then when I looked more closely, I noticed that he was carrying his coat as he used to do to keep his hands free. He folded his coat in half and put it on his left shoulder. I have never met anyone with that habit! So, this detail deeply disturbed me... I was stunned... Without hurrying, he entered a ladies' fashion shop. At that moment, I wanted to know for sure, I ran the short distance and entered the shop. Two customers were in the shop, and two saleswomen who assured me that they had never seen this tall man with the coat enter...! The coat is an important detail in this testimony. It was a habit, a bit strange, that he had taken in winter in France, in Annecy, when we lived there. But we left France for Florida. My husband died eight years after we arrived in the USA. In our little town in Florida, the coat was of course not necessary, the weather is nice all year round!"

I give the floor to our respondents for further descriptions:

"Looked as she did when I last saw her. She was wearing her favourite London Fog trench coat."

"He looked as he did in life; however, he was wearing the shirt he had on the night he died. I was so happy to see him I almost dropped my cup of tea. It was totally unexpected and was a month or so after his passing."

"He looked normally alive and was wearing a light grey 'leisure suit' that I'd bought him years before he died."

"She was sitting at her sister's desk, looking out the window. It took me days to realize she was wearing the clothes she had on when she died. This took place in the middle of the day."

"Saw my mother-in-law one year after she passed; saw her with her beloved dress and smelled her perfume very strongly, even after she vanished."

Occurrence and disappearance of visual ADCs

The *occurrence* of apparitions can take various forms:

1. The experient wakes up or is awakened at night by the apparition standing in front of him, e.g. at the foot of his bed;
2. The apparition is already present when the awake experient suddenly becomes aware of it;
3. The apparition is in motion and enters the experient's field of vision (e.g. a door opens and the apparition enters and moves around the room);
4. The apparition materializes in front of the experient's eyes, suddenly or gradually. Sometimes it is perceived as fog that suddenly takes shape and becomes recognizable.

The *disappearance* of the apparition is more abrupt than its occurrence. Experients use verbs such as: to evaporate, to disappear all at once, to dissolve, to dematerialize, to fade away, to vanish. All it takes is a blink of an eye or looking away for a fraction of a second and the apparition is gone. In the case of the perception of unknown deceased persons, the experients took them for real people until their dazzling disappearance made them understand that it was in fact an apparition.

We asked the respondents how the deceased had appeared to them. For a majority, the deceased were already present when they saw them, and for a minority, they materialized right before their eyes.

- **For 60% the apparition was already there when they saw it, for 29% it materialized before their eyes, and 12% were unsure**

After a few seconds, or a few minutes at most, the perception ends. We asked how the deceased had disappeared.

- Fading gradually: 14%
- Dissolving instantly: 28%
- Not there anymore when I blinked: 18%
- Unsure: 11%
- Other: 29%

The next reports refer to the way in which the perceived deceased had disappeared:

"About 12 hours after our son's death I saw his face (just his neck and face) appear sideways in a bedroom. He spoke to me and said, 'Don't be angry, don't be mad.' It was him in the room with me and he slowly faded away."

"She turned into bright white light as she started to vanish."

"My grandfather gradually faded away and turned into white smoke."

"One night, five months to the day after my father's death (the day before my birthday), while I was awake but with my eyes closed, I felt a presence and opened my eyes. My father, like a hologram image, was standing next to my husband, watching us. He looked very calm. In shock at seeing him, I sat up straight all of a sudden in order to talk to him. This caused him to 'disappear', but gradually."

The descriptions of the disappearance of the perceived deceased are manifold:

"At the time, I did not know who he was... He walked across the dining room and disappeared into a wall."

"I saw her before I ran out of the room, so I don't know when she disappeared."

"I didn't see him disappear because I turned around. I knew he was coming to tell me about a death in the family."

"He was no longer there when I looked in the direction he was at the start. I also got scared and asked him not to appear."

"When I left the room, the deceased was still there."

"Literally moved oddly upwards, not through the doorway or through the wardrobe directly behind it. But upwards and over the thin space between the ceiling and wardrobe. Really quite unlike anything I've ever seen before or since."

The next testimony describes the sudden disappearance of an apparition. As is often the case when unknown deceased persons are perceived, the participant was inconvenienced by this unlikely encounter:

"It was a sunny March in 2010, so, with a dear friend I'll call Pedro C., we decided to meet and the setting turned out to be a bar 'hidden between the streets'. Everything was going on as usual, when at one point I went to the toilet, completely unaware of what was going to happen... While I was washing my hands, to my right was a stall without a door, where there was a man standing and staring towards his feet. So far, I didn't notice anything unusual, but the strange thing was that this man remained completely still, with total indifference to my presence. But unexpectedly, I witnessed a surprising event, as this person suddenly faded away, disappearing completely from my sight in a fleeting manner... It should be noted that I experienced a feeling of strangeness and perplexity in my whole being, without understanding what had happened. Instinctively, I directed my outstretched arm towards the place in question, but obviously my hand met nothing but emptiness inside the cabin. Faced with this, I refrained from talking about this disturbing experience; the time will come to analyze it in depth, but later."

The following participant offers an explanation for the sudden disappearance of an apparition:

"I remember that a short time ago, I saw two or three times a person walking behind me and disappearing when he came up to my level. It was as if I was a boundary wall to that presence. This person or presence was unknown to me."

As with tactile ADCs, some participants reported that during the visual ADC they had a physical contact with the deceased and felt resistance or matter:

"I felt her 'physically'. She had substance."

"I ran my right index finger along her right cheek. It was warm and solid."

"We embraced (hugged). It was real. I could feel his warmth and his arms around me so tight."

"I felt his hand as it was when he was alive: the softness, the warmth, the tenderness of his skin and... the love he exuded."

"Just after his death, the first time, he held my arms, not wanting to believe he was dead. I was in shock at his apparition and the physical contact. I tried to free myself from his grip but I couldn't, he held me tightly."

"It was her who touched me, the movement came from her and I remember a sensation as if she had been in the flesh. This does not coincide with the image where she is in white but 'transparent' and so this material touch seems surprising to me in retrospect, but yet it was very real."

For some, the attempt to grab the deceased proved difficult:

"I felt him touching me but it was like an energy that I couldn't grab hold of."

"It was as though grabbing at wax; it wasn't a human feeling but still discernible as almost solid."

"I could touch him, but he was squishy. Like if I grabbed too hard, my hand would go thru him, although we did hold hands."

Interestingly, some participants reported that they could not or were not permitted to seize the deceased:

"I wanted to touch him, but I couldn't, it was like there was an invisible barrier, a veil that prevented me from touching him."

"He jumped out the way making it very clear not to touch him. As our vibrations weren't compatible yet."

"I wanted to touch Dad and I reached for him, but he stepped back from me and said 'no' in a kind way."

Did the experients have the impression that the deceased was conveying a message? This was indeed very largely the case for our respondents. Once again, we notice that the message — the information transmitted — is an essential element of ADCs, regardless of the type of contact.

- **For 80% the apparition conveyed a message, 9% were unsure, and for 12% no message perceived**

How was the message conveyed?

- In words I could hear (like a conversation among living persons): 26%
- As if telepathically: 37%
- By the expression of the face: 16%
- Unsure: 7%
- Other: 13%

The experiences of our respondents are multifaceted as illustrated by these testimonies:

"His face expressed concern."

"His presence was the message."

"It's not like listening with physical ears... more like what you might call 'listening with the ears of the soul' ... I could also say it was like a telepathic message, it's not heard but it's as clear as hearing it spoken out loud..."

"He came up to me with a distressed face. I couldn't hear what he said, but I understood that he was very sad that I was so desperate."

"A normal conversation as if they were alive."

"It's both telepathically and by the expression on his face. When I see him, he has a beautiful smile. It took me a while to realize that I was receiving words while his lips were not moving."

"There were those three words 'I love you' that sum it all up and the intense expression of love on the face."

"Two hours after I learned that my 21-year-old son had died in an accident at work, I saw him in the corner of my room saying, 'I love you, Mum. Mum, I love you.' He was insisting and he was a bit panicky because he kept repeating 'I love you, Mum,' leaning forward slightly as if to make himself heard because I was in shock and this vision didn't catch my attention, thinking it was my imagination."

One participant was able to describe precisely how she perceived the message:

> "Words, but which I seemed to filter through my brain, as I had to translate an 'impression' into words as I went along, but, yes, it was clear and precise, even if difficult to describe."

Smelling a fragrance

- **28% smelled a fragrance characteristic of the deceased**

276 of our respondents experienced an olfactory ADC, i.e. a contact during which fragrances associated with a deceased family member or friend appear.

Smelling a fragrance

Olfactory ADC	Men	Women	English dataset	French dataset	Spanish dataset
Yes	23%	29%	26%	30%	29%
No	77%	71%	74%	70%	71%

The following testimonies describe olfactory ADCs:

> "After I received a phone call from the respective doctor at the hospital where my mother died, I rushed to the hospital about 40 km from where I live. When I arrived in the town in which my mother died, the traffic lights turned red and I was forced to stop and wait for a while. There I sensed my mom's spirit: I smelled her. I could smell her presence. It was her unique smell and I knew at that moment that she was in the car visiting me. It wasn't just thinking she was there — it was knowing that she was with me in the car. So, I started crying tears of joy to be able to have her near me again and I spontaneously shouted joyfully:

'Mom, you are here. You are here, Mom, aren't you?' It was an unforgettable experience which led to my intense research about life after death and after-death communication."

"My son died very suddenly whilst we were on holiday, of pulmonary oedema. He was a smoker. Neither my husband nor I smoke. As my husband's job involved having clients in his car, it was a strictly non-smoking zone, usually smelling of air freshener. The day before my son's funeral, we went to the local [...] shop to buy wine, beers etc. for the wake. We loaded our purchases into the back of the car and made our way home. As we neared our house, I was aware of a strong smell of tobacco smoke in the car. My husband is extremely pragmatic, so I didn't mention anything, in case he thought I was imagining it. But when we parked on our drive, my husband remained in his seat, staring ahead. After about ten seconds, the car was engulfed in the smell and my husband asked me if I 'could smell it?' He was due to take my other son and daughter to the funeral parlour to say 'goodbye' later that day, but used my car, as it had unnerved him so much."

"My daughter passed in 2015, and I experienced her through both the sense of smell and touch. Starting the night after she passed, every night for at least 14 days I would smell a strong fragrance of flowers when I would lie down at night. It was so pronounced that I always inquired if my husband could smell them... he never smelled them. During this same time frame, I could feel her presence in our home and in the car. I had the sense of my hair being touched around the crown of my head (enough to make me turn and look behind me). Interestingly, her dog would seem to be looking at her just behind me or at the top of the stairs."

"Whilst sitting alone in my lounge watching TV, I smelt the distinct perfume my sister always favoured, which was

'Poison'. Unmistakable scent and I didn't have any in the house. I knew immediately she was there with me despite not being able to see her."

The following account is yet another example illustrating that the means of expression of the ADC — in this case the perceived smell of alcohol — are only the medium for the *emotions* felt, or even supposedly transmitted by the deceased. In other words, the message is inherent in the contact itself. However, we do not know whether the deceased communicated his own state of mind — a feeling of well-being, gentleness and peace — or whether the contact triggered these emotions in the participant:

"At home, as often happens to me in a little bluesy moment, I talk intensely to my partner, sitting with his picture in front of me. Then I pull myself together, go about my normal business, without thinking about him. And about 30 minutes later, I walk past a chair on the outside balcony where he used to sit, I smell a very, very strong odour of alcohol! My partner was an alcoholic. I really took a good look around me, but there was no one there. The smell only lasted a few seconds, but afterwards I was really carried away by a feeling of well-being, gentleness and peace. It was really impressive; I'll never forget it. I felt really good."

These olfactory ADCs occurred over a long period of time, with an intensification in a difficult period for the participant:

"My nan had a very specific scent that lingered in her house. There were at least four occasions over the first few months of her death where her scent would appear within an area of our home. It would last for about 20 seconds, but sometimes longer. It would then occur periodically over the next few years before becoming more prevalent six years later when my husband and I were going through a divorce."

The fragrances smelled are representative of the person's life. They can relate to their activities or their preferences. For example, experients can smell a scent that immediately transports them in their mind to the deceased's kitchen when she was baking her famous apple pie, just as they can smell the odor of the hospital room where their grandfather spent the last weeks of his life.

Fragrances often mentioned are those of a perfume, an aftershave lotion or a characteristic body odor, but the range of reported fragrances is wide. They can be flowers, but also food, drinks, tobacco, etc. Fragrances appear suddenly, for no apparent reason and out of context, indoors or outdoors, without any source being detectable. After a few seconds or a few minutes at the most, the fragrances dissolve.

Here are some examples of perceived fragrances:

"The smell of my parents' home mixed with a hint of her perfume — 'Mum'."

"It was a musty scent that was synonymous with Nan's home and clothes."

"The smell of my father's pipe."

"My father was a carpenter, I smelled sawdust."

"My father was a beekeeper. When he died, we inherited the family property, around which there were major property problems. I solved these problems so that I could put the house up for sale. The night after the sale was confirmed, I was awakened by a smell that stung my nose. When I was fully awake, I identified that smell. It was the one I smelled in the room where my father made his honey, a beeswax scent that I love. And at home I don't have any candles or furniture wax or anything that has that scent."

Sometimes the fragrances are indefinable because they simply correspond to the unique odor of the person, to no other comparable:

"It was just my mum's natural smell."

"A soft fragrance very characteristic of her. It was not her habit to wear perfume. There was a sweet scent emanating from her that I smelled every time she hugged me and that also permeated her clothes."

"A few days after my son's death, I felt the presence of his smell, as if someone was surrounding me."

And occasionally fragrances are linked to a significant location:

"It was the smell of the hospital room where she passed."

The testimony to follow nicely describes a set of perceptions, perceived by different sensory organs, leading to a coherent and peaceful experience:

"When at my Grandma's house, a few weeks after my Gramps's death, I sat in the living room on my own. My Grandma was in the kitchen making a sandwich. I was reading the newspaper when I experienced a strong smell of cigarettes — roll ups. My Gramps used to smoke roll ups. I absorbed the fact that I could smell the smoke and didn't register that I shouldn't be able to (my Grandma didn't smoke). I then heard whistling. My Gramps always whistled whenever he was busy doing something. Again, I didn't really register that I shouldn't be able to hear whistling.

The living room door, which had been completely shut (to keep the warm in), then opened fully. I looked up, fully expecting my Grandma to walk in, but she didn't. Instead, my Gramps walked in. I didn't see him in the physical form, but I felt him there — that feeling you get when someone walks into a room behind you; you don't see them but you know they're there. He crossed the living room to his chair and the smell of cigarettes grew stronger. He then disappeared, as did the smell and any sense of anyone being there."

This participant has perceived two contacts, one year apart:

"Three days after my dad had passed. I was in my bedroom 250 miles away. And just smelt him so strongly. My dad was a smoker and a bit of a drinker too. I'm neither. I don't believe I was even thinking of him at that particular moment. I was busy tidying, collecting washing, etc. Then I could just smell him, but only in one area of the bedroom. I was checking all around to see if the smell was everywhere, but it wasn't. It lasted for about 30–40 seconds. Then went. There were no windows open or anyone in the house who smoked. Besides it had a very specific smell, which was just like my dad. About one year later, I was at work. I work in a high school. I was walking down the corridor, lessons were on, so the corridor was quiet. Once again, I wasn't thinking of anything except the task I was doing. I walked around the coy corner and there was my dad. He appeared slightly translucent but looking exactly the same. He just smiled at me. I blinked and he was gone. It wasn't scary or upsetting, it felt like a confirmation that he was OK."

The following testimony describes a shift in the respondent's feelings during the contact, evolving from a state of sadness to a feeling of happiness:

"Months after my grandmother's death, I could not get over her loss. I often smelled her fragrance like a soft breeze on my face. At first, I felt like crying, but then the fragrance was accompanied by a feeling of happiness."

The olfactory ADCs described in the next narrative occurred over an unusually long period of time, with significant frequency. Did the widow have to recognize these odors as a message from her late husband for them to cease?

"My dad loved coffee, but when he was alive he couldn't drink it because he had liver disease. After he died, for 9 months, once or twice a week, in the early morning (5–6 a.m.), there was a smell of freshly brewed coffee in the house... for over an hour... I thought my mum who was sleeping downstairs smelled it too and knew it was 'Dad coming to make his coffee'. After nine months, when I went to wake her up in the morning, I said to her: 'Did you smell it? Daddy came to make his coffee again early this morning!' My mum was surprised. She said: 'Yes, I could smell it, but I couldn't identify it... now you tell me it's coffee! That's it! Yes, it's Dad!' Once Mum understood, it never happened again."

The following case is strikingly similar to the previous testimony: once again, the odors recurred very frequently and for a long time, and only ceased on the day the deceased's supposed wish was fulfilled:

"My mother passed away when I was pregnant with my first (and only) baby. It was very difficult to get over her death because we were very close. Some time after my son was born, I started to smell cigarettes, especially at night. It was so strong that it woke me up! But my husband didn't smell anything. I knew it was my mother because she smoked a lot. This happened for several months until we went to my mother's house (where they had already told me they had seen her spirit). Since the day we went to her house, the smell of cigarettes stopped waking me up, and the person who saw her spirit in her house called me two or three days later to tell me that she was 'gone'. Maybe she just wanted us to take her grandson to her home? It was impactful!"

A meaningful fragrance was perceived simultaneously by a couple and their young child on several occasions:

"Afterwards, I had the feeling that she was close to me. I didn't see her, ever, but my wife and I smelled her perfume, and my two-year-old son would sometimes point to a particular spot in the room and say hello, or he would smile, as if someone was playing with him. I don't know if it was my grandmother or another relative, but it happened often."

In the next account, our respondent was the only one to perceive the olfactory contact, although she was in the company of others:

"Mum died on 8 November. In December, with my sister, we had a personalized plaque made to put on her grave. It was my sister who collected the plaque. We took it out of its box at my father's house. All three of us were very emotional. As I unwrapped the plaque, the scent of mum stopped me dead in my tracks. I knew she was there with the three of us. Neither my father nor my sister smelled Mum's scent, that scent of perfume she had when she died in my arms."

This event was considered by the respondent as a support in a stressful situation:

"I'm driving home from a meeting and I don't like driving at night, it makes me anxious. Suddenly, I have this feeling of a presence in the car on the passenger seat next to me. I smell cigarettes (I've had my car for 11 years and no one has ever smoked in it) and soon after, like a feeling of being hugged. All this followed by a renewed energy to drive into the night with the conviction that Mum is with me in the car."

A majority of participants felt that the deceased was conveying a message to them through this fragrance.

- **60% perceived a message, 21% were unsure, and 20% did not perceive a message**

Let's have the respondents elaborate on their thoughts:

"Felt our son was assuring us he was still around and helping us through the dread of his funeral."

"Just a way of letting us know he was visiting."

"He wanted to let us know he was with us at the restaurant when I had dinner with his kids."

"I felt as if she was trying to make contact to let me know that she was OK and still near, as well as trying to bring me comfort."

"Letting me know he had survived the death of his physical body. Giving me personal proof."

"To comfort me. To show 'I am here. Nobody's really gone'."

"At that time, I was very sad about the death of my husband and I was weeping for him for a long time. When I noticed his odour, I stopped crying immediately and became calm. That was his message."

ADC during sleep

- **62% experienced an ADC during sleep**

618 participants had an ADC during sleep, when falling asleep or waking up.

ADC during sleep

Sleep ADC	Men	Women	English dataset	French dataset	Spanish dataset
Yes	52%	64%	63%	58%	72%
No	48%	36%	37%	42%	28%

There are three types of sleep ADCs:

1. Contacts that occur while the experients are asleep, but which they distinguish very clearly from an ordinary dream;
2. Contacts that take place when falling asleep, during what scientists call a hypnagogic state,[16] or upon waking, in a hypnopompic state;[17]
3. Contacts which wake up the experients. Once awake, their experience falls into one of the other categories: ADC of sensing a presence, tactile, visual, auditory, or olfactory ADCs. More than half of our respondents (52%) were awakened by the ADC.

The following account demonstrates the perfectly realistic quality of ADCs during sleep:

"About five/six months after my grandmother passed away, I had an experience while sleeping. I went into my parents' house where my grandmother lived long before they moved in, and there I saw my grandmother, smiling, sitting on the sofa in the living room. It was very strange, because I knew and was aware at the time that she had passed away, but there she was, as real as if I were meeting someone face to face. She stood up and hugged me and I felt the warmth and touch of her skin. She looked at me and said she knew I loved her, that I shouldn't worry (unfortunately I hadn't been able to say goodbye like I would have liked to). After that I woke up, but it was a strange feeling, I very rarely have any notion of what I had dreamt, I hardly ever remember it, but this event was as real as any daily event in my life. I don't know how to explain it. I doubt to this day that it was a dream as such since I have never had a dream experience of such a level of realism. In any case, I had a sense of tranquility and peace like I have rarely felt, both during and after this experience, as it allowed me to say goodbye properly."

Despite a certain degree of doubt about the reality of her encounter with her deceased husband, this participant was nevertheless consoled by this experience. Although experients frequently insist that this event was not a dream, the contacts occurring during sleep may make them at times less definable than those in the waking state:

"After losing my husband I experienced his presence within a dream. I had been hoping for some kind of sign from him. I cannot recall exactly how long since his passing I had the experience, however, the dream was clear and we spoke together in the kitchen of our home where everything looked as it did in reality. What struck me the most was that after we had hugged each other, he simply told me that there was something else (meaning after death) and that he shouldn't really be with me. He had someone with him who I couldn't see and my husband was not permitted to divulge their identity. At this particular time of my grieving I was so desperate to have some kind of confirmation that my husband was existing elsewhere and although part of me still wondered if this was simply a dream, I was still comforted and it gave me hope that it wasn't just the end for him."

In the following account, our participant tells us about the completely unexpected and very welcome change in her life initiated by her sleep ADC. It is not (only) a question here of coming to terms with the grief of bereavement but of a transformation that has led to possibilities previously unsuspected by our participant:

"My father-in-law passed away in May 2010. About six months later, I woke up from a 'dream' one morning, and told my husband I had had such a vivid dream about his dad. I was walking along a path in the woods and my father-in-law was walking behind me. I was mildly uncomfortable, not quite knowing where we were headed, but comforted by my father-in-law's proximity. I finally saw a tree house with a rope ladder ahead of us and I got nervous about having to climb the ladder. I was somewhat reassured with my father-in-law behind me and didn't want to show that I was nervous. When we got to the ladder, I effortlessly seemed to just fly up the steps of the ladder. When we got into the tree house, I sat across from my father-in-law and took note of how well he looked. He was in shorts and a collared, button-down shirt with the sleeves rolled up. We sat in silence and looked at each other. He seemed to be about 60 years old, but healthy and well. I then woke up. It was somehow very emotional for me. I told my husband about the dream and then went downstairs to get breakfast. While standing at the sink in my kitchen, I suddenly realized the date was November 6th — my father-in-law's birthday. I went back upstairs and told my husband how stunning it was that I would have this 'dream' on his father's birthday when we hadn't even been talking about it. Again, I felt very emotional. I again went downstairs when suddenly I understood my father-in-law's message to me — 'what you think you can't do, you actually can do.' I told my husband and was very choked up telling him. It was all very intense. About a year later, I suddenly felt very driven to do something artistic. Now to say that I had never been artistic at any point in my life is an understatement. As my husband said, 'You never even doodled!' Well, I ended up starting to draw and was somehow able to do it. I then started to paint and was somehow able to do it. My father-in-law was a wonderful painter. Oddly enough, my work looks very similar to my father-in-law's. Sometimes, my husband will see one of my paintings and tell me if he didn't know better, he'd swear his father had painted it! So, my father-in-law's message to me was true. Like climbing that ladder in my dream, what I thought I couldn't do, I actually could do."

This contact in the form of a last farewell was able to soothe our participant's regret at not having been present when his mother died:

"My mother died of motor neurone disease in April 1998. That summer, I had dozed off to sleep at night and then I met her in a kind of lucid dream. She was so real and looked so young, full of life. I told her that she looked beautiful and so young. She said that everything was fine and that was it. I was happy then and never had another ADC. I just wanted 'one last time' as I had missed her bodily death. It fills me up even now."

The experient claims to have learned something about the conditions of existence in the "other dimension" during this contact:

> "About two weeks after my father died, he appeared to me in a vivid dream. His appearance did not resemble my favourite pictures of him but as he appeared in his late '50s, which I believe was for him the prime of his life. He was attired in a suit and wearing his favourite Stetson hat — not the kind that cowboys wear but the kind that Wall Street bankers do. He came to me and said, 'Son, being dead takes some getting used to, but you'll like it.' This vivid dream was comforting to me, although before the dream I had no doubt that my father was in a good place. In the years since that experience, I have often thought about his words, 'Being dead takes some getting used to...'"

This "conversation" perceived during sleep appears to have continued after our participant woke up:

> "I dreamed that my mother had a conversation with me. She appeared much younger than the 94 years when she passed. She talked about her life regrets and how I should move forward with my own life. When I awoke from the dream and got out of bed, I could still hear her talking to me, so I continued to listen to her for around 15 minutes until she suddenly stopped, said goodbye, and then the whole thing ended."

This sleep ADC has initiated an unexpected rapprochement:

> "[I] dreamed about my deceased biological mother and felt as if she was encouraging me to reconnect with my biological father who left before I was born. I reconnected with him, and when I came home after speaking with him, I suddenly smelled flowers in my home, and felt as if she was with me."

The particularity of the following testimony is the fact that two people experienced an ADC during sleep on the same night with the same deceased, the night after an event that marked a new stage in their grief:

> "My husband's son (MN) died in 2002 of a heart attack at the age of 22. He was his only son. We have no children together. We have been together for 24 years now. We had cleaned out the small room upstairs where there was a bag full of MN's clothes and we took them and other things downstairs to make space in the small room upstairs. That night, I remember that while I was sleeping, I felt MN in the other room and then he came over to greet me. He felt so real, even while asleep, and I leaned back to kiss him. At that moment I woke up and saw my husband crying. It was 3 a.m. I asked him what was wrong and he told me that he had dreamt of his dead son... He had never dreamed of MN before, and neither had I, and we have never dreamed of him since. It was as if he had come to say good-bye... He was wearing a grey jumper, just like the one I had put in the bag containing his clothes."

The next testimony falls into the category of evidential ADCs since the respondent was able to easily verify, with relief, the veracity of the information perceived during this sleep ADC:

> "The most significant ADC occurred during sleep. I had lost an object [a ring] that was very important to me. In fact, my niece and her girlfriends accidentally lost it and my grandmother in a dream told me the exact location where it was..."

This rather disconcerting contact occurred in a sleep-like state. The participant could not identify the perceived deceased:

"I was in a relaxed state, about to fall asleep, when I saw a tall, skinny man come in as a shadow, walk around my bed and sit down next to me (I even felt the weight of his body sagging on the mattress). I thought he was a thief and while I was figuring out what to do, I realized that he was worried, sad, with his head down and looking as if he was saying 'no' with his head. I finally decided to confront him, but when I straightened up, he was gone."

This comforting experience took place during sleep:

"My son died in a dramatic way following a road accident. He was 22 years old and we were very close. On the third day after his death, he appeared to me in a dream. I could see him clearly as he usually was, both in terms of his clothes and his attitude and face. I saw him serene, happy, smiling, and he said to me: 'Don't worry, Mum, I'm fine.' I was in a lot of pain."

This contact was highly beneficial for the grieving process of the person surveyed:

"I was half asleep, but I knew I wasn't dreaming. It felt different. My mum was sitting on my bed looking at me with her eyes full of tenderness. She had the same facial features, but without the old age and without the illness. She has always been a beautiful woman, but now she was glowing. She was a resplendent beauty, more lovely than ever. She was wearing a long white dress. She took me in her arms. It was a gesture she liked to do when she was alive, but I was shying away from it at that time. Now, I really let myself go into her embrace, I could actually feel her. We didn't talk, but I felt that she wasn't angry with me for not being there when she died, for saying the last words to her in a hurried and annoyed tone. It totally soothed me and in a lasting way."

A bereavement process could finally be completed 17 years after the demise thanks to an ADC during sleep:

"My mother died in 1972: she was 42 and I was 17. My world fell apart. For the next 17 years, I dreamt about her every night (dreams and often nightmares where I saw her die again). In 1989, 17 years after her death, she appeared to me, again in my sleep, but it was not like my usual dreams. She was sitting on the floor, her knees bent under her, dressed in white, her face bathed in light. With a wonderful smile, she said to me several times 'look how beautiful it is here, look at this light, I am happy now, you have to leave me'. This experience had absolutely nothing to do with my usual dreams and completely transformed me. All my dreams and nightmares totally disappeared and the way I dealt with my grief changed entirely."

Respondents were asked if they were soundly asleep or about to fall asleep or wake up when the ADC occurred.

- Soundly asleep: 61%
- Falling asleep: 10%
- Waking up: 18%
- Unsure: 11%

The next question provided clarification: If you were asleep, did the ADC wake you up or did it occur while you were asleep?

- Woke me up: 52%
- Occurred while I was sleeping: 37%
- Unsure: 12%

Although 62% of our respondents experienced an ADC during sleep, when falling asleep or waking up — and sleep ADCs rank first in our classification by type of ADC[18] — it is important to bear in mind that of these, 52% *were awakened by contact* and their experience then fell into one of the other categories of ADCs.

Experients sometimes explain that they were dreaming when the deceased popped into their dream, as illustrated by the following short descriptions:

"I was dreaming and the dream I was having suddenly stopped as if I had gone 'somewhere else', and then I saw the deceased person."

"Because it was clearly not a dream. For example, I felt the dream was interrupted when my mother appeared. I realized that I was already awake but with my eyes closed."

Contacts during sleep are qualified by the experients as being completely different from an ordinary dream. They would therefore have the same characteristics as ADCs in the waking state. These contacts are clear, coherent, memorable and felt as real and do not have the complex, symbolic and fragmented character of dreams, which are quickly forgotten when waking up.

Some participants clarified how this experience was different from a dream:

"It's very difficult to explain the feeling of the dream. It's like experiencing an actual event with an energy that is very different from a 'regular dream' or something produced by the subconscious. She seems to be completely in charge of what's happening."

"We have the impression that they want to show us something, but that at the same time, it is important that it should not really be made known, otherwise the mystery will no longer be there... so we are plunged into a semi-consciousness between dream and reality, which is what makes it totally confusing!"

"At the same time, it was like a dream, but so much more real and with such intensity that I can talk about it now (12 years after it occurred) with almost as many details as feelings."

"When I wake up, I understand that I did not dream because I remember all the details of our exchange. I can clearly see the difference between a real memory like our exchange and the vague memory of a dream that evaporates with time."

"I had very strong feelings and I saw him as if he were real. He came to comfort me. I told him, 'But I didn't have time to say goodbye,' and he took me in his arms. We were in my room at home, I could see us. And I woke up with this feeling of being at peace, light and happy, whereas I had been depressed for several weeks. I clearly differentiated this contact during sleep from a mere dream, because I experienced every emotion in a real way. He had come to say goodbye to me when I expected nothing."

Those who have had both dreams involving deceased significant others and ADCs during sleep make a clear distinction between the two types of experience:

"The times I have been 'visited' are totally different than a dream. Much, much more vivid and I remember every detail, even now — years later."

"Visitations are clear, vivid, detailed. Dreams make no sense and are hard to remember after a while. Visitations you'll never forget. Not even details."

"On occasion, I have dreamt of people who are dead. There is a subtle difference between a normal dream about someone who is dead and a message dream from someone who is dead."

"Completely different!!! He could have been alive. He has answered many questions through [gesticulating] and me lip reading. Also joking and laughing a lot."

"It was a distinct physical presence, not at all like any dream I've ever had."

"It wasn't a dream, because I had already dreamt about my father after he died, and this was completely different, it was real."

"It was very real, I know very well the difference between a dream and reality."

In this section, we have reviewed the different types of ADCs, namely ADCs of sensing a presence, auditory, tactile, visual, olfactory and sleep ADCs. The large number of questions put to our respondents has allowed us to deepen our knowledge of the nature of these types of ADCs. Several insights can be drawn from this. The data show that contacts have the same impact on experients, regardless of the *type* of the sensory perception. It appears from the testimonies collected that sensing the presence of the deceased has as powerful an impact on the experients as seeing an apparition. The type of the contact is not important since it is only the medium for the essence of these experiences, namely the emotions felt and perceived by the experients, as well as the information obtained.

ADCs occur in a wide variety of forms and situations and each experience is unique, because it is intended for a particular person. The vast majority of experients are grateful and delighted to have experienced this contact, which they did not expect at all and consider to be an expression of love and solicitude on the part of their significant other.

ADC at the time of death
* **21% experienced an ADC at the time of death**

206 of our participants have experienced an ADC at the time of death, also referred to as *crisis ADC*. These experiences usually occur at or shortly after death. In a few rare cases, they may occur shortly *before* death, particularly when the person perceived had fallen into a coma and had not regained consciousness before dying.

Experients claim to have been informed of the death of a family member or friend **by the deceased himself or herself.** These experiences **precede** the announcement of the death (by the hospital, the family, etc.). Experients can, for example, see or hear their significant other announcing his or her death with serenity ("I've come to say goodbye, I'm leaving now"). It should be noted in passing that they often seem to use the verb *to leave*, as if they were about to embark on a journey. Sometimes the apparition does not transmit a message, but the experients immediately understand that this is a last farewell.

By virtue of their evidential nature, these ADCs are particularly interesting for research because the experients received information during the contact that was previously unknown to them — the information of the demise of the significant other. The fact that experients are not (yet) in mourning at the time of contact argues against the hypothesis that ADCs are nothing more than a self-generated phenomenon of individuals deeply affected by the loss of a loved one.

How can one experience an ADC at the time of death? Here are a few examples:

"I was 15 and was sitting in my room, drawing. Last night my mother had a terrible headache and early in the morning she went to the hospital with my stepfather. I was listening to *Heaven Can Wait* — an Iron Maiden song — now I see a synchronicity in this. It was exactly 9:50 a.m. when I looked at the clock and heard her voice: 'It was terrible, an awful pain, but now I'm calm and can rest' — something like this by meaning, not in exact words. And in the afternoon, they told me that this was the exact time of her death. [...] We were very close, she was not only my mother, but also a friend. When she was alive, we had a kind of agreement — if there is something beyond, the first one of us who goes there would inform the other one."

"About midnight, sitting on couch. Felt a presence. Saw reflection on TV and saw a human shape walk behind me and down the hallway. I just knew it was my great-grandmother. I was hyperventilating and my phone went off. It was a text from my mom saying that my great-grandmother has just passed, 1,000 miles away. I went to bed with my door cracked open. Lying in bed, not yet asleep, and my door opened all the way. I felt a warm squeeze on my hand. No one was there. I knew it was her saying goodbye."

"My mother was not anticipated to live more than a few more days. I was in bed around midnight, suddenly sensed her presence at the side of my bed. She spoke my name and patted my shoulder. I felt Mom had passed. Within 10 minutes, my brother phoned to tell me she had died a few minutes before his call to me."

"I was 23 years old. At that time, I lived in Lyon. My grandmother lived 80 km north of Lyon. We were very close, we had a great relationship and friendship. I had been seeing her a lot less lately because I had a very busy job. I didn't come home very often at weekends to see her and my parents who lived in the same small town. My grandmother was very ill and we knew that the illness would soon take her away. My mother asked me to come that weekend and we all went to the hospital (many sisters on my mother's side). On Sunday evening in the hospital we were all around her bed to say goodbye. I was the last to leave... trying to comfort her and telling her not to be afraid, that she would be reunited with all the people she loved. I left knowing in my heart that it was the last time and, strangely enough, I was not sad!
On Tuesday night I wake up attracted by a strong presence. I am sitting in my bed overlooking a large open loft. And there, right in front of me, only two or three meters away, slightly higher, I perceive her presence without seeing her! A sort of luminous white haze and above all an incredible sensation invades me, of happiness, of peace, of Love. I smile at her. I know at that moment that she has passed to the other side and that she has come to say goodbye and reassure me. I go back to sleep soothed and the next day leave for work. The telephone rings at my workplace in the middle of the morning, it's my mum. She tells me with emotion that my little grandmother has died!"

A candle was the vector of this experience at the time of death:

"Grandfather was known to be dying. He was heavily sedated and had terminal cancer. I was informed the previous evening that he had gone downhill and was started on the morphine. I was in another country, a four-hour plane journey away and was distraught at being unable to get there. The earliest flight was the next day. That night I lit a candle for him and went to bed. I didn't sleep well and awoke about half five. The candle was still burning steady, there was no breeze in the room. I was telling myself off for leaving an unwatched candle burning. I was still upset, wishing I was home with my family, just wanting to be there… I remember just sitting watching the candle thinking it was way too early to phone home. I was also thinking I should blow the candle out. It was about five ft away from me when the flame flickered for a few seconds, went still, then went out… I got a smell of medicine, hospital disinfectant and immediately knew my papa was there with me saying goodbye. I felt a pressure across my shoulders and back like a hug. He was at peace and I was too. I was no longer upset. A short time later I phoned home to be told the news. He had died a few moments before the candle went out."

The testimony of this contact, which occurred in tragic circumstances, commands respect for the mother's presence of mind:

"He didn't know what was happening to him, he was panicking, he kept saying, 'They've murdered me, Mum, they've murdered me, Mum.' I told him to calm down and breathe and to go towards the light, that I was here and that he had passed and he needed to go to the light… I wasn't the only person in the room who heard him either."

Our data collection includes very few cases of ADCs that occurred when the perceived person was in a coma but had not yet been declared dead. It is important to note that these persons did not regain consciousness before they died. The following testimony describes such an ADC:

"It is about my paternal grandmother, to whom I was very close. When my 'dream' came up, my grandmother was ill. It was about 5 o'clock in the morning when my grandmother appeared to me in this dream, but it is a dream of a quite special nature, very real. She was radiant in the midst of other people around a table and she said to me with a smile, 'You can't imagine how happy I am!' I woke up and went to her sister's house where she was staying and to my surprise, my grandmother was in a deep coma, and had been for a few hours without us being informed. My grandmother died without regaining consciousness."

ADCs at the time of death considerably dampen the shock caused by the passing of a loved one. Being informed of the demise **by the significant other himself or herself** consoles the experient since this experience seems to imply a continuity of some form of existence. By the time the official announcement of death reaches the experients, either through the hospital, the family or the police in the event of an accident, they are already informed. The shock will have been softened by the ADC, but they will of course not be spared the sadness of the loss.

When the demise was unpredictable and therefore unexpected, for example in the case of an accidental death or cardiac arrest, the protagonists did not have the opportunity to say goodbye, nor, if relevant, to settle outstanding relationship issues. We asked whether our participants had had the opportunity to say a final farewell to their loved ones and, where appropriate, to resolve unsettled conflicts.

- **38% had the opportunity for a final farewell, 6% were unsure, and 56% did not have this opportunity**

We inquired whether our respondents had immediately and without hesitation recognized the identity of the deceased. As with other types of ADCs, this was the case for a large majority:

- **85% immediately recognized the deceased, 3% were unsure, and 12% did not immediately recognize the deceased**

The ensuing testimonies further illustrate contacts at the time of death:

"My uncle died of cancer at about 5:30 in the morning. At that time of night, I was coming out of the toilet and came face to face with him. He smiled at me in an angelic way. Shaken, I decided to wait until 7:00 a.m. to call my cousin and tell him of my uncle's passing. At 6:58 a.m., my cousin phoned me to tell me that he had died."

"My aunt passed away in the middle of the night, at about 2:30 a.m. At that moment I was woken up by a caress on my cheek, like a breath of air. The window was closed, there was no draft in the room. Ten minutes later, the hospital phoned me to tell me that she had died."

A draught, occasionally combined with a drop in ambient temperature, sometimes appears to be the vector of ADCs, as was the case with this experience that took place at the precise moment of death:

"I had a very powerful experience when my mother-in-law was dying of cancer... I was on a farm in the mountains, in a room that was hermetically sealed because of the cold weather up there. At 00.34 (I looked at the clock immediately after this event), I felt a gust of wind enter the room and blow my face in the darkened room where I was lying in bed. The wind made a delicate swirl and I realized it was leaving through the inner door as it slammed shut as if by a violent gust of wind. I was amazed by this strong breeze that could not enter anywhere… 15 minutes later, my ex-wife called to tell me that her mother had passed away at 00.34."

This account is interesting since the deceased seems to have gone through one of his daughters to give a last kiss to his mother-in-law at the very moment of his passing, while asking her to take good care of his family:

"My son-in-law spoke to me right after he passed with leukaemia. I was in the room next to his ward in hospital looking after his two girls aged eight and ten. I sat next to the youngest girl. Suddenly she sat bolt upright, leaned over and kissed me gently on the cheek, and I heard my son-in-law say, 'Lisa' (my name is Elizabeth), 'look after them.' My daughter (his wife) came into the room we were in, crying. He had just passed over. When I asked my granddaughter if she remembered kissing me, she said she didn't."

Exceptionally, I present here a second-hand testimony which is particularly noteworthy, because Alzheimer's disease has obviously not diminished this elderly person's ability to perceive the ADC:

"The day my grandfather died, and before we were informed of the demise, we were in the living room with my grandmother who has Alzheimer's disease. She told us that my grandfather had just come into the living room and walked through it, then headed out to the patio. She got up to follow him to the patio and asked us to go with her because, she said, he was about to leave. We thought she might be saying this because she missed him, but a few minutes later an uncle came in in tears to inform us that our grandfather had just passed away. Apparently, his soul had passed through his house, perhaps as a farewell."

This testimony sounds like a last-minute attempt at reconciliation:

"I was estranged from my uncle and had no contact with him. One day, in the early afternoon, I had the strange impression of receiving what seemed to me to be a thought not modulated in human terms. A thought that I was receiving, and that I had in no way generated. In this thought, my uncle was addressing me, and saying 'this is so stupid'. I dismissed the idea and went about my business. The next day I learned of the man's death, and based on the time of his death (heart attack), I understood that this strange contact had taken place at the time of death."

Unusual noises were heard at the very moment of a demise which had occurred in a different location:

"The most significant ADC was the first one. I was in bed with my partner. We were both wide awake owing to hearing a banging on the wall behind our heads. The room behind us was the garage. I presumed, as had happened before, that I'd left an entrance door to the garage unlocked, and perhaps it was windy and the door had swung open and was banging on the wall intermittently. However, that would normally create a banging in one place. The bangs were coming from all over the wall. Something as heavy as the door would have been required to create such a sound — like a hammer. It was around 6:30 a.m. I was reluctant to get out of bed to investigate, but for what little time we had left to sleep I wanted to try and do it in peace. I first got out of bed and looked outside the window to the garden. It was light. I opened the window and leaned out to look to the back entrance door to the garage. From what I could see, it was shut. I also noticed that no trees or bushes were moving. It wasn't windy. It was a silent morning with only the sound of the odd bird tweeting. The banging had stopped but I went outside to check. The door was in fact locked. Unlocking it, and checking inside the garage, nothing was out of place that could have caused such banging. I went back to bed after briefly discussing it with my partner. She then went to work at 7:15 a.m. On her drive out, she went passed my parents' house and noticed — oddly — that they were getting out of their car and returning home. She realised something was wrong. Before she could call me, my mother rang me to say they had just returned from the hospital. My grandmother had died in the hospital at around 6:30 a.m."

The two testimonies to follow also occurred at the very hour of death:

"I awoke suddenly for no reason from a good sleep and saw my grandfather standing at the side of my bed. He seemed slightly younger, healthier and radiating pure love. He smiled at me and said, 'I'm going away, my wee dove' (his pet name for me). I smiled back at him and looked at my alarm clock, it was 06.00, then he was gone. It didn't occur to me to ask my grandfather where he was going or why he was in my room at 6 in the morning. I just slipped back into a peaceful sleep. I was later wakened by the telephone ringing and my grandmother sobbing on the phone that papa was dead. His death certificate later stated approx. time of death 06.00."

"I was in Boston and I was woken up at 5:30 a.m. in the morning by my smiling husband. He told me he was gone and that he loved me. It wasn't a dream. I found out later that he died on December 1 at 5:30 a.m."

The next testimony refers to a contact experienced in childhood at the very moment of an accidental death:

"I was about ten years old when one night I had just gone to bed and was not yet asleep. I felt a hand tapping me on the top of my shoulder. I turned around and there was no one there. A few minutes later the phone rang and we were told that my paternal grandmother had died in an accident. I will always remember this because it was a strange feeling, as if someone was trying to tell me 'I am here'. I never had an explanation for it."

It is not always easy to determine whether the ADC coincided exactly with the time of death, either because the experient didn't check the time when the contact occurred, or because the official time of death was not available.

Nonetheless, more than half of our participants were able to corroborate the perfect match between the time of the ADC and the time of death.

We asked whether the time (hour/minute) when they experienced the ADC was later confirmed as the actual time of death of the person.

- **For 60% concordance between time of ADC and time of death was confirmed, 17% were unsure, and for 23% concordance was not confirmed**

The ensuing account describes an ADC during sleep. It is noteworthy that our participant felt a compelling need to take a nap, which allegedly allowed this contact to occur:

> "I was on the balcony of my house talking with my husband when I had a very strong, overwhelming attack of fatigue. So much so that I told my husband I had to retire to go to bed. I lay down on my bed with all my clothes on and fell into a deep sleep. I then saw my room and at the door of my room was my grandmother who had been hospitalized as she was very ill. She told me that she had to go now, that it was her time. That I shouldn't worry about her, that everything would be fine. She also reaffirmed her affection for me and that she would always love me. We talked about several more topics and at that moment I woke up. My sister was standing at the door of my room and she said to me, 'Have you heard yet? Our grandmother has just passed away.'"

The next testimony describes a contact during sleep on the night of the demise:

> "My childhood friend who was ill and doomed by a rare disease came to visit me the night she died. I didn't know it at the time when I saw her walking again, smiling, happy and relaxed, even though she was suffering and paralysed. She told me that she was fine, that I had nothing to worry about because she was at peace and happy. We were 20 years old and she had her childlike face as when we were at our carefree age, and I was happy for her. My mother came to wake me up, it was about 8 a.m., and told me that Christine had passed away during the night. I realized that she had come to tell me not to be sad because she was happy.
> Years later, I had the opportunity to share this moment with her younger brother who seemed so saddened by not

having any conversation with his parents about his sister's passing. He hugged me, moved but comforted. I thought very strongly of Christine who was probably also touched by the sharing of this moment when she left soothed and had come to tell me so."

This contact served as a warning of a suicide which, nonetheless, could not be avoided:

"A close colleague of mine had died of cancer a few months before my ADC. Not only was he a colleague, but a very dear friend. One night he appeared in my dream. He didn't speak, just made eye contact and gestures. I asked him if everything was alright and he just shook his head. There was darkness all around us. The next day I found out a colleague of ours had killed himself. It's like he had appeared to warn me."

This experience, which preceded the announcement of the death of the participant's grandfather, undoubtedly made it easier for her to come to terms with this irreversible act:

"A few hours before I was told that my grandfather had died, I felt a heavy and affectionate hand on my shoulder. This happens to be the time when he took his own life."

This participant, whose son was abroad, had been informed of his death long before the official announcement of his passing reached her:

"When my son died abroad, it was around midnight. I was half asleep and I found myself above him, face to face, and I kissed him on the forehead... In the morning I got up and, as I put my feet on the floor to get out of bed, I felt a great emptiness, nothingness, an imbalance, something had been taken from me, I knew it was my son... Two days later I was informed of his death. It was the same night I kissed him on the forehead."

In some cases, the death was not foreseeable because the person was not ill and had, for example, died in an accident or succumbed to a heart attack. The **expectation** of the imminent death of a very ill or elderly significant other could therefore only act as a trigger for the ADC in certain cases.

The data collected support this hypothesis. For many of our respondents the death was foreseeable, so they may have expected it, but for a significant number it was not predictable.

- **For 48% the death was predictable, 8% were unsure, and for 44% the death was not predictable**

Cases of suicide in particular are often not predictable and yet some experients perceive the drama that is unfolding, as the following case illustrates:

"My boyfriend George, with whom I was very close, died on 5 November 2016. That evening I was staying with friends. Around 11 p.m., I dozed off in the middle of a conversation. I didn't realize that I was falling asleep, and I saw, as if in a vision, my dead boyfriend who had hung himself. When I woke up, I had a strong gut feeling that didn't leave me. I tried to contact him but couldn't get hold of him. It was only two days later that they found his body hanged."

A large majority of our respondents were physically distant from the place where the person was dying.

- **75% were physically distant, 1% were unsure, and 25% were not physically distant**

The classic definition of an ADC at the time of death — or crisis ADC — indicates that the contact must have occurred within 24 hours of death. We discussed at length within our team the time frame taken into consideration for a contact to qualify as ADC at the time of death. It seemed to us that the 24-hour criterion was not entirely relevant because the crucial element was that **the experient was not informed of the demise** at the moment of the ADC.

Let us imagine the case of a person who accompanied a significant other during his last moments. He would have been at the bedside when his loved one took his last breath. An hour later, he would have experienced an ADC with that person. According to the classic definition, this would be an ADC at the time of death since it would have occurred within 24 hours of death. However, this person would obviously have been aware of the death since he would have been present when it occurred. From the point of view of temporality, it would indeed be an ADC at the time of death since it would have occurred within the predefined period of time, but an essential criterion would be missing: **the fact that the experient is informed of the death by the deceased himself or herself.**

If, on the other hand, the experient was unaware of the death and was informed of it by the deceased himself or herself — even after the 24-hour time limit — then this contact would qualify as ADC at the time of death under our revised definition.

In the description that follows, the person has perceived information that was not previously available to her, which classifies this ADC as an evidential experience:

> "One evening, I felt a presence on the first four steps of my staircase, a tall, male person; he was watching me and stayed for at least 15 minutes... The next evening, we are told of the alarming disappearance of my husband's cousin to whom he

is very, very close. At the time, I didn't make the connection, and in the night that followed, I dreamed of him. He showed me a place in our town. In the morning, everyone started looking for him and, alas, he killed himself at the place I had dreamed about."

Sometimes ADCs are simply a last thank you, as was the case for this female doctor:

"The most striking ADC concerns a patient with advanced cancer. A very spiritual person. I was head of department and we treated her for three months. We were close, with a strong therapeutic relationship. I said goodbye to her before leaving on holiday to Egypt, convinced that I would not see her alive again. I had a wonderful 12-day cruise on the Nile. On the tenth day, I remember perfectly leaning on the railing of the boat's deck watching the landscape go by very slowly, the children jumping and playing in the Nile, the villages passing by. I was relaxed and perfectly calm. Suddenly, I feel a warmth in my plexus that spreads into my heart, and then triggers a wide smile... immediately, I know that it is the patient who has come to greet me because she has passed away. I speak aloud to her, thanking her for coming to say goodbye and telling her that she can go in peace to the Light. An intense joy and a communion of hearts invaded me. Then I went down to the cabin to see the day in my diary and the time, as I never wear a watch. It was a Wednesday afternoon. Back in France, I received confirmation of the day and time of death of this patient... with one hour difference from the time noted which corresponds to the time difference!"

Some participants report feeling the pain and discomfort in their bodies that their loved one would have felt during the dying process. These sensations cease at the precise moment of death and are often replaced by a sense of peace and serenity.

The two next testimonies illustrate this type of case:

"It is about my mother who lives 20 km away from me. It is towards the end of the night, I find myself in my mother's body, I am her, I have various pains in my body and feel some distress. Then I wake up around 5:30 a.m. At 9 a.m., I learn that she has been taken to the emergency room for respiratory failure. 48 hours later I wake up with an unusual headache (I never have headaches), then around 10:30 a.m. a big black circle dances in front of my left eye. One hour later I have the beginnings of nausea (nausea that doesn't resemble indigestion or pregnancy nausea) that grips my stomach. This stops around noon. At 2:30 p.m. I learn that my mother died at 12:15 p.m."

"My dad was in hospital. We knew that the medication that was supposed to support him had been stopped as there was no hope. At 19.00 I called the hospital and a nurse confirmed that he was stable and that I should not worry for the next few hours. At 21.20 I tell my husband that I feel a strange nausea. I take an herbal tea. At 21.40 I tell my husband that this tea must be miraculous because my nausea has stopped and I feel calmed down and relaxed, despite the circumstances. At 21.50, the hospital calls me to inform me that Dad had passed away ten minutes earlier. I took this as a gift from him. While he was alive, our relationship was very conflictual and difficult despite all the love we had for each other. For a long time after his passing, I often had the feeling that he was by my side, that he was supporting me."

The case to follow is particularly noteworthy because our participant had not had any contact with her former boyfriend for a very long time:

"It was early morning. I had a cup of coffee and was mindlessly going through some papers on my desk at home. I felt odd for several seconds and then it passed, I thought. Suddenly I felt that I may be having a heart attack because of feeling immense chest pressure and I didn't know what to do as I was alone. After several seconds, a voice in my head said, 'Marvin is dying,' and a few seconds after that, the pressure released. I felt relieved but then the same voice said, 'Marvin is dead.' Marvin was a former boyfriend that I hadn't had any contact with for close to forty years! I didn't know anything about his life."

The following account describes a temporary state of confusion of our participant coinciding with the moment of her grandmother's death. What happened during this event that was so strange and destabilizing for our respondent? Could her grandmother have found a way to share with her how she felt during the dying process — a moment of confusion followed by a state of happiness? And the sadness for those who remain and weep for their departed loved one? It is a hypothesis.

"It was February 1998. I was at a restaurant with my husband and friends. When I was asked: 'Have you chosen your dish?' I answered, 'I have to go there in April.' From that moment on, I made increasingly incoherent remarks. My ideas were clear in my head, but the words that came out of my mouth had neither tail nor head! The more I wanted to explain myself, the more I was talking nonsense! My husband and our friends were crying out with laughter and I didn't understand what was going on. Then it stopped as suddenly as it had happened! And then I was able to express that I didn't understand what had just happened to me. I was very intrigued and I repeated it several times during the evening... what a strange event! The next morning, I received a phone call informing me that my grandmother had died the night before at exactly the same time as I started to make these incoherent statements. The connection between the two events immediately became clear to me. It's very strange how strong this feeling was! And what was very paradoxical at that moment was that I was so sad and at the same time so happy for her."

The ensuing account describes not a physical sensation but emotional distress felt at the moment when the participant's mother was fighting death. This moment of panic was largely compensated by the ADC she experienced after the passing:

"My mother died suddenly, following a heart attack. At about 3.30 in the morning I woke up in a state of panic. An anxiety that I couldn't explain. I felt that something grave was happening... I couldn't get back to sleep. At 5:15 a.m. my sister phoned me and told me that our mother had died at 4:30 a.m. Mum had woken up at about 3:30 a.m., she was feeling ill. Dad was with her. He told her that he was going to the corridor to phone the ambulance, she held his hand, she refused to stay alone... Seeing that her condition was not improving, Dad decided to make the phone call. He returned only five minutes after the phone call to the ambulance, and mum had already died. An hour after she woke up she had passed away. It was very hard, it was the first time I experienced the loss of a loved one. I was full of anger! I was angry at the whole world for taking my mum away from me when she was only 70! I went to see her, I spoke to her at length. I told her that we hadn't even had a chance to talk on the phone that weekend, that we still had so much to share... At the time I had a book project that I had not yet told her about. The next morning, I woke up from my sleep and I felt that she was there... She hugged me tightly. It was almost daylight, I looked around my room to see if anyone was there, but I didn't see anyone. I just felt her presence and she whispered in my ear 'I'm fine, sweetie, don't worry, I'm here and I'll help you with your book,' then I felt a caress of infinite tenderness on my cheek. Tears were running down my cheeks and, paradoxically, I had an incredible inner peace! Since her death, I have become much more spiritual! She opened a path for me. A year later my book was published on the anniversary of her death. She accompanied me a lot, I often felt her presence in my dreams. This experience was overwhelming!"

I will close this section with a description of an event that occurred in the childhood of our respondent. Children seem to have a special sensitivity to perceive this type of phenomena:

"I was eight years old and we went with my aunt to do the Christmas shopping, as we were going to spend the festivities at my grandmother's house in Mendoza. When we were leaving, a sparrow fell dead at my feet. I told my aunt that my grandmother had just passed away... When we got home, my mother opened the door crying with the telegram in her hand."

ADCs at the time of death are particularly interesting, including for research purposes, because of their evidential nature. According to experients, and as attested by the testimonies cited above, they have been informed of the death of their significant other by the deceased himself or herself. This circumstance of occurrence of the contact excludes a perception based on the desire to receive a sign from the deceased loved one. Therefore, psychological needs cannot be the trigger of the ADC in this context.

The fact of having been informed of the death by the deceased themselves mitigates the shock of the announcement of the demise and gives the experients the subjective conviction that their loved ones are still able to manifest themselves to them, thus implying the survival of a part of these persons. The sadness of the loss, however, is not spared to the experients. The testimonies quoted show nonetheless that the grieving process can commence in better conditions than if this last farewell had not taken place.

Comparative graph by type of ADC

The following graph shows the number of occurrences by type of ADC of our sample.[19] The large amount of data collected — 1,004 completed questionnaires — allows for a fairly significant ranking.

In line with our expectation, ADCs during sleep top our ranking. However, more than half (52%) of our respondents were awakened by the contact and the rest of the experience fell into one of the other ADC categories. Visual ADCs, which are very striking, rank higher than expected, as the literature does not report such a high number of occurrences.

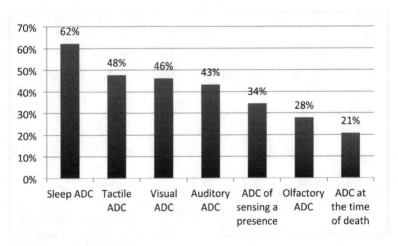

Table by type of ADC

Shared deathbed visions and death experiences

In our data collection of 1,004 cases, we have four cases that seem to be quite exceptional and rare, namely two cases of shared deathbed visions and two cases of shared death experiences. I will present these two phenomena in some detail.

Deathbed visions

At the end of their lives, people may have a "deathbed vision" shortly before (or sometimes days or weeks before) they die. "Deathbed visions", also called "End-of-life Dreams and Visions (ELDVs)", are much more than the traditional representation of an apparition at the foot of the bed. They are part of the broader concept of "End-of-life Experiences (ELEs)" and refer indeed to the subjective experience of perceiving a deceased significant other that dying persons have while asleep or awake, but also to other phenomena at the time of death, as described by Fenwick, Lovelace and Brayne: "ELEs included deathbed phenomena (DBP) such as visions, coincidences and the desire to reconcile with estranged family members. These experiences seemed to comfort both the dying and the bereaved. Interviewees described other phenomena such as clocks stopping synchronistically at the time of death, shapes leaving the body, light surrounding the body and strange animal behaviour."[20]

Two American palliative care nurses, Maggie Callanan and Patricia Kelley, have elaborated a concept that integrates deathbed visions into the broader context of "Nearing Death Awareness" (NDA), also called "Near Death Awareness", of which they are an essential component. This phenomenon concerns people who die slowly — from illness or old age — as opposed to those who die suddenly in an accident or during cardiac arrest. Broadly reported testimonies and several case studies suggest that up to 50–60% of people experience some form of NDA prior to their death.[21] This concept, which describes a specific state of consciousness inherent in the proximity of death, is presented in Callanan's and Kelley's book *Final Gifts*.[22] The *need for reconciliation* and the *conditions for dying in peace* are also components of this enhanced state of consciousness associated with the proximity of death. Another element of the NDA phenomenon, the *awareness of the proximity of death*, allows people at the end of their life to know instinctively that their death is near, even if their state of health does not predict an imminent fatal outcome. This certainty grips them approximately in the last 72 hours before death. Dying people often express themselves in symbolic language, as if they did not want to upset their loved ones by speaking in plain language about their impending death. They say, for example, that they have to pack their suitcase, look for their passport and book a plane ticket for a trip they are about to take.

The Swiss-American psychiatrist Elisabeth Kübler-Ross, a pioneer in death and dying and near-death studies, has identified three languages the dying use to communicate their knowledge of their impending death: plain English, nonverbal language, and symbolic verbal language, in adults,[23] and in children.[24]

As with ADCs, it is important that family and friends, and in this case also health care professionals, be informed of the NDA phenomenon in order to ensure that the dying receive the appropriate attention: "The language patients use to communicate NDA may be symbolic and if caretakers are not aware that NDA can occur, patients may be ignored, treated condescendingly, or inappropriately medicated for delirium."[25]

A phenomenon researched over time

Deathbed visions have been reported for centuries and, unlike ADCs, have been the subject of quite extensive scientific research over time. At the beginning of the 20th century, there was a great deal of interest among both researchers and the public in the so-called "psychic" phenomena. The first systematic study of deathbed visions was conducted by Sir William Barrett, Professor of Experimental Physics at the Royal College of Science of Ireland. In 1926, he published a milestone book entitled *Death-Bed Visions*.[26] He concluded from his research that deathbed visions were not simply a by-product of a dying brain but occurred when the dying person was lucid and rational. Furthermore, he presented several cases where medical staff or relatives in the room had been able to share the patients' visions.[27] Sir William Barrett was the driving force behind the establishment of the *Society for Psychical Research (SPR)* in 1882, which is still a highly respected institution today. In 1884, he founded the *American Society for Psychical Research*.

Years later, Erlendur Haraldsson, professor emeritus of psychology at the faculty of social science, University of Iceland, and Karlis Osis, a Latvian-born parapsychologist, studied deathbed visions over several decades. In 1971, they published the benchmark book *At the Hour of Death*[28] describing their research into deathbed visions in the United States and India. They concluded that deathbed visions are more consistent with the hypothesis of a "transition experience" rather than with the "extinction hypothesis".

More recently, in 2006, the results of a pilot project on End-of-life Experiences were published. This study was conducted by Professor emeritus Peter Fenwick, neuropsychiatrist and neurophysiologist, King's College, London, and his colleagues, in collaboration with a palliative care team from the Camden Primary Care Trust, London. The findings indicate that death is a transitional process that can be heralded by various phenomena, including visions that comfort the dying and prepare them spiritually for death. The researchers in charge of the pilot project found that patients regularly reported visions at the time of death as an intrinsic part of the dying process they were engaged in, and that they were generally more serene when in the company of their "secret visitors". Another finding of the pilot project was that deathbed visions are not caused by pathologies or drugs and that dying people prefer to talk about them to nurses rather than doctors. Furthermore, the researchers assume that people at the end of their lives do not necessarily talk about their visions, for fear of not being believed or of being ridiculed, of worrying their significant others, or for lack of public recognition of the phenomenon.[29]

In a paper published in 2010, Fenwick and Brayne state that "Our end-of-life experience (ELE) research suggests that deathbed visions (DVs) and deathbed coincidences (DCs) are not uncommon, and that the dying process appears to involve an instinctive need for spiritual connection and meaning, requiring compassionate understanding and respect from those who provide end-of-life care."[30] The nature of ELE, and in particular of deathbed visions, and their beneficial impact on the dying are described in the excellent book by Peter and Elizabeth Fenwick entitled *The Art of Dying*.[31]

How do deathbed visions unfold and what is their impact on the dying?

According to data collected by researchers, people at the brink of death allegedly perceive significant deceased persons and communicate telepathically with them. Like ADCs, these visions typically feature deceased spouses/partners, family members or friends with whom the dying persons generally had had strong emotional bonds during their lifetime. Apparitions are sometimes described as surrounded by a halo of light. Occasionally, the object of the apparitions represents a religious or mystical entity, shaped according to the religious affiliation or the spiritual beliefs of the dying person. More rarely, visions of paradisiacal environments are reported, described as sublimated earthly landscapes.

These visions, which are usually quite brief, tend to be recurrent and to accompany the persons throughout the dying process, namely during the hours or days before death.

A case reported by Peter and Elizabeth Fenwick exemplifies this point:

"At around 3 a.m. the night before he died, three people entered his room whom I could not see. He became very animated and even moved his arm that he had not been able to move for over a year. I asked him who was in the room and he replied, 'Thomas' (a good friend who had passed on), 'Elizabeth' (an auntie that he was very close to) and 'Phyllis' (my mother, who had also passed on). These people stayed with him for three hours and he laughed and was very happy. At around 6 a.m. he waved them goodbye (and blew kisses) and his eyes followed them out of the door. I asked him if he would have a sleep then and he said 'Yes'. Immediately, his face lit up and he watched them enter the room again. They stayed a further one hour, then left. He passed away at 2.15 p.m."[32]

Like people who experience an ADC, the dying do not question the reality of these apparitions. Despite their diversity, their personal belief system, their unique biography, they give them a surprisingly homogeneous meaning. According to those on the brink of death, the role of the apparitions is to welcome them at the threshold of death and to guide them towards the invisible world. They welcome these apparitions with naturalness and joy and describe them to those around them, aware that only they can perceive them. They are neither surprised nor frightened that a deceased loved one appears and speaks to them, and they explain the intention of the apparition in all simplicity: "Jason is here, he came to help me cross over to the other world!"

Deathbed visions have a spiritual dimension that goes far beyond the mere fleeting perception of a deceased significant other. They generate an essential comfort and certainty that sweeps away in a few seconds apprehensions that may have been present throughout a lifetime. A transfer of knowledge seems to occur during these visions that free the dying person immediately and completely from the fear of dying. The anxiety and agitation often present in the dying process disappear instantly. Serenity, and even anticipated joy, take hold of the dying person that would have been unthinkable a few minutes before. The impact of the vision is extremely powerful, immediate and liberating. It is a profound psychic transformation. Following the deathbed vision, people are ready to die, ready to depart on a mysterious journey, perhaps.

The following case illustrates this sudden awareness:

"Suddenly she looked up at the window and seemed to stare intently up at it... She suddenly turned to me and said, 'Please, Pauline, don't ever be afraid of dying. I have seen a beautiful light and I was going towards it... it was so peaceful I really had to fight to come back.' The next day when it was time for me to go home I said, 'Bye, Mum, see you tomorrow.' She looked straight at me and said, 'I'm not worried about tomorrow and you mustn't be, promise me.' Sadly, she died the next morning... but I knew she had seen something that day which gave her comfort and peace when she knew she had only hours to live."[33]

As with ADCs, pre-existing beliefs seem to have no impact on the probability of having these visions. Let us imagine an individual, agnostic or atheist, who has rejected all his life any idea of survival of consciousness, convinced that only dissolution and nothingness will be at the end of the road. At the time of his death, his deceased father appears to him and speaks to him. He does not doubt for a second the reality of this apparition and converses with him with naturalness and pleasure, while describing the apparition to those around him. This would be a typical reaction.

The following experience is a good illustration:

> "I was nursing my friend who had definitive views that there was no afterlife. In her last couple of hours, she became very peaceful and arose from her unconsciousness periodically, saying clearly and happily such phrases as 'I will know soon', 'Come on, get on with it then, I am ready to go now', and 'It is so beautiful'. She would immediately lapse back into unconsciousness after uttering these phrases. She was very obviously content, happy and at peace. It was a wonderful experience for her partner and me."[34]

In some — perhaps rare — cases, it seems that the dying patient's caregivers and relatives can also perceive the deathbed vision. In a recent survey, the Shared Crossing Research Initiative (SCRI), Santa Barbara, CA, USA, stated: "Anecdotal evidence suggests that some loved ones and caregivers of dying patients undergo a type of end-of-life phenomena known as a shared death experience or SDE, whereby one feels that one has participated in a dying person's transition to a post-mortem existence. Anecdotal evidence also suggests that SDEs can have a range of profound psycho-spiritual-emotional effects. [...] Analysis revealed four distinct though non-exclusive modes of an SDE: remotely sensing a death, witnessing unusual phenomena, feelings of accompanying the dying, and feelings of assisting the dying."[35]

Let us now go back to the accounts collected in the framework of our survey. The testimony to follow is one of the above mentioned two cases of shared deathbed visions, experienced both by our participant and presumably by her dying mother. It also illustrates perfectly that, in an objectively short period of time, very contrasting emotions can be felt. Our participant describes a dynamic evolution of her feelings, from deep despair to a sense of peace and acceptance:

"In a clinic, at my mother's bedside in a very serious condition, I was watching over her at night when I saw a ray of light at the door. I thought it was a visit from the nurse, but this light moved, stopped at the foot of the bed, and inside this white glow I saw very clearly my son, Jean-Pierre, who had been murdered seven years earlier. I couldn't see his legs, but he was quite distinct up to his upper thighs, the white light made him a little blurred. He ignored me, all concentrated on his grandmother. He held out his arms to her with tenderness. I knew at that moment that he had come to fetch her and inside me I collapsed, like a building being demolished and falling into ruin all at once. Then he went around the bed, came and stood behind me, my neck and head were touching his body, I could feel him. He put one hand on my left shoulder and the other at the base of my neck and he filled me with peace, as if he was pouring it into me with a funnel. I squeezed my hands, nails in my palms, to make sure I wasn't dreaming. When everything in me was filled with peace, Jean-Pierre disappeared. I got up in one bound and went to the toilet to look at myself in the mirror, I was really awake and what I had just experienced overwhelmed and soothed me. I sat back down, my mother was breathing softly but I knew she was leaving us."

We obviously do not know if our participant's dying mother perceived her grandson, but this testimony suggests that Jean-Pierre would have "come to fetch his grandmother" and at the same time he would have comforted his mother.

Another of our participants also had an ADC that seems to have occurred simultaneously with an alleged deathbed vision experienced by her dying mother. This testimony eloquently highlights the essential element of deathbed visions, just as it is the essential element of ADCs, namely *the emotions* inherent in this type of experience. The perceptions, which in this case are visual, are merely the medium for the very essence of these experiences: a sense of boundless and unconditional love, of pure joy, of profound comfort, and of confidence for what lies ahead:

"This particular ADC happened in July 2007 when my mum died, aged 77. She had been generally physically and mentally unwell for some time and had been admitted to [...] Hospital after a fall. She was only in hospital for a few days and at first, she seemed to be recovering as her mood had picked up, but I think it was all part of getting ready to die, as her last conversations were very much like warm, cheerful goodbyes. She then deteriorated quickly as her organs began to fail and she was put on a ventilator. A day later my brother and I agreed to switch off her machine and we sat vigil at her hospital bedside for several hours, waiting for her to go. To set the scene: we were in a side ward of about six beds, three on each side. Mum was in the middle bed on the right-hand side of the room and the other beds were empty. My brother sat on a chair at the foot of her bed on the left, and I sat on a chair at the foot of her bed on the right. There was a curtain pulled down the right-hand side and around behind me, but not across my brother's side as there was a big, light window on that side. The ward was also well lit. At some point during the afternoon, my brother suddenly decided that mum needed more pain relief, although she was just lying there unconscious. As soon as he had left the room, I became aware of several presences coming into the space around me. It happened in a matter of seconds. They seemed to materialise from around behind me and then gathered as a group to the side of me on my right. They appeared to be watching my mum. I could see (or sense?) the vague outlines of maybe six or seven people of varying heights, their heads and shoulders being the clearest. I did not notice anything below the knees, so I suppose they were in effect just hanging there, but at the right height above the ground. They were sort of shadow-like but not shadows and with no real substance, but in 3D and with the curtain as a backdrop. There were no distinguishing features other than their classic humanoid shapes. As these presences were gathering, the most incredible thing then happened — a powerful presence moved over to me and I suddenly felt enveloped in the most wonderful, beautiful, profound sense of love, peace and comfort, such that I shall never forget! It was a virtual embrace of such joy, positivity, hope, warmth, wellbeing... quite beyond words really. I started to sob as I was overwhelmed by a feeling of euphoria in that moment, and then sadness as I realised that it must be time for my mum to leave. As the beautiful presence and the others all moved closer to my mum, I got just the very slightest sense of her spirit/consciousness leaving her body as she lay there face up, and then a moment later they were all gone. They all just sort of blended and dematerialised, disappearing upwards to the front and right of me. I was alone, the room felt empty, and I felt a strange mix of happy-sadness. And I was struck by how her whole appearance had changed. It was clear to me then the difference between a living body and an empty dead one. I don't remember there being any sounds, smells, or physical touches during this ADC. Only the one presence connected with me, the attention of the others was on my mum. I am not sure how long it took, but it couldn't have been more than a few minutes and I stayed in my chair the whole time. No sooner had they left when my brother returned. I told him what had happened, and he was so surprised, and sad of course, and rather disappointed that he had not been able to share in that extraordinary experience. Throughout the whole strange and unexpected event, I never once felt afraid or threatened, just alert. The euphoria is the most stand-out moment for me and if that was what my mum experienced when she died, and if those were familiar faces (perhaps her parents, sisters, son, my dad) that had come to meet and greet her, then I am so happy for her. I've heard that often people who have had a near-death experience report seeing deceased loved ones and experience euphoria. I feel privileged to think that I may have witnessed that from a different perspective."

Near-Death Experiences (NDEs)

We have two cases in our data collection which are of particular interest because they refer directly to another death-related phenomenon, namely a Near-Death Experience (NDE). An NDE is a phenomenon that people can experience when they are at the threshold of death (and more rarely also without actually facing death). In a near-death episode, a person is either clinically dead, near death, or in a situation where death is likely or expected. 10 to 20% of people who have suffered a cardiac arrest remember having experienced an NDE. Zingrone and Alvarado state that: "An analysis of the incidence of NDEs among critically ill patients as documented in nine prospective studies in four countries yielded an average estimate of

17%."** Current knowledge about NDEs is solid, as it is based on 50 years of rigorous and diversified international scientific research.[36]

The persons who undergo an NDE (near-death experiencers or NDErs) have the sensation of leaving their body **(out-of-body experience)**. They view their bodies and the surroundings from an external vantage point at some distance, usually from above (scene of accident, resuscitation efforts, hospital ward in case of surgery, and so on). Typically, they memorize the ongoing events, words and gestures which can be subsequently corroborated. NDErs immediately experience a feeling of absolute well-being, notice the absence of pain and lose interest in their bodies which they leave behind without any regret.

At this stage, NDErs have the impression of being "sucked" into a dark **tunnel** and of moving at an extremely high speed toward a brilliant light beckoning at the end of the tunnel, still very far away. They approach this light, which attracts them like a magnet, at dazzling speed and finally enter the light with a sensation of infinite joy and awe.

Next comes the encounter with a **being of light**, which is described as the vision of a superbly beautiful light, personifying unconditional love and absolute knowledge, more intense than any earthly light, yet not blinding. NDErs say this being knew everything about their life and their good and bad deeds, and loved them (nevertheless) unconditionally. Communication between the being of light and the NDEr happens instantaneously

---

** Zingrone, N.L.; Alvarado, C.S. (2009). Pleasurable Western adult near-death experiences: features, circumstances, and incidence. In: Holden, J.M.; Greyson, B.; James, D. (Eds.) The Handbook of Near-Death Experiences: Thirty Years of Investigation. Santa Barbara, CA: Praeger/ABC-CLIO, pp. 17–40.

and without words, like by telepathy. Many make the analogy with "coming home" or "having reached their destination". The encounter with the being of light produces a feeling of absolute bliss, total knowledge, and profound peace.

According to NDErs, **guides** and **guardian angels** were welcoming them in order to reassure and guide them. They also encounter **deceased loved ones** which they identify more by recognition of spirit rather than by the perception of their bodies which are often described as translucent or fluid, or indeed as a pure center of energy, but nevertheless immediately recognizable. A telepathic communication can occur during these encounters.

At this stage, a **life review** might occur. NDErs witness a three-dimensional review of their whole life, from the most significant to the most banal events. In the presence of the being of light, they relive the events from their own perspective, but also from the point of view of the persons who were involved in the action which is analyzed. This NDE feature has a strong didactic connotation, as it allows the NDErs to simultaneously feel the emotions of all the participants of the scene which permits them to fully understand the significance and implications of their own actions, words, and even of their thoughts. Sometimes, they are informed of future events in their lives that actually do occur later on.

NDErs may report seeing a **limit or boundary**, symbolized in various ways, which, if crossed, would make returning to the body impossible. The near-death experience terminates with the **reintegration of the physical body**, more often imposed than desired, and rarely defined in a precise manner. The return to the physical body is described by NDErs as emotionally painful, limiting and constraining on all levels. The reintegration of the physical body is frequently associated with an imperative feeling of having a mission to fulfil on earth.

It is important to stress that one rarely finds all the above-mentioned phases in a single near-death experience. Each NDE is unique and can include any combination of phases, and the phases can occur in any order, and no one feature is common to all NDEs.

Just as it is the case for shared deathbed visions, it seems that some persons have been able to witness/share the experience of a dying person in the very first phase of the NDE, or, if the person had died during the episode, in the very first stage of his or her dying process. Raymond A. Moody, the American philosopher, psychiatrist, and author, most widely known for his best-selling book *Life After Life*,[37] has described shared NDEs in his book *Glimpses of Eternity: Sharing a Loved One's Passage From This Life to the Next*.[38]

The following short testimony of our data collection is evocative of the typical unfolding of a near-death experience. It can be stipulated that our respondent would have perceived the injured person in the first phase of the NDE — the out-of-body or decorporation phase — i.e. at the moment when the person was dying/had just died. To be precise, it should be stressed that this is in fact a "death experience", rather than an "near-death experience", since the person perceived during the ADC had actually passed away:

> "I witnessed a traffic accident in which a person was dying, and I saw that same person beside his body, kneeling, watching himself die."

A certain number of NDErs report that they were given the choice of crossing this perceived boundary and entering the realm of death, or returning to their physical bodies. When they chose to return, it was often out of an imperative sense of responsibility to their loved ones, for example to take care of their young children. Others state that they had wished wholeheartedly to take that ultimate step and leave their physical bodies behind, because they were so irresistibly attracted to the indescribable bliss they believed awaited them on the other side. However, those who returned to their physical bodies against their will report that they had been told that their time had not yet come and that they still had a mission to fulfil or complete in their lives. For those who left, we obviously do not know whether or not they had this choice to make, although the following testimony gives us perhaps some insight into this. It seems to be indicative of the crucial decision made by the person perceived during the ADC (in this case a friend of the participant) who apparently decided to enter the realm of death and leave her family behind, despite the dilemma that this choice seems to have implied for her:

"It happened in late autumn 2016, in October or November. A friend, Carole, a 47-year-old great athlete, for whom I had much affection, suffered a cardiac arrest during a festive family meal in which she was showing her joie de vivre. While she was dancing happily, she suddenly collapsed to the ground. Her husband Robert, a highly experienced lifeguard, started CPR until the fire brigade arrived. The fire brigade took over once they were on the scene. After 45 minutes of resuscitation efforts, Carole could be transported to the hospital where she remained in a coma for two or three days from which she did not emerge. One afternoon, during my daily nap on the sofa in the living room, I had a dream, but I wasn't really asleep, as if I was in a 'in-between' state. I see Carole. She has a face that reveals a serious situation. She looks gravely at her family, which I cannot see, a husband and three children. Then I see her turn towards a light that I also see shining behind her. Her face lights up with a wonderful smile, the one she used to show so often. I understand that she has a choice to make and prefers to leave. My 'vision' stops when my mobile rings. It is Dominique, Carole's mother, who calls me in tears without being able to say a word. I understand, and I knew, that Carole had just passed away. I am struggling to find my words, but I manage to express my empathy and affection to Dominique. My wife, who was napping in our room, was awakened by the phone conversation. As soon as she enters the living room, I tell her the bad news and she says, 'Look, I just saw her in my dream, dressed in her usual casual clothes, and she told me she had to go.' I say, 'Yes! She came to see me too.' After that, we never 'saw' her again."

Before concluding this section, I would like to share two rather intriguing testimonies that give us some insights into this supposed separation of the consciousness from the physical body, either temporarily during an out-of-body experience (OBE) or permanently at death.

In our survey, we did not ask about contacts that allegedly occurred while the experient had temporarily left his or her body, in other words, during an OBE. We do have a few cases, however, where our participants report having met their deceased significant other in an "other space" after having momentarily left their physical body:

"My father passed away on December 19, 2017. Since his passing, I have felt his presence on several occasions, including through gestures he had towards me when I was a child. I felt his presence a couple of times. In the month of October 2018, around the 20/25, I went to bed and during my sleep which seemed light, I experienced a splitting of my body. I went out of my body to float in the room. I saw my partner sleeping, I saw everything there was. And I felt the presence of my father. I looked on my left, and there I clearly saw my father sitting beside my bed, looking at me. I wanted to approach him to touch him, to hold him close to me, but it was impossible, there was like an 'invisible barrier' that prevented me from touching him. I saw him very appeased, smiling as he used to be. Then I fell back into my physical body, and I looked around."

Information about the dying process appears to have been obtained during the ensuing ADC. The previous testimony described how our participant had apparently temporarily left his body when he perceived his deceased father. The following case depicts this same process, i.e., the alleged separation of consciousness from the body, but this time at the time of death, and described by a deceased person to his son during an ADC:

"I was 18 years old, my Dad had died about six months before. I was woken up in my bed. He was sitting there, light filled the room. He spoke for what seemed a while, but I was so fascinated by his eyes which seemed to glow with white light that I missed most of his conversation. However, I will never forget what happened next. He said to me, 'Don't be scared of dying, it's easy, this is all that happens, watch.' He then separated into two and both sat on my bed. He said, 'Now your turn.' He reached out and I felt myself tingling and separating from my body. Then he got up and walked out the wall."

This concludes this section on shared deathbed visions and shared death experiences, those seemingly rare phenomena that give us the unique privilege of learning, from different perspectives, about the experiences that seem to take place as we leave our bodies to, perhaps, continue our existence in an unknown and unimaginable elsewhere.

Other forms of expression of ADCs

With regard to the types of ADCs, our questionnaire was designed to collect data on ADCs perceived by four of the five sensory organs: hearing, touch, smell or vision (the sense of taste is not concerned by these contacts). In addition, we included ADCs during sleep, when falling asleep or waking up, as well as ADCs of sensing a presence. We also added a series of questions on ADCs at the time of death, which are of particular interest because of their evidential nature.

At the beginning of the questionnaire, we invited our participants to describe their ADC in as much detail as possible in a free text dialogue box. I will draw on these descriptions of the English questionnaires, with the addition of a number of cases of questionnaires in French and Spanish, to present other forms of expression of ADCs that have already been identified (Guggenheim classification[39]). However, I cannot present any statistics because we did not ask our respondents any questions on this subject.

Psychokinetic ADCs are common. The term *Psychokinesis (PK)* (from Psycho-Kinesis: Greek for "movement based on the psyche") was coined in 1914 by the American author Henry Holt and presented in his book *On the Cosmic Relations*.[40] One proposed definition of psychokinesis is the "movement of physical objects by the mind without use of physical means".[41] In the field of parapsychology, the action of mind on matter, in which objects are allegedly caused to move or change as a result of mental concentration upon them, has been extensively studied by renowned researchers such as the American parapsychologist Dean Radin, PhD, Chief Scientist at the Institute of Noetic Science (IONS) and Associated Distinguished Professor of Integral and Transpersonal Psychology at the California Institute of Integral Studies (CIIS).[42] In his book *The Conscious Universe:*

The Scientific Truth of Psychic Phenomena,[43] he presents the results and implications of a large number of experiments conducted in the field of psychokinesis, remote viewing, and related phenomena. These experiments are of course carried out with living subjects.

In ADC accounts, we also observe psychokinetic phenomena, such as temporary apparent malfunction of electronic devices, e.g. of (mobile) phones, as well as the spontaneous turning on or off of televisions, music equipment, etc. Lights that turn on or off, or flicker for no apparent reason, are frequently cited. Objects such as photos or pictures are turned over, moved or found undamaged on the floor. In addition, there are many accounts of watches and clocks that have stopped at the time of death. Unidentified and recurring night-time noises are often reported. Experients interpret these events as messages from their deceased significant other.

I have made a representative selection of this type of ADC reported by our participants and start with apparent *electrical and luminary malfunctions*.

The testimony to follow is beautiful in its simplicity. We can feel our participant's desire to do well, her wish to write a perfect speech, and the love of her father who, as any father would do when he sees his child struggling with a task, releases her by putting an end to her strain:

"When my father died, I was writing the eulogy for the funeral, and the computer and all the lights failed. I got them back on again and continued writing, trying to get it really perfect. Again, all the lights and computer went off and I thought I might have lost all my writing. I continued after I got the electricity on, then I felt a presence and I looked up to see my father standing in the doorway and he said, 'Stop it now, Mary, you have done enough.' I did and the electricity stopped shutting off."

The meaning of this temporary electrical malfunction was immediately obvious to our respondent and her sister:

"When my mom died, and the funeral director came to the house to bring her to the mortuary, my sister and I left the room as we were very sad. Suddenly all the lights went off in the house and came back on without a sound. Our next door neighbor came over next day and told us that her power did not turn off at that time. She was awake because they saw lights on in our house and were concerned about us as my mom had been ill. My mom always used to have a habit of saying, 'Did you turn the lights off?' And also saying 'make sure you turn the lights off when you leave the house'. The moment the lights went off was right after the mortician closed the door and she was outside the house. I knew my mother was saying 'your mother has left the building'. It was a happy communication, we knew it was her."

A lamp that continues to function after being unplugged is the subject of the following testimony:

"Six or so months after my father's death, I was cleaning the house. I pulled a lamp's cord out of the wall with the lamp being turned on. It took me a few seconds to understand that the light... even though unplugged... was still lit. I was shocked at first. Then I felt my dad. And I remembered. My dad was an electrician. When I was a child, sometimes he would explain the way electricity worked. He taught me that our bodies have electricity inside and that when we die,

that electricity is drawn into the air; that when he died...
he would show me a sign that life does continue... through
electricity. When the lamp incident happened, I knew this
was my dad's electrical energy. I just knew."

The following account mentions a momentary malfunction of a
light bulb, a "classic" for this type of ADC:

"In 2008, my grandmother passed away at 93 at home. I was
there when she died. Once we had prepared her body, we all
went to bed because it was late. As I couldn't sleep, two–three
hours later, I went down to the kitchen and sat on a stool.
There I shed all my tears thinking about my grandmother
and the fact that I won't see her anymore. All of a sudden,
the light bulb in the kitchen lamp started to flicker. I couldn't
say how long (maybe 30 seconds?) but it seemed like a
long time. Completely surprised, I looked at the bulb and
then I felt my grandmother's presence. It's hard to explain
because it was an inner feeling, but connected to the outside
(the kitchen) and I couldn't say why, but I knew it was my
grandmother. Not weak and ill as she was in the last weeks
before her death, but in all her strength and splendour. And
she was communicating to me (... telepathically? At least not
with words but with a kind of 'direct inner communication')
something like: 'Don't cry, life goes on!' Then it was over and
I was alone again in the kitchen."

Our respondent experienced manifestations of various kinds,
simultaneously perceived by her husband. Her son also noticed a
manifestation, which suggests that the deceased was apparently
trying to make contact several times and in a number of ways.
However, he did not obtain the forgiveness he seems to have
yearned for with some urgency:

"My ex-husband, whom I had divorced, died in San Diego of pancreatic cancer. At the time of his death, around three o'clock in the morning Costa Rican time, the lamp on my bedside table went on. This lamp is not one that you touch to turn on, but you have to push a button to turn it on. I woke up, and I woke up my current husband, and I pointed out to him that it was strange that this lamp had turned on by itself. That had never happened before. But I turned it off and went back to sleep. Two hours later, my ex-husband's sister called to let me know that he had passed away. Days passed and at night, when we went to bed, I began to hear footsteps in the room, which has a wooden floor. The footsteps moved around the room and came back next to me. My husband also heard them and thought that it was my first husband who wanted to communicate with me. Sometimes when we were watching television it would go off and I would say to him, 'That's funny' and then it would come back on. I also heard one evening that someone was knocking on the door of my son's room, who was 15 years old. He was playing on a PlayStation with a classmate and I heard him say: 'Go on! Come in!' because he thought it was me knocking on the door, but it wasn't me. He opened the door, but there was nobody there. So, he came into the kitchen to ask me if I had come to knock, and I said no. I then phoned a woman who was a psychic and told her about these events. She asked me to send her a picture of my ex-husband, that she was going to invoke him. I sent it to her and the next day I called her. She told me that my deceased ex-husband wanted to contact me to apologize for everything he had done to me. I started to cry with rage, and I felt that he was in the hallway, even though I didn't see him, and then I told him that I wasn't going to forgive him, that he should go away, that he was already dead, that he didn't belong here, that he should leave, and, from then on, I never felt him in my house again."

Inexplicable *movement, displacement, and breaking of objects* are the subject of the next testimonies.

The following long description by a medical doctor is of particular interest. The baffling physical manifestations were observed by our participant and his mother, classifying these experiences as shared ADCs. The meaning of such explicit manifestations became apparent to the participant over time and had essential therapeutic consequences for his sister:

"[These ADCs relate to] my maternal grandfather, with whom I had a very close relationship from the age of 7 to 19. The week after [his passing], one afternoon when I came home from school, I found my mother watching television in a room on the second floor of the house. I sat down to keep her company and soon after she said, 'Son, I have to tell you I'm worried, I've been alone all afternoon and something very strange has happened in my room.' We went to her room, the door of which was closed. We opened the door and my mother showed me that on the floor, next to her bed and on the side that faced a window that in turn looked out onto the street, there was a picture frame with a photo of my little sister. The photo was on the floor, a little less than a meter away and in front of the desk, where the solid wooden photo frame with a stable base was usually located. The fact is that a few minutes before, my mother had already picked up the photo frame from the same spot on the floor and placed it on the desk more than 10 cm from the edge of the desk where it was usually placed. So, this was the second time that my sister's picture had fallen on the floor. My mother didn't want to put it back again because she got scared and wanted to talk about it and show someone what had happened. I remember we made jokes about it being a huge rat, or an unknown animal hiding somewhere in the room, or maybe a 'percussive spirit' playing a nasty game...

I personally picked up the photo frame from the floor and put it back in its place. I stress that this was a heavy wooden photo frame made of only two pieces. A rectangle where the photo fits and a triangle assembled at the back to form a T-shaped base. The pieces were about an inch thick, the rectangle about 15x12 cm, and the triangle with which it formed the base T, about 10 cm. This gave it enough stability that it could not fall easily, let alone jump to the front of the desk. Once I had put the photo frame back on the desk, we left the room and closed the door to continue watching television and commenting on the event.

Not even five to ten minutes had passed, when suddenly we were interrupted and greatly surprised by the resounding sound of a glass breaking. The noise came from my mother's room... We thought it might have been a stone or some other object thrown from the street or a ball kids were playing with that accidentally broke the glass. We got up from our chairs and headed for the bedroom. We opened the door and were surprised to see the lower part of the left-hand curtain sticking outside the window through a completely broken window. This two-piece curtain was normally drawn and completely closed in the centre of the window. [...] The air conditioner was on and the curtain was fluttering outside the window, making the unmistakable sound of tapping fabric. We walked very frightened to the foot of the bed, only to be much more shocked when we saw my sister's photo thrown on the floor again, in the same place where my mother and I had previously picked it up, each on a different occasion. But what was even more surprising is that there was not a single piece of glass inside the room, all the broken glass had fallen on the open parking side of the street. Needless to say, we felt a chill from head to toe and started praying for protection...

At that moment, we could not find any explanation for this... However, in this state of alarm and almost panic that we felt,

I personally had a moment of equanimity and it seemed to me that I saw the image of my grandfather in full body but very small, like a miniature figure, on the pillow on this side of the bed, where my little sister, the one in the photo, slept for many years. Somehow, I could perceive the image of my grandfather's face coming off it, telling me to 'take good care of my darling granddaughter', in the manner of a recommendation and concern he had for his granddaughter. I understood that he had felt the need to point this out to us by throwing my sister's photo on the floor three times, but the third time he had to break a glass to attract our attention in a more obvious way in order to manifest his request.

Surely, we had not yet understood the meaning of insisting on the photo of my sister. Without this vision I had of my grandfather, I would not have thought or perceived the message. It would have remained perhaps as a warning of something very negative about my sister. I can even say that I couldn't help but have the intuition that this was what it was all about, but I couldn't discern more at that time. My grandfather, as a homeopath and practicing physician, knew that my sister was suffering from something serious... She had been suffering from epilepsy since she was two years old, but there was no etiological diagnosis. She had been examined at a medical center in Houston, Texas, USA. But her illness had only been classified as grand mal epilepsy and she was receiving anticonvulsant treatment [...]. I continued my medical studies and always had a special interest in my sister's case and always associated it with this inner 'voice' I felt from my grandfather who was worried about her.

It was in 1985 — when I was studying for the selection exam for a medical specialty — that I was able to recognize my sister's illness by gathering all her stigmata. Finally, she had Bourneville's disease or tuberous sclerosis... but in a variant without mental retardation. This made it possible to predict a complication that could have appeared years later, namely the Wünderlich syndrome, which could be treated with great expediency by embolisation of abnormal arteries in her right kidney with angiomyolipomatosis."

What is the factor that turns the simple failure of an electronic or electric device — or any other inexplicable physical manifestation — into a significant event for experients? We are all regularly confronted with malfunctioning devices that we replace with a newer model without giving it a second thought, or with night-time noises that we fail to identify but to which we do not attach any importance, to mention just these two cases. These are the small annoyances of everyday life and yet they are sometimes invested with a strong meaning by the experients who interpret them as a sign, sometimes as a warning, or even as a message of love beyond death. Where does this immediate conviction come from? It is obviously the *emotions* associated with these trivial events that give them their full meaning. The experients feel the presence of the deceased family member or friend and perceive their *intention*, which they interpret as an expression of love, a desire to comfort them in their grief, or the transmission of crucial information.

The following account describes the malfunctioning of a gate that suddenly takes on an unexpected meaning. Our respondent speaks of a "feeling of energy", which others might call "a presence", that transforms this event into a significant message, likely to change the course of her life:

"It's a summer afternoon. It is about 5 p.m. when my partner, with whom I have had a tumultuous relationship for several years and who no longer lives at home, comes to my house for the umpteenth time to talk. This person is no longer entirely in my life, but also refuses to leave it for good, which is a very painful situation for me. We are in my yard. By the time he decides to leave, about twenty minutes have passed. The weather is beautiful and clear, no wind or even breeze in the atmosphere that day. So, he gets into his car, opens the driver's side window and we continue our conversation. He is driving at a walking pace, I am walking next to him. The gate is now facing us. It is made of wood. The left-hand gate is closed and the right-hand gate is open, attached to a cypress trunk by a strong rope that goes around the trunk several times and ends in a sailor's knot. Once again, I would like to point out that despite living in a windy region of southeastern France, the weather is very calm that day, no breeze, the sun is shining and the air is rather stifling. Suddenly, when the car is at a short distance from the gate, the right-hand door comes off in a fraction of a second and closes so violently that it goes over the bumper with a shattering sound. We are both shocked by what we have just witnessed. He, very surprised, laughs nervously and asks me what has just happened? I don't have a logical explanation for it, as the only thing that could have explained this phenomenon would have been a strong gust of wind. But there was none of that.

I feel a special atmosphere at this very moment. I have a feeling of energy flowing at full speed around us. Then nothing. Everything calms down and he goes home after having managed, not without difficulty, to get the right side of the gate on the right side of the bumper. I always thought that on that day, my grandmother, who had died some twenty years earlier, had come to tell my ex-partner that he was no longer welcome in my house. My grandmother was a strong woman who had suffered a lot from men during her life. I didn't know her well because she died when I was only 15. Ironically, I never felt closer to her since I became an adult [as I did that day]. My ex-partner was an abusive and toxic person, and I experienced what happened with the gate as a sign of protection from my grandmother. A sign for me not to let him into my life anymore, and for him to get out of it for good."

The range of ADCs expressed by psychokinetic phenomena is wide:

"It was 18 years ago, I was starting to study psychology. It was the day before school started. I was sitting on my bed with my paper pad on my lap and I was making margins so as not to waste time doing them during class. I heard a strange noise behind me. I turned around and saw my drawer open, with my late grandfather's watch inside. I was very surprised. I walked out of my room and a cold draft ran through me. I perceived: 'no, you have nothing to fear'. Since then, I have no doubts about life after death."

This account involves a music device. The material element, the CD that was inexplicably placed in the device, is typical of this type of ADC:

"My father-in-law passed away. We had agreed that he would give a sign of the afterlife if he died (he had a heart condition and had recently had surgery). One afternoon I was getting ready to go out when my stereo (CD player) started up by itself, although perfectly switched off, and Bach music filled the room with the words in German 'Jesus, have mercy on me'. I had to switch it off after a while and inside the device was the CD I had not put in. Another night, a plug in the living room was pulled out which is very hard and cannot be removed without great effort."

The perceived sound of a music box has triggered a beautiful experience:

"It was the night before my birthday and for some unknown reason I asked my mum, in my head, 'What are you getting me for my birthday? It must be something extra special considering you're dead' and instantly thought 'why have I just said that, what a strange thing for me to think'. Then I walked into my room and lay in bed ready to sleep (still awake as I had only just lay down and had my eyes open), I heard the sound of a musical jewelry box that I had when I was a child. It sounded clear as anything, like it was playing in my room, without it actually, physically, being in my room... and I just felt my heart expand to the other side of my bedroom — it's difficult to explain, but it's like I could feel my heart beating more than what I'm usually capable of feeling it beat in my chest, but it felt like it was also on the other side of the room at the same time, and all the space in-between! And I just got all these flooding images in my vision (eyes were open and I could see my room at the same time) of memories of times I had with my mum that were so happy and beautiful, which I had completely forgotten about somehow. I was seeing picture after picture of happy times with her I had had, that I had forgotten about, like a slide show. It was really beautiful and I felt like it was a gift from my mum, like she was with me."

A toy is the medium for the following two experiences:

"My father died in September 2002. At the beginning of November 2002, when I was invited to my nephew's (one year old) birthday party, I said with tears in my eyes, 'It's a shame Daddy can't be here for his grandson's first birthday.' Just as I was finishing my sentence, one of my nephew's musical toys that was no longer working started to ring and play its little music. At that moment, no one was near the toy and no one was touching it. My sister-in-law confirmed that the toy had not worked for a while. I knew then that my father wanted me to know that he was there with us."

"The night after the funeral of a friend's son (who died at the age of eight), a previously non-functioning toy of my son's turned on by itself (at around 2 a.m., my son was sleeping soundly). This toy had been non-functional for months and my friend's son, while alive, often wanted to play with this little remote-control car."

Televisions are sometimes the vehicles for psychokinetic ADCs:

"My only son died in an accident when he was 25. Several months after his death, I would often get up at night having trouble sleeping, waking up frequently. One night I got up at about one o'clock in the morning to drink a glass of water, my husband was already in bed, nothing special, the silence of the night. An hour later I woke up again and got up, and then I heard the sound of the television being turned on. How did it turn on by itself? Scientific explanation? Weird… No one else was up but me. I burst out laughing as I was sure it was my deceased son who had turned it on and said, 'Thank you, my angel'."

"A few months after my mother's death, the television would turn on by itself at night. It wasn't every night or at the same time of night (but always at night). There was no alarm clock or timer set on the TV. This happened five or six times over a month."

"It had been about nine months since my mother had died suddenly. One night, while I was sleeping at my father's house with my husband and children, I had to get up to prepare a bottle for my then 20-month-old son. Then I went to bed and I clearly heard knocks on the wall. It was as if someone was punching the wall... I tried to find a rational reason for what I was hearing, but really, I couldn't find one. Also, in this room there is a TV on standby and the button started flashing... I immediately thought of my mother, of course, because I often asked her to show me signs... except that it scared me and I asked her to avoid doing it at night."

ADCs manifesting through a *(mobile) phone* are relatively common. Experients notice an apparent malfunction in their mobile phone before contact is made. Sometimes the landline or mobile phone will ring, and when the experient answers, they will hear the voice of the deceased communicating a message or a two-way communication may even be established. The physical aspect of this type of contact — the ringing of the telephone — is noteworthy. Sometimes communication is established indirectly. For example, a person calls a company or an administration. When he has chosen the number of the internal service he wishes to contact and the hold music starts, this music is interrupted by the voice of the deceased who transmits a message. Then the hold music resumes.

The next case refers to a public telephone:

"Two weeks after my daughter's death by suicide I went to a coffee shop she always went to and she used to get a really foul-smelling coffee. And I was going to get the same thing and say, 'Here's to you, honey.' As I parked the car and walked past the phone booth outside, the phone started ringing and I absolutely KNEW it was for me, but I refused to pick up the public phone. It rang and rang and rang and any normal person would have hung up by now. I said, 'Nope,' and went into the store. Just as I stepped back out with my coffee and walked past the phone, it rang again. After about another 15 rings with everyone at this busy coffee place ignoring it, I finally picked it up. The line sounded open with swishing and echoing, can't explain the noise, but it sounded empty. I said, 'You have reached a public phone,' and my daughter's voice said, 'Hello.' I just went to my car and leaned on the door and cried."

The next contact occurred via a mobile phone:

"I lost my dad on August 8, 2017 to cancer. I was with him until the end. I was close to him. A few days after the ceremony and the cremation, I was on the phone (mobile) with my aunt. The moment I entered my dad's house, communication suddenly became blurred. A very intense whistling, sizzling on the line for three to four minutes. I could no longer hear my aunt. The whistling and sizzling stopped all at once when a loud and fast breathing was heard in the phone. I asked who was on the line, no answer but only that breathing which came back several times during this event. I knew this breathing, because my dad had had this strong, fast jerking breath a few days before he died. I was drawn to the breathing, but also scared. I didn't want to hang up although I was shaking, so I opened the blinds because the house was in darkness and then... nothing. Communication with my aunt became fluid again. On her side, my aunt had heard the whistling and water flowing, splashing (my dad's ashes had been cast into the sea two days before). Since then, I think about this event very often."

These luminous apparitions were supported by another medium, the mobile phone, as if to reinforce the meaning of the initial manifestations:

"On the day my sister died, at night, I saw a sphere of white light hanging in the air in the bedroom. I was relaxed. The next day, also at night and in the bedroom, I saw several flashes of blue light. That's when I got scared and called my partner to come over to my house. When he arrived, I asked him to lend me his mobile phone to check my emails. As soon as I opened the email application, an email from my sister from two months ago opened by itself, without me touching anything. She was on a trip and said she was doing very well and that everything was going beautifully. Then the email message closed itself, the icons on the mobile phone screen disappeared, the screen was black and the mobile phone reset. Stunned, I looked for a technical explanation for what had happened, but I couldn't find one. My partner said that it was probably a message from my deceased sister."

This account describes a lengthy scenario which had to be in place before the contact could happen:

"I attended to an old gentleman at the end of his life with whom an emotional bond and companionship had been established. One day when I was going to visit him, he had just passed away. Beyond the sadness, my greatest regret at that moment was to think with all my heart, 'My God, I would have liked so much to say goodbye to him, he passed away without me being able to say goodbye!' A few days later it was time for the funeral which I had planned to attend. As I prepared to leave, I was troubled by the idea of whether or not to take my mobile phone. I remember being annoyed, going back and forth saying, 'I'll take it,' and then, 'No, I won't take it.' This attitude was all the more disturbing because I never, ever, take a mobile phone to a funeral! Even switched off, I'm too worried that it will start ringing in the middle of the ceremony, so this question shouldn't even have been considered! Slipping it into my pocket, I eventually decided to take it, turn it off (and I remember checking that it was switched off) and leave it in the glove compartment of the car. Except that on the way from the house to the car I left it in my pocket, not thinking about it anymore, because with my hesitations I was running late. Before blessing the coffin, I stopped to greet the family, in silence, and then I approached the coffin. The funeral director passed me the aspergillum and just as I raised my arm to start blessing the body, I heard a beep from my mobile phone, as if I had received a message! I thought to myself 'oh gosh, my mobile phone!' and then I hurried to my seat. It was then that I discreetly wanted to turn off the mobile phone that had emitted a signal so as not to disrupt the ceremony, except that the phone was completely switched off! Beyond the words, which are only pale representations of what happened that day, it is the feeling in the depths of my heart and my soul that made me understand that this gentleman whom I liked very much, was telling me at that moment what I had so much wanted to tell him: 'Goodbye and thank you.' I caught myself smiling and found myself at peace."

The inexplicable display of photos of the deceased on a mobile phone is also frequently mentioned, as described in this testimony:

"After taking four pictures of my car with my mobile phone, when I looked at them, I noticed that one of the four pictures had a person in the vehicle. When I looked closely at this photo, I immediately recognized my father's face in the driver seat, which seemed to be smiling in a light fog. My father died at the end of December 17 at the age of 88. He loved cars, it was his passion. His face was the same as when he died suddenly."

A photo made its way into a painting, unbeknownst to the artist and much to her surprise:

"In the very last conversation with my father who passed away seven months ago, he wanted me to do a painting for him in resin which is a very fluid medium and does not allow for any other art than abstract. He passed away before I could do it. After many ADCs, including one where my phone was calling, by itself, in the middle of the night, my resin supplier, I set about the task. After three days of working on this painting destined for my deceased father, I considered it finalized. I placed it at a distance to see it in its entirety and decide where to place my signature. Taking a few steps back I staggered... My father's portrait was in the painting... Not just any portrait, but a very specific photo that was the one he used as an identifier on his emails, a photo I kept close to me. As if the picture had slipped under the resin. That painting was framed, I knew I had to keep it, and I put it in my house. My husband, my children, all my relatives and friends who knew my father always see him [in the painting]."

Another form of expression of spontaneous contacts with a deceased person are named **ADCs for protection** which occur in situations of crisis or imminent danger and result in the avoidance of a dramatic — potentially even fatal — event, such as an accident, a fire, an assault, a drowning, etc. There are reports of young children in danger who were saved in extremis thanks to a warning transmitted by different types of ADCs. Sometimes undiagnosed health problems were identified in time thanks to the contact. These experiences do not occur when a danger has already been identified by the person concerned. For example, an individual who has realized that his house is on fire and is running to get a fire extinguisher or is calling the fire brigade will not have this type of experience. These ADCs are not about *managing* a crisis situation but about *becoming aware* of it.

Here is an illustration of an ADC for protection:

"I was crossing a street without paying attention, probably distracted by my thoughts. I felt a hand pulling me back as a vehicle was about to hit me. I attributed this hand to my husband's, who had died a year earlier."

The following testimony describes a very similar situation of imminent danger that was narrowly avoided. In contrast to the previous case, our participant was unable to identify the deceased who was/were allegedly at the origin of this salutary gesture:

"I have been physically pulled back from danger by someone in spirit. I was extremely tired and almost walked in front of a car with my youngest son in his buggy. The unseen pulled us back. It would have been catastrophic had they not. This was 17 years ago."

The ensuing account is succinct, but nevertheless allows us to understand the significance of this perceived warning:

"My brother tapped me on the shoulder and told me to slow down whilst I was driving. Very clear."

A warning during sleep was not enough and a second intervention was apparently needed to avoid a dramatic outcome for this respondent:

"Several years after my mother's death, I dreamed of her one night. She was very present, I could feel her close. She was visibly concerned, and told me that she was worried about me because she was afraid I would have a motorbike accident (I ride both a motorbike and drive a car). I told her, 'I'm careful' (I am, 40 years of two-wheelers, zero accidents). But she insisted, repeating that she was worried despite my answer. The contact ended there. A few days later, in the morning, I needed to go to a work meeting which made me take an unusual route. I went to the car park where my motorbike and car are parked, which is five minutes away from my house. When I arrived, I realized that I had made a mistake (this had never happened to me), I had taken the car keys instead of the motorbike keys. So, I had to go back to my house and then return to the car park, which made me lose ten minutes. Then I took the road to my destination, and a few kilometers away, at a junction known to be very accident-prone, there had been a very large pile-up that took up the whole width of the road. And obviously this accident had just happened, probably ten minutes before, the ten minutes I had lost getting my key. That morning I didn't feel my mother's presence, but I'm sure it was she who created this unusual absent-mindedness in order to delay me and probably save my life."

This participant received two warnings from his deceased grandfather, one of which was of paramount importance. He reported that he had left his body momentarily during these encounters, what may have been out-of-body experiences (OBEs). Skeptical at first, our respondent was able to verify immediately the veracity of the perceived information:

"I lost my grandfather in December 2009. I was very close to him and his death was very unsettling for me. I had just moved into a new house which he never saw because he was hospitalized the day before he was to come to my new home. He knew nothing about my house (this is important for the rest of my account). Five days after his death, I was visited by my grandfather in my sleep and I found myself in a magnificent place, indescribably beautiful and full of love and kindness. He said he wanted to communicate with me to assist me in my grieving process and to help me develop an extrasensory gift, but that is not the subject here. Being skeptical by nature and thinking that I was dreaming, I asked him for proof of his real presence and of the veracity of our exchange, which was unusual to say the least. He smiled at me and with an amused look he told me to be careful with my boiler and that a pipe was not insulated from the cold, that I might have problems with the winter coming. (My grandfather was a heating engineer.) When I woke up, I understood that I had not been dreaming because I remembered all the details of our exchange. I can clearly tell the difference between a real memory like our exchange and the vague memory of a dream that evaporates with time. Still skeptical, I decided to check my boiler which I had never inspected before. I had to lie down on the floor of the garage to look under the hot water tank and realized that one of the water pipes had no insulation. I was shocked because I understood instantly that I had indeed communicated with my grandfather. Actually, I had never looked under this hot water tank. I could therefore rule out that I had constructed this encounter from memories."

[During another contact] "He suddenly stopped me in our exchange to tell me to go back and check on my son (he was three months old) who was sleeping in the next room because he had an object in his mouth and was in danger of choking. I immediately found myself back in my body. I woke up my wife to share this information with her (I hadn't told her about my encounters with my grandfather). We went to see our son who actually had a piece of the mobile in his mouth that normally hangs above him, with the risk of choking."

The following experience suggests — as do all ADCs for protection — that our deceased loved ones watch over us at all times and intervene when necessary to warn us of potential or even imminent danger. Our respondent hardly knew her grandmother as she was a small child when she died, but she nevertheless seems to have spared her a serious problem during this intriguing event:

"Five years ago, I was working on a stone cutting site. It was at the end of the day on Friday and I was responsible for cutting several pieces of stone for a construction site that was due to start on Monday. I was under a lot of pressure from my client to finish this order before the weekend. To go faster, I decided to use a large disc cutter instead of the small one (I'm not very tall and being a woman in this job, some tools are not really adapted to my size). To go even faster, I chose not to move the stones to my work surface and I started working them directly where they were on their pallet at ground level. Here I was in a very uncomfortable position, with a machine in my hands which, when it started up, made me take a step backwards because it was so powerful, with time pressure and the week's fatigue in the body. It was very hot, there was a lot of dust, what was left of my face and hair was as white with dust as the entire space of my workshop, you couldn't see more than a metre. It was at that very moment that I received a very clear message from my maternal grandmother, who died when I was two years old (I have no conscious memory of her). This message told me very clearly (it was staggering) to put down that disc cutter. She told me to calm down and that if this order wasn't ready, it didn't really matter. How, at that moment, could I think of my grandmother whom I didn't even know? The message was so clear that I stopped my machine immediately, took off my protective breathing mask, my gloves and my hearing protection helmet and sat there for a while, shocked by what I had just experienced. Like a child who has done something stupid and is given a little slap on the back of the head to set his mind right. I didn't know my grandmother and so I never mourned her. The message was auditory, I would say, well, it was in my head. With the noise there, it was as if I had perceived it inside my head. A bit like when you think, except that it wasn't coming from me."

During this ADC, a potential car accident was avoided thanks to a warning:

"9 p.m., on a country road in winter. I had just finished my work, it was dark, no radio. Suddenly, in my left ear, I heard a voice saying very, very quietly, 'Watch out, my daughter, on your right-hand side.' I wasn't driving very fast but I found myself putting on the brakes anyway and about 20 metres further on the right, two big black cows crossed the road. They were as dark as the night and I couldn't have made them out. I can't explain why I know it was my father who had died a few months earlier, but beyond the fact that he always said 'my daughter' when he spoke to me, I know it was him. Tears came to my eyes. I had often felt him around me quite soon after his death and it's true that it helped me a lot in my mourning because, in my view, he is just on another level. I thanked him very much."

In this case, it was not the car accident that was avoided by the ADC for protection but its potentially serious consequences:

"My father died in April 2005. The following month I turned 18, got my driving licence and bought my first car. Less than a week after I purchased my car (at the very beginning of June 2005), I had a serious car accident. As the car began its wild ride following the loss of control of the vehicle, I then felt and had the vision of two hands pushing hard on my chest, securing me to the seat of the car as it rolled over and slid down on the left side of the car onto the road. Those two hands were my father's hands. The sensation is still distinct 14 years later, his raspy fingers, the shape of his broad fingers, and the size of his hands. I came out of that accident unscathed, with only a large scar on my left cheek (the windows had shattered during the impacts) but no haematomas (no seatbelt lacerations, no stiffness or blockage of the cervical vertebrae), much to the astonishment of the firemen and doctors who examined me in the aftermath of that accident."

The next account is interesting — our respondent made only partial use of a perceived warning. Generally, the experients follow the recommendations perceived during the ADC and avoid performing the action which could put them in danger, thus, they will never know if the harmful event would have actually taken place. In the following case, however, our participant has only partially taken into account the warning and the announced accident has actually occurred:

"Before a car accident I got a message in my head: you are going to have an accident. It was very strong. Because of this message I did not take my daughter in the car. And I had this very serious accident. If I had listened to the little voice… the car was classified as a wreck and I was very badly injured. I don't know who warned me."

For this case as well, several warnings were not enough and a more substantial intervention was needed...

"One of the most striking experiences I had in relation to my late husband occurred about three months ago. I woke up in the morning and felt him right beside me, on the left-hand side — a slight cool breeze seemed to accompany his presence. I never see things with my physical eye, it's a sensation in my mind's eye, as it were. He warned me to be careful that day, and as I continued with chores around the house, this warning did not leave me, and I felt he was still very much around. Anyhow, later in the day I decided to start painting the ceiling in the kitchen — a friend offered to help me over the weekend, but I wanted to make a start. I put a chair on the floor in the kitchen to climb up, but couldn't reach the area I wanted to paint, so decided to lift myself up with my hands onto the board next to the kitchen sink (which allowed me to reach the ceiling, as it was higher up). I spread paper across the board, to prevent it from being slippery, and started the painting with a brush. Once again, I felt my husband was around and told me to leave it, but I mentally replied I would only do a small area. I painted for a little while, but got really tired and fed up with it, and as I was about to finish, I slipped and fell. I thought 'oh no, this is going to end badly', and then I seemed to almost lose consciousness for a few seconds, when suddenly I felt two arms/hands lifting me up and literally dropping me onto the chair, upright. I was disorientated for a while and of course a bit in shock, but when I was put into the chair I immediately knew the arms belonged to my late husband, and he had literally saved me from what could have been a very nasty fall. To clarify, I was standing sideways on the board by the sink whilst painting, and there is no way I could have ended up sitting straight in the chair, considering the chair was a little distance away too. It hurt a bit when I landed on the chair (due to the hard impact) but I had no after-effects whatsoever. I sat on the chair for a while, as I couldn't quite take in how/what had happened, but realized my husband had tried to warn me right from the time I got up and then intervened to keep me safe. Later in the evening, I sort of relived the whole experience and I felt more shocked/awed then as to how things unfolded earlier in the day. Needless to say, I thanked my husband profusely."

Under the name **practical ADCs** are grouped the experiences in which the deceased seem to pass on practical information to their significant others of which they were not previously aware. Thus, these contacts fall into the category of evidential ADCs. The subject of these contacts may include the location of a family record book, a life insurance policy taken out without the knowledge of others, investments in the stock exchange kept confidential, or any other documents urgently needed by the family or friends of the deceased. These contacts may occur when the experient is frantically searching for a document that he cannot locate or, conversely, when he does not suspect anything.

Our data collection contains only a few such cases. This account is interesting: our respondent did not trust her perception, the veracity of which has, however, been confirmed by her brother who was not aware of this event:

"My father and I were like twins. We were very close during his lifetime. A few days after his passing, my brother and I were looking for the registration papers of his car, which we were going to sell the next day. The papers were nowhere to be found where they were supposed to be: in a safe where my father kept all the important papers. By digging into this safe, I found a file with my name on it, in which my father had carefully kept all the papers that concerned me. I felt a wave of love and tenderness towards him when I discovered these papers and that's when it happened: suddenly I saw him — an image in my head — both real and unreal. He was wearing a navy blue jumper and, scratching his head nervously, he said to me in a loud voice: 'You're looking in the wrong place! The car papers are in my laptop bag!' And the vision disappeared. I wasn't afraid because it was an image there and not there. But my rationality won out and I chose not to look in the place he told me. Besides, as we were in my brother's flat, I thought that the laptop bag belonged to my brother and that there was no way that papers belonging to my father would be in it. So, I went out of the room without looking there. A few hours later, my brother called me: 'I finally found them! They were in his laptop bag!' I was in shock. 'But isn't it yours?' 'No, in fact, he had bought the same laptop bag as mine because he thought it looked fashionable!' I smiled and I gave my father a conspiratorial wink. I knew he could see me..."

Yet another form of expression of spontaneous contacts are **ADCs for a third person**, when the experient, who is not grieving for the perceived deceased or doesn't even know him, receives a communication intended for a third person who is bereaved. The messages to be transmitted usually serve to inform the recipient that the deceased is alive and well. It is not always easy for experients to carry out the request, as this mission entrusted to them is so completely out of step with the endeavors accepted in our societies. I have in mind the case of a woman who wrote to me to tell me about an ADC during which her deceased neighbour had asked her to inform his widow that everything was going well for him and that she should not be so sad anymore. It seemed inconceivable to her to knock on the door of her neighbor, whom she hardly knew, to deliver the message. After a few exchanges of e-mails, my correspondent found the courage to go see her neighbour who welcomed her message with gratitude and relief.[44]

Why do the deceased not contact the recipients of their message directly? We don't know, of course, but one might assume that a direct contact was not possible, for whatever reason, and that the deceased manifested themselves where they could be perceived.

ADCs for a third person occur relatively often in the context of a sudden, e.g. accidental, death, when the passing was not expected and a final farewell was impossible.

This was precisely the case for the testimony to follow:

"A man who died in a truck accident came to see me. He didn't believe in this type of manifestations when he was alive but he needed to send a message to his wife... It was very moving, especially for his wife. After giving her the message, she told me that he had offered her the best present he could have possibly given her."

In the following case, the respondent did not know the perceived deceased, although a family connection would soon be established:

"I was dating my future husband, and I felt a presence in the room. I was used to hearing spirit from time to time so I asked: 'Have you something to tell me?' I heard a voice, partly in my head and partly a whisper, saying it was my future mother-in-law that had passed a year ago, whom I never met. She said that her husband was unwell and to let her son know (my boyfriend). I answered that I was unsure about telling him as we were not dating long, and he wouldn't believe me. I was told to say something only her husband would know, when my boyfriend and her husband return from their trip to Italy. I was to say that her husband had taken her handbag to Italy with him, and the reason was because this was the first time he had travelled without her. I didn't say anything for over a week, as my boyfriend was a sceptic. But it was confirmed, his father took his mother's handbag, and he became unwell with cancer within the year. My husband is still a little sceptical, although he does tell people how I got that message."

A car accident is at the origin of the following experience:

"I received a message from a friend of my son, who died in a car accident, asking me to tell his mother not to be angry with him, that he had to leave and that he was happy and at peace."

In the cases of suicide, the deceased sometimes seems to contact a third person with a certain urgency to deliver a message to their family:

"He needed to explain why he had done what was not meant to be a fatal act and apologize to his mother."

"She asked me to write to her son what she would have wanted to tell him to explain her fatal act."

Symbolic ADCs are subtle experiences that are considered by experients as a sign or a wink from the deceased and only take on meaning through their *interpretation*. Although these are events that are commonly regarded by their entourage as mere coincidences and are not taken seriously, they are nevertheless very important to the experients. The range of symbolic ADCs is wide. It may be the seemingly unusual behavior of a pet, a bird or an insect, clouds gathering in the shape of a heart, a sudden ray of sunshine on a gloomy day, or any event of this type occurring at a significant time that, in the eyes of the bereaved, symbolizes a message of love and support intended for them personally.

Our data collection does not include many descriptions of symbolic ADCs. This may be due to the fact that we asked respondents to describe *only the most significant ADC* in case they had experienced several contacts. Since 80% of our participants had indeed experienced multiple ADCs, many of them had to make a choice among their experiences. They may have decided to describe their most striking or even spectacular ADC, which would exclude from the outset symbolic ADCs because of their very subtle nature.

Symbolic ADCs often occur on a significant date, a birthday or death anniversary, or, as in the following story, on Mother's Day:

"It's Mother's Day, the first without my son, who died a few months before... We go down to the pool for a swim and suddenly a dragonfly appears. It is circling around my son's diving mask, which was left on the edge of the pool after I had used it to clean the bottom of the pool the day before. And then, I have no doubt, I know it's him! I say, 'Are you coming to check that I'm taking care of your mask?' I call the dragonfly by holding out my finger... it comes and lands on it! I am calm, I have no doubt that it is him... I tell him to go and see his uncle who is swimming. The dragonfly takes off and lands on my brother's head. I tell my brother to hold out his finger... it lands there! My mother, in tears, also holds out her finger... it flies away and lands there! Fortunately, I took pictures of all this, otherwise I would think I was dreaming!"

The account to follow involves a butterfly, a recurring theme for symbolic ADCs:

"My grandmother died three hours after I had seen her for the last time in hospital. My mother called me to tell me about her death. I was at my night-shift as an ambulance driver. When I heard about my grandmother's death, I went to an empty conference room in order to be alone for some time. This room had no windows. Suddenly a butterfly came flying towards me and landed on my shoulder where it rested some time. It then flew to a painting which hung on the wall. It was a painting of the hometown of my grandmother and myself. The butterfly landed on this painting. I wanted to catch it, which was really easy. I just took it off the painting, went to another room and put it out of the window. It was such a surreal situation. It wasn't summer and there were no butterflies outside. Never before had a butterfly landed on my shoulder. I somehow 'felt' that this experience had to do with my grandmother, who had just died some moments earlier."

The shared perception of a rainbow coming out of nowhere was soothing for this grieving father:

"I was standing in my front yard smoking a cigarette with my daughter-in-law (because we don't smoke in the house). I was talking about the hospital and how I thought the nurses weren't paying attention to my son, and I was beginning to vent and get very upset about the memories of the last week of his life and what I thought were obvious errors in the care my son received. It was a sunny day, but suddenly a downpour of rain came out of nowhere, and looking all around I could see the sky was still blue. And then a rainbow appeared right in front of us in the road; it stretched from the road and up into the trees, it was about 20 feet tall — it didn't go higher, it wasn't connected to a rainbow in the sky. A rainbow just simply materialized in front of us. For a moment we were stunned into silence, and then my daughter-in-law looked at me and said, 'James is here,' and I said, 'I know.' I had my phone with me and I captured it on video and have pictures of it. In my mind it was as if I could hear my son's voice telling me, 'Chill out! I'm OK!' I felt his presence, and I felt like he wanted us to calm down, to not go to the dark place in our minds where those bad memories were. It was amazing."

The previous testimonies illustrate this — symbolic ADCs are often so subtle that they only make sense to the experient. The testimony to follow reminded me of the words of wisdom sent to me many years ago by Allan Kellehear, Professor Emeritus of Palliative Care at the University of Bradford, UK: "*You can attribute meaning to any event. There is a fine line between self-deception and personal meaning, of course, but never let others decide that for you. Only you know who loves you. And some love letters are, and always will be, a secret code. Some messages are meant only for you. Even in death.*"[45]

"The first few mornings after my husband's death, when I was sitting in his chair, on the sideboard facing me I saw his picture lit up with a ray of sunlight, centred on his face (photos to prove it). This went on for about ten days. In my view, this was a sign. I felt good, but I didn't like this photo (showing him when he was already sick) and I don't think he would have liked it either. I put another one on, and I haven't seen that ray of sunshine again, not in the next few days and not for three years."

This concludes the presentation of the different forms of expression of ADCs. The accounts presented in this section clearly show that these contacts can occur in a wide variety of situations and take many forms. They are tailored to the context of the experient's life, and the inventiveness and creativity of these contacts is often striking, even delightful.

The contacts expressed by an inexplicable physical manifestation — the *psychokinetic ADCs* — are at first sight quite banal events. A displaced object, a malfunctioning mobile phone, a photo of the deceased found on the floor in the undamaged photo frame, the stereo that turns on by itself and plays a significant tune... the event is certainly inexplicable, but no more unusual than other strange events to which we do not pay much attention. And yet, a seemingly banal event is suddenly invested with a meaning, a message is associated with it, and the agent behind it is immediately identified, as was the case for our French participant who interpreted the unprovoked and unexplained closing of her gate as a message from her deceased grandmother advising her to exclude her partner from her life for good — quite surprising indeed.

ADCs for protection are frequently not only impressive but also extremely important for the experients as they have been spared a serious problem, or even a potentially fatal outcome, thanks to these warnings. In cases where experients have heeded the warning, we obviously do not know whether the announced potential danger would actually really have occurred. In some cases, however, the experients did not, or only partially, make use of the warning and the dangerous event announced during the ADC did take place, albeit often mitigated so that the experient suffered only limited damage.

As with the testimonies presented by type of ADC in the previous sections, the contacts in which information previously unknown to the experient is perceived are among the most remarkable, due to their evidential nature. *Practical ADCs* fall into this category, allowing experients to easily, and often immediately, verify the veracity of the information perceived.

With regard to *ADCs for a third person*, experients are not the direct recipients but the designated messengers to deliver a message to a bereaved person. Conveying the message to the addressee is not always easy, as the experients do not know how it will be received. Indeed, communicating a message from a deceased person is not considered a trivial matter in our materialistic Western societies.

Symbolic ADCs are subtle experiences that are considered by the experients as signs from the deceased significant other and only become meaningful through the interpretation they give them. Although these are events that are commonly regarded by their entourage as mere coincidences and are not taken seriously, they are nevertheless very important to the experients, especially if they are bereaved. The form of expression of symbolic ADCs is broad, often based on a shared memory or preference of the deceased. Animals — insects, birds or pets — that seem to behave in an unusual way are often considered by the bereaved as secret and efficient messengers of their deceased loved one. Natural phenomena are sometimes invested by experients with a symbolic meaning, such as a rainbow forming at a significant time that they believe is meant for them alone. The experients are immediately convinced that those manifestations are signs addressed to them personally and the prevailing skepticism cannot dissuade them from attributing meaning to them.

Identification of the deceased

- **85% immediately recognized the deceased**

Do the experients instantly identify the perceived deceased? Even if they only sense their presence, without seeing or hearing them, without smelling a characteristic fragrance and without feeling physical contact? We asked the participants if they had recognized the identity of the deceased "immediately and beyond doubt" and the response was very significant, since **833** of our 1,004 participants answered in the affirmative. Occasionally, experients say that they had perceived apparitions that they did not recognize. Later, by consulting a photo album, they identified them for example as a great-grandfather or a family friend who had died when they were children or not yet born, as exemplified by the following short testimony:

> "He appeared suddenly and I didn't recognise him until I looked at some photos and it was indeed him, because he looked like a familiar face."

The following ADC — which occurred when our participant was in her teens — illustrates the issue of identification:

> "When I was 12 years old, I was resting in the bedroom of my grandparents' house and, during a storm, I turned over in my bed and saw a woman in front of me who was sitting on a bed on the other side of the room. This woman looked at me and said that she was not feeling well, that she needed my help. She looked a lot like my maternal grandmother, but it wasn't her. I knew that because I had already seen my deceased grandmother on other occasions and I've never seen her like this before. I was a bit scared because her appearance

was very sad and her face expressed great pain. She kept insisting that I help her, I was petrified and got very scared. I hid my face with my blankets but I kept listening to her. I wanted to shout to my mother to come and get me because I was feeling increasingly frightened, but although I tried, no sound came out of my mouth. After about five minutes, I decided to run out into the patio to go to the other side of the house where my mother was. I set off and when I stopped, the woman was still sitting on that bed looking at me. I took a swing and opened the louvered door that separated me from the patio. As I did so, there was my mother who had come to see me because it seemed to her that I had called her (again, I should point out that I had never been able to call her because no sound had come out of my mouth). I hugged her and we went to the kitchen. When I told her what I had seen, she said that the woman I was describing was her aunt, the sister of my maternal grandmother, who had died in that room and bed about five years before I was born."

This testimony describes a rather disconcerting experience:

"A man came to my workplace (shop) wearing a light-coloured outfit. I greeted him, without really paying attention to him. When I didn't see him come back, I went to the back of the shop to ask where the man was. My colleagues replied that no one had entered. And for some unexplained reason, I told them that it was certainly a dead man who had come to see me. On my way home, I felt that someone was following me. Someone was either beside or behind me. It was a bit oppressive. When I got home, I had a strange feeling and I understood 'in my head', I don't know how, that the person who had followed me was an elderly gentleman I had known and not seen for several years. He was telling me that he had died. I felt that I had to look at the pages of death notices (something I never do) in the local newspaper and indeed, there was an announcement that this gentleman had died."

However, a number of experients perceived a deceased person whom they really did not know. How can one imagine a contact with a stranger? And what could be the meaning of it? Contacts with known deceased persons serve to reassure and console the experients, as is evident from the testimonies presented in the previous pages. But what could be the meaning of a contact with an unknown deceased person? Bringing comfort to the experient is clearly not the reason.

It could be presumed that in these cases it is the *deceased* who needs contact with a living person. Perhaps they are not aware that they are dead? Perhaps they are in a state of confusion, or suffering, and are seeking contact with the living, as if there were an urgent need for them to materialize wherever possible, wherever they can be perceived, even by a stranger? The question remains (for the time being) unanswered.

Contacts with unknown deceased persons are sometimes considered by experients as uncomfortable, oppressive or even frightening. At the very least, these experiences surprise and intrigue. Unlike ADCs involving deceased loved ones where the benefit is obvious, ADCs with strangers are of a completely different nature, as they lack the bond of love and tenderness between the deceased and the experients that make them such profoundly moving and beautiful experiences. In this chapter, we will focus on the perceptions of unknown or ambiguously identified deceased persons.

The following case, unusual in its duration and characteristics, takes us on a different track. It suggests that this contact was necessary not only for the murdered young woman but also, and perhaps most importantly, for her family left with so many open questions regarding her death:

"I was driving one afternoon having just left a visit with my middle daughter. As I approached a traffic circle, there before me was a full-body apparition of a young woman. She was in color and 'looked' almost as if she was alive. She raised her hand and waved at me. Though I didn't know her, I knew her name somehow (she didn't tell me; I just knew it). When I got home, I searched her name online. She was a young woman who was murdered not too far from that traffic circle. Over the course of months, I kept being given images, and visits from her psychically. I would make notes of what was relayed. Sometimes it was about the people involved. Sometimes it was purely feeling or events from her life. I connected with another woman who was psychic and contacted the family of this young woman. We spoke and I shared what I had been given from her regarding her murder. This kept going for several months, but the contacts from her began to end with her handing me a large orange flower (in vision). This made no sense to me but I would make note of anything I was given and share them with the family (mostly the father of this young woman). We agreed to meet at a restaurant as he was driving through my town. As I parked at the restaurant and opened my car door, there on the ground was a large orange flower, right where I would step out. It hadn't been there prior to my pulling in as I would have seen it. I shared it with the father. Many of the things I relayed were validated as facts known about her murder. Some things have not been validated as well. Unfortunately, the murder case remains unresolved for now."

Sometimes the identification of the perceived deceased is not immediate or obvious and gives rise to interpretations and questions:

"On 16 July 2015, I was returning from a holiday in the Camargue with my daughter (I live in Switzerland). We were driving on the highway, it was around 1 p.m., my daughter was reading and I was concentrating on driving. The traffic was very smooth, nobody behind us and just a car a few hundred meters ahead. I got closer to the car and started to overtake it. When I was about 20 meters behind this car, on the left lane, there was a movement on my left, coming from the centre of the highway, which attracted my attention. I turned my head slightly in that direction to see that the form was a man, about 40 years old, wearing jeans, a red jumper, a beard, brown hair and carrying a black rucksack, who was walking across the highway. I braked abruptly, gave a slight jerk of the steering wheel to my left (on the right was the car I was overtaking) and let out an exclamation shout, all of which took place in one or two seconds, whereas it seemed to me to last for minutes. As a result of my quick reaction and a lot of luck, there was no shock, which confirmed to me that I had avoided this imprudent man. At the same time, I looked in my right-hand rear-view mirror, in which I saw my good fellow on the emergency lane. He had stopped and gave me a friendly wave of the hand, as if to say to me 'the situation has been perilous, but I crossed without harm and you can continue your road serenely', and he walked away. Still a little shocked, I asked my daughter, who was 13 at the time, if she had seen this man cross in front of our car. She looked at me quizzically but did not answer. I still had one more surprise left, which later became a question, 'Where was the car I was overtaking?' ... Indeed, I could not see it in my rear-view mirror and it was not in front of me either (visibility was good and the field of vision extended over a kilometre), the road was empty, we were alone.

While being immersed in my thoughts and asking myself if I had dreamed or if I had just lived an extraordinary experience, I continued my journey. I should point out that on the day of this experience, my father was at the end of his life (I did not know it at the time), he was to die three days later. Since that day, I wonder if this apparition was the soul of my father who announced his forthcoming passage into the invisible world by saying to me, 'My son, this crossing was risky, but I managed it without difficulty, you can continue your journey with a peaceful mind,' or if I had just seen the soul of an unknown person (unknown to me) who had perhaps had a mortal accident at this place and who crossed this invisible door exactly at the time of my passage. The only thing I am certain of is that I was not dreaming, not hallucinating, but simply experiencing a particular situation. This confirmed what is my belief (I am not at all religious or attracted to any cult), namely that there is something behind the mirror."

This visual ADC, experienced by a child, was very disturbing for her, especially since the father failed to listen to his daughter and to support her:

"I was seven years old, we lived in a house, I had my own room. One night, I was woken up by an older man with straight grey hair staring at me and not talking to me. I felt like I was being watched… I'll let you imagine my fright. I remember it as if it was yesterday, even though it was 34 years ago! I screamed, but my father, who had to get up very early for work, told me to be quiet. I was wide awake! So, I put my head under the sheets and turned to the other side of the bed. I heard a noise. I thought it was my sister coming to comfort me, so I lifted the sheet and there he was again, staring at me. I screamed again… It was scary. No, I wasn't dreaming, I was wide awake. I remind you that my father replied by reprimanding me, saying that I had to sleep. To this day, I remember perfectly this man dressed in white and staring at me…"

We learned a little more about this frightening experience with our question "Did you feel that the deceased tried to communicate something by his/her sheer presence?" to which this participant replied:

"This elderly man whom I saw at the age of seven, although he did not speak, I strongly believe that he wanted to tell me something, but because of my fear I did not hear anything..."

Some ADCs are clearly linked to a *place*. This phenomenon is known as a "haunted house", "spook house" or "ghost house". These manifestations usually occur in old houses and the objects of the apparitions — which the experients do not know — often are people who lived there long ago. These contacts can be frightening because the apparitions sometimes appear to be in distress or angry. Some experients feel the need to help the perceived deceased, for example by praying for them or inviting them to go into the light.

The following account describes a location-related ADC — a haunting case — involving an unknown deceased:

"At the end of August 2018, I visited a friend who lives in Paris. My friend's twin sister invited us to her home — a beautiful 100-year-old house. I was reluctant to visit the house, but at my friend's insistence, I let myself be convinced. When I arrived upstairs in the guest room, an immense sadness overwhelmed me to the point of having to hold back my tears. In the corner of the room, I saw a beautiful woman, tall, thin, with her head bent forward. I was obviously the only one to see her. I couldn't take my eyes off her. She told me (telepathically) that she had given birth to a baby girl and that she was immersed in a depression from which she could not escape (hence the immense sadness I felt when I entered the room). I distinctly heard the name 'Henriette'. I could also describe her clothes (small blue cotton waistcoat, spring-like, and a classic skirt). I hastened to tell the lady of the house what I had just seen. I asked her if she knew the history of her house, because a tragedy took place there, a tragic death. I saw her turn pale and she ended up telling me the history of the house. This house was sold to her by a widower who lived there with his daughter. The widower sold his property in Paris to move to Lyon. A year after the purchase, neighbours told my friend's sister that the former owner of the house had committed suicide after many years of depression. She left behind her husband and a seven-year-old daughter named Adèle. The guest room was in fact the room once occupied by the child. I understood that this poor woman was waiting to see her daughter again and had been haunting the room since the date of her death. I explained to her that she had to go into the light. According to the current occupants (my friend's sister and her husband), the sense of presence is no longer there. After doing some research, we found her date of death: Friday 13 April 2007. Last detail: the deceased was named Henriette..."

The next experience also took place in an old house:

"A few years ago (in 2002/2003), something very strange and not really nice happened to me. My husband and I were restoring a very old house that was two hundred or even three hundred years old. This happened in the bedroom. The bedroom was the only room not yet restored at the time, but we inhabited it anyway. One morning hanging out in bed, I'm daydreaming, my thoughts are wandering, but I insist: I am not sleeping! It is 8:15 a.m., I connect my electric blanket because I am a little cold and at 8:20 a.m. exactly, several people located at the end of the bed pull me by the feet, they are very angry and I see them! In the foreground I see a woman with her mouth wide open, dressed poorly... full of anger.

At this moment, I feel my body lifting up... I am levitating. I cannot move, I cannot speak, I am completely paralyzed, my eyes see since I saw the time on my alarm clock but I just endure the events and then everything stops. I get up without really being afraid, but my heart beats nevertheless a little faster! In my head only one question: 'What was that?' Just the obvious... these people wanted to chase me away. I have the feeling that it happened yesterday, it is still so very present in my mind, despite all these years passed, and very strong in intensity... no equivocation, I was disturbing them!"

The insight gained in this section is that an overwhelming majority of our respondents (85%) immediately recognized the perceived deceased, regardless of the type of ADC experienced. However, a number of our participants reported perceptions of unknown or ambiguously identified deceased persons. ADCs involving strangers are sometimes not very pleasant experiences, as the perceived deceased may appear to be confused, distressed, or angry. The latter often refers to contacts in old houses reputed to be "haunted", as if the deceased, who died a long time ago, still inhabited these places and did not wish to be disturbed by newcomers. These people are often known to have succumbed to a violent death or their passing had otherwise unfolded under tragic circumstances.

ADCs involving strangers lack the bond of love and affection between the living and the deceased that make them such consoling and beautiful experiences. The question naturally arises as to the *meaning* of these contacts, and, above all, who benefits from them. It is obviously not the experients who may be intrigued, sometimes inconvenienced or even frightened by these contacts. Some feel compassion for the perceived deceased who seem to be in trouble and seek a way to help them, for example by praying for them. The question of the purpose of this type of ADC must remain unanswered for the time being.

Messages perceived

A large majority of our participants perceived a message during the ADC.

This participant explains in a few precise and concise words how he perceived the message:

"He only came once. He said goodbye to me and never came back. He came to give me a very clear and precise message. I saw him, I heard him, just as you see and hear any living person."

The table below shows the occurrence by percentage for all types of ADC. For auditory contacts, we phrased the question a little differently.

Messages perceived

Did you receive a message from the deceased during the ADC?	Yes	Unsure	No
ADC of sensing a presence	74%	15%	11%
Tactile ADC	80%	10%	10%
Visual ADC	80%	9%	12%
Olfactory ADC	60%	21%	20%
Was the perceived communication different from a thought?	Yes	Unsure	No
Auditory ADC	87%	6%	7%

In the eyes of the experients, the fact of having an ADC is in itself a message: the message that the deceased significant others apparently still have the capacity to manifest themselves. As the experients interpret it, the very fact that they seem to be able to make contact with the living implies that the deceased continue an existence — elsewhere — the nature of which is beyond our understanding. The greatest impact undoubtedly comes from this apparent ability to make contact, a revelation for some, a confirmation of a pre-existing belief for others (that some form of consciousness survives physical death).

In addition to the message inherent in the very occurrence of the ADC, a large majority perceived a personalized message, as mentioned in the table above. Each message is obviously unique because it is addressed to a particular person and shaped by a common history. However, the contents can be schematized because, in their essence, they are relatively homogeneous.

The most important message is the information that *they are alive and well*. In addition, the messages are usually infused with love and reassurance. The perceived deceased persons encourage the bereaved to come out of their grief, and some may ask them not to hold them back with their suffering; sometimes they offer the prospect of a future reunion. When the relationship between the experient and the deceased was conflictual, the contacts serve as a request for forgiveness, sometimes as an explanation or justification for past relationship issues.

Messages can be summarized by the **4 Rs**. They are:

Reassuring: I am alive and well, don't worry about me, the troubles I had at the end of life are now behind me;
Resolving: Settling old conflicts, allowing space for apologies, providing closure;
Reaffirming: Continuing bond, affectionate, I love you, I will always be by your side, we will meet again one day;
Releasing: Don't be sad, pursue your life, don't hold me back by your suffering.

It should be emphasized that the messages contain no information about the alleged new form of existence of the deceased and reveal nothing about their "new home", which, incidentally, may not be a *place*, but rather a *state of consciousness*. Only the mindset of the deceased significant other is briefly described ("I am alive and happy").

The message to follow is typical in its straightforwardness and its perfectly clear recommendation. Our participant does not describe how she perceived the communication but rather speaks of an awareness triggering this perception.

"[I] experienced a gentle awareness from Dad that said 'take care of Mom'."

The theme of the following message is a classic one in that it reassures the experient about the well-being of the deceased and assures the bereaved that they will get through this difficult time:

"When my father-in-law passed away, he came to me several times to let me know he was OK, that he was with Mom and that we were going to be OK. He stressed the fact that we need not worry about him, or Mom, and that he was with our family in the heavenlies."

This comforting message was perceived at a moment of hardship:

"In June 1999, I was having problems sleeping due to issues within my relationship (I suspected my partner was cheating) and I had recently suffered a miscarriage at 25 weeks. I got up to use the bathroom and as I opened the bedroom door my grandfather stood in front of me (he had died just before I was born in 1974). He was smiling at me and placed his hand on my cheek, it felt slightly warm, just above normal body temperature. He said, 'Do not worry, things will always work out for the best, even if we don't think so at first. Everything will be alright and you will be happy again soon. I am always watching over you.' I heard someone in the [distance] call his name Anthony. He smiled again and turned away and vanished. I went back to bed and although I didn't sleep any better, I felt a real sense of calm and reassurance."

As illustrated by some of the testimonies mentioned in the previous pages, ADCs sometimes serve to announce a forthcoming death, as described in the following testimony:

"I was 14 years old. Five days in a row, I dreamed that my piano teacher was dying. She was reaching out to me in my dreams, telling me that she was dying and/or had died. After five nights of these dreams, I woke up on Saturday morning and my Mom showed me the newspaper obituaries, which told of her death a day or so earlier. I later learned that she had been rushed to the hospital on Monday afternoon, after my piano lesson with her."

Sometimes contacts only make sense through events that occur later:

"I saw my grandfather at my side several times. He wanted to tell me something and I didn't understand him. Soon after, my uncle, his son, passed away and I understood what he wanted to tell me. He appeared to me later in a dream with my grandmother and my cousin (who had passed away and whom I never knew) to say goodbye and to tell me that he would come back to see me. To this day, he has not yet come back."

Apparently, a genuine information transfer can take place through this type of message. The experients are alerted not only to the imminent occurrence of a death, but more specifically to the identity of the family member or friend concerned. What is the usefulness of this information, given that the demise cannot be avoided anyway? One can imagine that the experient thus warned could take the opportunity to exchange last words of love and appreciation with this person, words that would have been lost forever in the absence of this announcement. Moreover, prior knowledge of the death of the significant other can help the experient to prepare mentally and emotionally for the ordeal ahead.

Here is such a description. This death was probably neither expected nor foreseeable, since the person died of a stroke:

> "The most significant contact was meeting my father. I always felt his presence from the beginning. He passed away when I was 23 years old. At first, I saw him in my dreams. We would talk, he would help me to make the right decisions. He appeared to me the first time while I was cleaning my kitchen. I felt his presence. I turned around and he was just a foot away from me. He appeared to me dressed in white. A halo of light surrounded him, but I was not dazzled. I knew why he was coming. He was coming for my uncle. It was a Thursday. The following Sunday, my sister called to tell me that our uncle had died. He had been rushed to the hospital on Thursday for a stroke."

The message perceived by this Swiss respondent was very specific as it indicated the precise hour of the forthcoming demise:

> "After my father passed away in 2011, I always felt his presence. On Wednesday morning, March 20, 2013, his energy came to me strongly when I was between sleep

and waking up in the morning. Telepathically, he told me that my mother-in-law (my husband's mother) was going to die. Since there were no warning signs, I assumed that this event could happen within a week or so. He told me, 'No, today at 10:00 p.m.' I was stunned by this news. I told my mother about it, as proof of the contact I had had with my dad. Then at 7 p.m. I asked my husband for news of his mother and he told me that everything was fine. When he returned from his office at 8 p.m., he told me he had received a phone call from his mom's retirement home. I interrupted him to tell him the message I had received from my dad. That's when he added that according to the staff of the retirement home, his mother would not pass the night and they asked him to come to Cannes to stay with her. She indeed passed away that evening. During her funeral, the undertaker told me that she had died at 11 p.m. I did not try to clarify the time difference, having received absolute proof of the information received by my dad."

Some contacts simply announce an imminent death, while others console and reassure experients about the fate of the person who was about to leave them:

"My parents appeared to me together, united, radiant, smiling, serene. They let me know that they were 'there' ... and a few hours later, my brother, who was very ill, passed away. I guess my parents came to tell me not to worry, that they were there to welcome him and that everything would be fine."

How can we imagine a "dialogue" between the deceased and the experient? Here is an example:

"I suddenly feel a very great emotion with immense love; I cry but I don't know why. I know that the person is there. I can ask him questions and I receive the answers immediately, internally. I perceive, I feel a tremendous amount of love."

The content of the messages is mostly focused on the experients and serves to console them and ease their sadness.

"I am by your side and will remain as long as you are suffering."

"I'm here, don't worry. Everything is going to be okay, I'll help you."

"That I was loved and would always be loved, that I was not alone."

"It was my dad holding my hand and saying, 'It was a pleasure to have shared this life with you'."

"Everything is well. Don't be so sad."

"That he was at home with us like he used to be."

"I am right here with you. Death does not exist, don't be afraid and pass on this message."

Other messages offer advice of wisdom, which has been gained throughout a lifetime:

"Don't worry as I have done all my life, don't make the same mistakes, be at peace, don't worry, everything will work out fine."

ADCs suggest that in times of great distress, our deceased significant others are by our side, even many years after their death, perhaps implying that they continually keep an eye on us and intervene when we need them:

"Person perceived at a specific and important time in my life. My son was suffering from a cardiovascular disease and I asked myself many questions about his open-heart surgery… And that's when, one evening, my grandfather, who had passed away in 1981, came to talk to me and told me that everything was going to be fine. A person I knew very little about because I was too young when he died. He was standing there in front of me with his halo of light around him, talking to me. It was not a dream. He told me that everything was going to be fine, that he was proud of us and that my father, who had also passed away, was fine. Then he left. My son's surgery went very well."

A dramatic situation, on the verge of being unbearable, is instantly converted into an absolute conviction that everything will be fine, despite the adverse circumstances and potential dangers still ahead:

"My son was born… I had to have an emergency C-section due to foetal distress and a double cord wrap. I was in a great deal of stress. I was in pain, discomfort, and very, very worried about what was going on with my newborn. I have medical training as a nurse and I understand the ramifications of such a thing occurring. My son had a foetal heart rate drop more than once from 140 down to about the 96 range. I was worried about his cognitive ability, his Apgar score was 5, at five minutes after birth. I was worried about him going blind, oxygen absorption in the NICU. I was worried about mental retardation, all sorts of stuff. I was in a great deal of pain. I was on my left side — the nurse in the room was getting on the phone because the synthetic they had given me for pain was not working at all to dull the pain, and she got on the phone with the doctor. While I was laying on the gurney being on my left side in almost a foetal position it hurt so bad... my dad suddenly walked in the room. Which was impossible because he had died 18 months before, and I remember thinking 'but visitors are not allowed in the recovery room'. My dad came up to the side of the bed, and all I could see of him was the bottom of his tie, and his button up shirt and the bed rail of the gurney. He paused a moment as he stood beside the bed and he said very clearly, very distinctly, 'He's going to be fine.' And from the second I heard his voice say that — my pain disappeared, my stress disappeared, my fear, my anguish, my internal turmoil, my questioning thoughts — it all stopped. I knew from that moment forward my son was going to be just fine, and I had nothing to worry about. So, I didn't. I blinked and my dad was gone from my bedside, gone from the room. I remember sitting up slightly and looking around for him. Which in my prior condition would not have been possible for the amount of pain that I had been in. The doctor had ordered a Demerol shot for my pain and I was given that post ADC, and by the time I was released from the hospital four days later... I was on nothing but Tylenol. I remember deciding not to tell the recovery room nurse what I had just seen... because I was afraid she might think I was going into a psychiatric shock or something from the surgery I had undergone. And that was going to cause a lot of drama and issues that really didn't need to be happening. So I was happy but I stayed mum. From that moment forward no matter what they told me about my son in the NICU, about a shunt in his head and IVs and blood testing, I would just nod and smile and pat their hands and say, 'It's going to be fine, it's going to be OK.' My son was released from the NICU in perfect health five days after he was born."

Other messages are more focused on the deceased who inform their loved ones that they are still alive and well, like a traveler informing their family that the trip went well and that they can be reassured.

"I'm alive, everything is fine."

"My mom told me that she was doing great, that I shouldn't worry, that where she was everything was just fine."

"Don't worry, darling, I'm alive and with you."

"Call the family and let them know I still exist."

"That she had never been happier."

"A message of peace, of acceptance of death, of assurance that he was alive elsewhere and concerned for those he loved."

"He told me, 'I'm alive', and another time he told me he did everything he could to stay with me."

"The time had come for me to leave. Don't worry about me. Everything will be fine for me. I love you and will love you forever."

The "dialogue" that seems to have taken place between our respondent and her grandfather suggests that the deceased are concerned beyond their death with the fate of their loved ones. In this contact, it was the grandfather, not his granddaughter, who most needed reassurance and comfort:

"A few weeks after my paternal grandfather passed away, I walked into my parents' living room and felt a very sudden and severe fatigue. I decided to sit in the recliner by the window. I closed my eyes to rest but I did not fall asleep (I know this because I could distinctly hear my parents talking). All of a sudden, I 'felt' my grandfather on my left, right between the window and the recliner. And, I can't explain how, I perceived what he wanted to tell me. It was as if his thoughts were in my head! And I was answering him with my thoughts too. He was worried about my grandmother and was afraid to go and leave us alone. I reassured him and then I opened my eyes and it was over. Two hours later I was in the bathtub and just as suddenly I 'felt' my grandfather's presence again next to the bathtub. The difference is that I definitely did not have my eyes closed at that time. He had the same concerns and I remember responding to him out loud to reassure him again. I also remember urging him to 'go' to the other side and trust us to take care of our grandmother. From that moment on, I knew he was gone… I can't explain how I knew, but I knew. It took me several days to remember the bathtub episode, while the living room episode was very clear in my mind. I was never afraid and it really made a positive impression on me. It was a very pleasant contact, very reassuring for me too."

The *way* in which the messages are transmitted remains a mystery, as does the occurrence and very nature of ADCs. Some messages, however, contain bits of information that may offer some clues:

"I'm fine, I can't stay any longer because it takes a lot of energy to be there."

It is clear from the many testimonies presented in the previous pages that the deceased can help the living. What about the reverse? What can the living do for their dead? The testimonies of ADCs allow us to understand that the deceased can indeed need us, and this is probably a surprise for many. We can in turn help them by doing our best not to hold them back too long with our grief and our tears. It is not easy, obviously, but it is perhaps the last proof of love we can give to our loved ones who have preceded us in death.

Indeed, the deceased sometimes ask their loved ones not to mourn them for too long and to let them pursue their new existence of which we know (almost) nothing, as if our sadness were paining them and hindering their evolution.

The following few excerpts from testimonies illustrate this point:

"My mom told me she was happy and asked me to let her go."

"I'm doing well, please let me go."

"I love you and I need you to let me go."

"To ask me to stop crying, he was weary of seeing me crying all the time."

"He told me not to cry for him anymore, that he was fine where he was and that he was very happy."

"Because I knew I had to be strong and get through his death because he was so sad to see me so devastated over his death."

The perceived request from the deceased was perfectly plain. The sense of reality of this contact was reinforced by some practical elements:

"It was early morning right before I woke up. I was in a state somewhere between sleep and being awake. I saw myself going to a house and going in, my deceased fiancé was there with friends that he served with in Vietnam who were also deceased. They were there kind of protecting him. He came and hugged me and it felt like the old familiar hug that I remembered. It was so intense and felt so familiar that I knew I was really feeling his energy. We spoke, but not in words. Our communication was kinetic, but we could understand one another perfectly. He asked me to try to stop grieving for him. He said that my grief was holding him back from moving forward on the other side. He wanted me to know he was fine. I told him I would do anything for him and I agreed. He told me that he would send me a sign that would validate our reunion. He hugged me goodbye and he and his friends left. I woke up and discovered that my watch on my nightstand had stopped. I also had a tape cassette on my nightstand that had been completely erased. There was an energy and a humming right in the middle of my forehead. As further validation, that afternoon, my Godson (his nephew born after he passed) walked into my office out of the blue. I hadn't seen or heard from him in months."

The following message falls into the category of an ADC for a third person, since the participant received a message for two mourners. The request from the deceased could not be any clearer:

> "My best friend's aunt had passed away and I stayed with the family for the night. We slept in my friend's room, her in her bed and me on a mattress on the floor. During the night I woke up and under the bed a hand was holding my arm. I saw the deceased — my friend's aunt — who asked me to tell her sister and niece to let her go because they were preventing her from leaving."

Conflicting relationships that were unresolved at the time of death sometimes seem to be sorted out during these contacts. These messages suggest that a dynamic relational bond persists beyond the death of the body and that there is still a chance to mend a relationship. ADCs imply that the bond between the living and the deceased is not broken; it is transformed and sometimes strengthened in death. Apparently, love can still spring forth in a rare and brief, but so very precious, interaction — during an ADC. These contacts teach us that it is never too late to understand, to repair, to forgive and be forgiven, and to express love.

The messages to follow are of this nature:

> "I had an argument with my dad on the day he died, just before his surgery. It soothed me to feel his presence. I think it was a way to make peace."

> "[Without that contact] I would not have known that he was sorry for what he had done in his life. I would have stayed full of anger towards him."

> "Because he apologized for what he had done to me. So I think he finally realized that I didn't hurt him, that I

wasn't mean to him and that he was the one who wanted to hurt me, and he apologized. That gave me peace of mind because I felt like he realized I wasn't a bad person."

"My father was crying a lot and asked me to pass on his message of regret to my older brother."

"I am fine, I am with my brother Charles. Don't worry about me, I apologize for what I did to you, live your life now."

"My father-in-law wanted me to forgive him for his behaviour with me."

"That he was sorry for having said hurtful things to me."

The ADC allowed this participant to begin her grieving process in good conditions:

"I was able to forgive myself and let go of my guilt and get through the emotions of grief."

Apparently, death does not necessarily freeze a relationship. An argument, a disagreement, need not necessarily remain unresolved but can find a resolution beyond death. This ADC during sleep allowed our respondent to come out of a grief marked by guilt:

"My father had been dead for ten months. A few days before he died, I got angry with him and asked him not to come to my house anymore. After his death, I was frozen in guilt and unable to feel my sadness. I lived like an automaton, a prisoner of confused, unrecognized and destructive emotions under a social mask that did not let anything show. I was devastated. One night, more precisely at the end of the night, I heard the front door of the house open and I saw my father coming up the stairs to my room. He sat down on a step and I joined him. I asked him for forgiveness and he told me that there was nothing to forgive, that I was not guilty of anything, nor was he. That the only thing that mattered was the love that united us and that could not disappear. That beyond our personalities, our life stories, souls and love are eternal. I 'woke up', my face flooded with tears and sitting on the edge of the bed, I heard the door close. I thought I had been dreaming, yet I was convinced that I had experienced something very real. A tremendous peace came over me and I was able to truly begin my grieving process. I was not able to start talking about this experience until about ten years later. It happened in 2006. Today the memory is still as vivid as ever, I have not forgotten any detail of that encounter and I just have to connect to it to feel unspeakable peace and love."

For the case to follow, however, the relationship problems could not be entirely resolved in death:

"My biological father died and less than two weeks later he was in my dream begging me to forgive him. You see, while he was in human form he was a fairly worthless father. He knew he was in the wrong for putting me aside for all those years but refused to apologize or make amends when alive, but I figure that once he died he was scared of what was to come. I wasn't very happy to see him, however, I did feel sorry for him because he seemed so desperate grabbing at my legs and refusing to let go unless I would forgive him. I finally relented and agreed to do so if he would only leave me alone for the rest of my existence while here on earth. I hate to say it, but he doesn't seem to believe in keeping promises to this day as he still does pop in every once in a while. You know what they say 'as they were in life so they be in death'. I hope one day he just moves on completely."

In the painful cases of suicide, the deceased are sometimes able to explain their act during the ADC. Reason alone did not allow our participant to understand her partner's suicide; she had to feel the ravages of Parkinson's disease in her own flesh to accept his voluntary departure. It was indeed a message she received during this ADC, but a message in the form of physical sensations rather than in verbalized form. This experience allowed her to understand and accept the seemingly inevitable choice of her partner. The powerful impact of ADCs on the grieving process comes through clearly in this testimony:

"This happened a few days after my partner's suicide. He had Parkinson's disease and a very strong tremor that could be recognized by hearing. His illness was the primary reason for him to commit suicide. However, still young and talented, happy in his relationship with me, I could not admit that he could decide to stop fighting against the disease that suddenly worsened. Yet, he could not imagine living without me, we were so strongly bonded. After discovering him lying lifeless, I could not accept the idea that he could, after overcoming all his sufferings with determination and courage (he was a surgeon), end his life. He literally made me 'feel' his illness. For a few minutes, I had the same symptoms as he had with his Parkinson's disease. He had a brain implant (cause of the accelerated degradation of his condition), he made me feel it in parallel. Also, I heard his shaking on the sheets and floor at that moment. After this brief moment of completely feeling his illness as if I was also affected, I could begin to forgive him and understand what a hell he had been living for the last 10 years and felt ashamed to be angry with him for abandoning me. Since then, I know in my flesh what it is like to be affected by this disease. It is unbearable and it is therefore understandable that he didn't want to endure it anymore."

The next testimony describes an experience of both physical sensations and awareness, resulting in the transmission of crucial information to the deceased's son:

"I learned of the death by suicide of my father's cousin whom I liked very much. I felt the need to talk to her. I asked her why she had done such a thing when she was such a wonderful person, had just become a grandmother, etc. and I felt very bad, deep blues, difficulty breathing. It lasted all afternoon and suddenly, without being able to explain it to myself, I felt soothed and I seemed to understand what she had experienced, what she had felt, the fact that she did not love herself. She wanted me to experience what she had gone through before her suicide, her suffering and her deliverance afterwards, and what she wanted me to tell her son. She was someone who wrote a lot, very long letters, and without explaining it to me at the time (I also like to write), I wrote a letter to her only son explaining to him that he had to forgive his mother, that it was her choice, that she didn't love herself and didn't see herself the way we saw her, that she was proud of him and of being a grandmother, that he should be happy, all the things I could have said to my son if I had been in her place."

In the two previous accounts, the participants learned from the ADC the reasons that made the suicide inevitable in the eyes of their deceased loved ones. This *post-mortem* information allowed them to understand and "forgive" this act that is so difficult for family members and friends to accept.

The following account does not describe the difficulties of the last moments of the deceased's life, but rather a burst of joy and energy seemingly completely out of sync with the sad circumstances of our respondent's father's death. One could hypothesize that it was the emotions *of the deceased* and not her own that this respondent felt at these moments:

> "Just after my father passed away in 2014, I felt an intense joy that lasted three and a half days, hence abnormal right after a death. It was an unusual joy because it was very intense and I also felt an inner serenity that I had never felt to such an extent before. I was enveloped by an energy of love during this period and I felt energy on me that moved along my arms and fingers. On the seventh day of the death, I accompanied the coffin in the hearse and I again felt this energy of love invade me, but it was different. This energy was not on me, it came from above, like I was showered by this energy. This lasted the time of the ride in the hearse, about an hour."

The ensuing account is similar to the previous one. In this case also, a feeling of heaviness and hardship has been replaced by a feeling of liberation at the very moment of the passing:

> "My grandfather was dying of cancer. On the day he died, before he died, I did not see him but spent part of the day feeling as if I was carrying a ton weight on my shoulders. It was a horrible feeling. At exactly 2:00 p.m., the weight suddenly lifted and I felt really elated as if I was getting carried upwards. It was an amazing feeling. When I got home, my mother phoned to tell me my grandfather had

died at exactly 2:00 p.m. I am convinced that I experienced my grandfather's passing over. Months later, I saw him, just standing, looking through a shop window."

The following testimony also evokes feelings of joy and even of bliss felt by the widower, quite out of sync and seemingly incomprehensible given the sad circumstances of his wife's burial. Again, it would seem that the experient was sensing his deceased wife's *current state of mind*, which radically changed his own mindset. The distinction he makes between the suffering of grief felt by his body and the absence of suffering in his mind is particularly noteworthy:

"The day of my wife's funeral became one of the most beautiful days of my life for me. My wonderful perceptions began early in the morning, and they increased as the hours went by. That day everyone was sweating, not only outdoors, but also in the church, because it was an unusually hot June day. I felt it was hot, but inexplicably I was surrounded by a pleasant coolness that seemed to envelop me like an aura or cloud. This coolness accompanied me until late afternoon. Something else surrounded me, and at the same time it penetrated me: the presence of my wife. I felt her presence clearly and intensely and had not the slightest doubt. It was stronger than if she had been physically present; I consciously perceived it all the time. This presence is not easy to describe. My wife was 'there'. I could not say that she had been standing invisibly to my right, or in front of me. Most likely I could say that she was present around me, but also inside me. Inside I felt very light, and also physically I felt almost as if I was floating out of sheer lightness. I also perceived feelings: her feelings. I felt a deep inner peace and an indescribable joy. Perhaps the word 'bliss' is the right expression here. And I felt an immense love, her love for me. All the time I knew my beloved wife was with me. This state lasted the whole day. It was clear to me that it was not due to medication, drugs, alcohol or anything like that, because I had not taken anything like that. During the funeral service my heart pounded violently. But this 'mourning' of my body did not penetrate into my soul; I took note of it indifferently. It was as if all suffering, even the suffering of my own body, was shielded from me. When relatives and friends cried at the grave, I felt sorry for them, because they did not know how well my wife was meanwhile."

Information that was previously unknown to experients

We asked respondents whether they had received information during their ADC that was previously unknown to them. This was indeed the case for almost a quarter of our respondents. The evidential nature of this type of data makes it particularly suitable for qualitative analysis, which one of our teams is currently carrying out.

- **24% perceived previously unknown information, 7% were unsure, and 69% perceived no previously unknown information**

What kind of previously unknown information are we talking about? A large number of our participants wrote in the free text dialogue box that the most important previously unknown information was that their loved one had survived the death of their body, that they were alive and well. However, it is obvious that this is not verifiable information and, therefore, it is not evidential.

Here are a few examples:

"That he was happy after death."

"You don't die — life continues."

"No reason to fear dying or death."

"That there is an afterlife. Neither of us believed it until he came to me."

"I did not know that she is living and happy."

"I felt he was sad, but with a level of peace as well. My father was not religious or spiritual but somehow I felt he was understanding all of it."

It is not unusual that experients perceive information about the circumstances of the passing that they did not know beforehand.

"My son told us how he had passed."

"How she came to be hit, that she was aware of what had been going on since she left. [...] She had been killed instantly by a truck and I did not feel I had gotten to say 'goodbye' to her. In the dream visit, which felt like real life, we got to hug and communicate about how the accident happened and about how things were now. It was amazing and very healing."

"The place of death had a traffic camera which the police initially denied the existence of."

Sometimes the perceived information is truly unexpected...

"She said that my son had something to celebrate. I later learned that he had secretly gotten married."

Some experients say that they have perceived information about events that were going to occur in the future and that were indeed confirmed with the passage of time. This type of message is rather rare.

"There were times when I had a dream about my deceased grandmother, and we were both aware of it in the dream. We talked together and she gave me explanations. She also told me about things that were happening now that I didn't know about, and things that were going to happen in the future [still in the family circle]. In other words, these were not strange prophecies or apocalyptic events. In my humble opinion, and based on my feeling, I feel that these were real encounters."

"Messages were given to me that I did not know about, but that made sense when given to the person I was instructed to give them to. Predictions were made that came true later."

The unusually long duration of the contacts described in this account raises questions:

"I lost my mother when I was 30 years old. I lived with my husband more than 100 kilometres from my parents and our work took up a lot of our time. I regretted not being able to see her more often during her illness. The day she passed away, I never felt her so close to me. On the day of her funeral, I really felt that her coffin was an empty shell. I perceived her differently. For years I had a dialogue with her, and still do, through my thoughts, which I distinguish from my own reflections. She gave me, during a difficult period, information about my future that turned out to be accurate, with amazing details such as dates."

A forthcoming illness or death of a significant other may be revealed, as we have already seen in several testimonies quoted in the previous pages:

"A prediction of a future event that I was not expecting to see happen as there was nothing to logically indicate my dad would die that year."

"My deceased mother told me that my husband was going to die. It was a year before it happened."

And sometimes the predicted future events are happy ones.

"My sister's pregnancy."

"I didn't know my daughter was pregnant, in fact she didn't know either because she didn't want to have any more children."

"The little one will be born on December 28th. My deceased grandfather told me in a dream, or rather in an astral encounter, the date of my daughter's birth. And it was right! One week in advance! The date of birth of the 'little one' was scheduled for later."

The messages may be practical and provide information that the bereaved need. The information thus collected can be verified easily, if not immediately, by the experients.

Here are some examples, including excerpts from previously cited accounts:

"The place where a ring that was very important to me had been lost. In fact, my niece and her little friends had lost it unintentionally and my grandmother in a dream told me the exact place where it was."

"We were told where the hidden documents, important to the family, were located."

"But why are you looking in the safe? The car's papers are in the laptop bag in front of you!"

"The location of the vault in the cemetery."

"Information about administrative and legal matters."

"A few weeks after the funeral, he told me that someone had put something in his suit pocket and that he always had it with him. I learned that my mother had slipped in a religious medal. He also showed me what was in the envelope my sister had put in the casket."

This immediately verified practical information was a great relief to the experient in this second-hand account:

"My husband has had several experiences of contact [with my mother] whilst totally conscious; he has heard the voice of my mother on several occasions. One occasion was when he was worried when a box of controlled drugs (we own a pharmacy) went missing and he spent days searching the stockroom and controlled drugs cabinet. He went in on a Sunday for one last look before having to report it. He was upstairs, just staring at the cabinet, when he heard my mum say, 'Look behind the radiator' — he reached down behind and wedged in there was the box of Diamorphine!"

The main lesson to be learned from this section is that the fact of having an ADC is in itself a message: the message that the deceased loved ones apparently still have the capacity to manifest themselves. The most important information allegedly transmitted by the deceased is that they are alive and well. In addition, our respondents perceived a wide range of personalized messages, predominantly messages of support, love and assistance in a painful period of bereavement. Sometimes specific themes are addressed and advice or guidance is provided. Relationship issues unresolved at the time of death may be brought to a closure during these experiences.

According to the data collected, the perception of personalized messages varies according to the type of ADC, ranging from 60% for olfactory ADCs to 80% for tactile and visual ADCs. It should be stressed that for 87% of respondents with auditory ADCs, the perceived communication was clearly different from a thought.

Nearly a quarter of our respondents (24%) perceived previously unknown information during the ADC. Often the imminent death of a significant other is announced, but the message may also refer to a happy event, such as a pregnancy of which the expectant mother and her family are not yet aware. Practical information needed by the bereaved (such as a life insurance policy taken out without the family's knowledge or hidden savings) is sometimes communicated during these ADCs. The precise circumstances of an accidental death may be disclosed during these contacts, as well as any other practical information useful, or even necessary, to the bereaved. These cases are of particular interest because of their evidential nature. They can be verified instantly by the experients, or their veracity will be confirmed by the passage of time in the case of messages referring to events that will occur in the future.

Circumstances of occurrence of ADCs

A series of questions gave us information about the *circumstances* in which the ADC occurred.

The duration of the contact was the focus of our first question. The data collected confirms previous research — these experiences are indeed very brief:

- Several seconds: 45%
- Several minutes: 33%
- Longer: 11%
- Unsure: 11%

Despite the brevity of the contact, experients often have the impression of a much longer duration, as if the ADC had occurred outside of time or in a different sort of time. A parallel can be drawn with the Near-Death Experience (NDE), and in particular with the "life review" which is one of its essential elements. It is during this stage that NDErs claim to have obtained a very large amount of information in an objectively short period of time.

Our respondent clarified her impression of the time elapsed during this ADC:

"Actually, I didn't expect to experience such a phenomenon at all. I was surprised, moreover because it woke me up so suddenly. But I didn't feel any negativity, just Mom's sadness and the compassion of the other 'supposed' person, as if she was preventing her from touching or grabbing me. I often wonder if my mom just wanted to say goodbye by taking my hand or if she wanted to take my hand to draw me to her so I would actually follow her, or for me to retain her close to me,

I couldn't tell. It's weird because it only lasted, I would say, maybe two seconds, but I had time to feel it all."

Other participants also commented on this topic:

"I couldn't say how long it lasted (maybe 30 seconds?), but it seemed like a very long time."

"Time seemed to me to be decomposed."

"It only lasted a few moments, but I was completely submerged in this very powerful feeling. I have the impression that time had stopped, that nothing was moving..."

What time of day or night did the contact occur? One could imagine that night is particularly conducive to the occurrence of these contacts and it is true that a small majority of the ADCs in our collection occurred in the evening or at night, but many had occurred in the morning or afternoon when lighting conditions were better and experients were awake and active.

- In the morning: 21%
- In the afternoon: 21%
- In the evening: 16%
- During the night: 39%
- Unsure: 3%

Was the location where the ADC occurred lit or in the dark? Although many of the ADCs collected took place at night, this does not necessarily mean that they occurred in the dark.

- Illuminated by the light of day: 31%
- Illuminated by an electric light: 15%
- Dimly lit by twilight, an outside light, etc.: 12%

- In the dark: 31%
- Unsure: 3%
- Other: 9%

We asked about the health status of the respondents at the time of the ADC (more than one option could be checked).

The vast majority of respondents were in good health. Only a moderate number of people were depressed or on medication, which is not surprising given that many of them were grieving.

- Good health: 79%
- Sick: 1%
- Depressed: 14%
- Under medication (antidepressant, etc.): 3%
- Under the influence of substances (recreational drugs, alcohol, etc.): 1%
- Unsure: 2%

We now examine the alertness of the experients when the ADC occurred. A majority of them were fully alert.

- Completely awake and active: 39%
- Completely awake and resting: 13%
- Somnolent/half asleep: 7%
- Asleep: 25%
- Falling asleep/Waking up: 7%
- Unsure: 1%
- Other: 8%

In an open-ended question with a free text dialogue box, we asked our participants what they were doing when the ADC occurred. The answers provided are of course as varied as our participants are, since they were all rooted in their own unique daily lives at the time of the contact.

Some were on their own, focused on an activity:

"I was painting and listening to music."

"Sitting on the patio doing sudoku."

"In the bathroom brushing my cat."

"Sitting in the living room, reading a newspaper."

"Working on business — preparing tax forms."

"Had started a puzzle."

"Preparing for my teaching assignment for the next day."

Others were in the company of other people:

"Walking and talking to my sister."

"My brother's friend Terry and I had just finished eating lunch and were getting ready to leave the coffee shop."

"Getting my children ready for school."

"Talking to my girlfriend on the phone."

Falling asleep or waking up is a favorable moment for the ADC to occur:

"I was waking up. Actually, I was awake, just thinking about a project."

"I was falling asleep but was still awake."

And here are some descriptions of the moment when the deceased was perceived:

"Walking into my bathroom and looking at my reflection in the mirror when I saw her behind me."

"I was coming down from the second floor, I walked into the living room and there he was."

"I was asleep and I woke up to get a drink of water and she was there when I turned on the electric light."

Did the experience happen instantly or gradually? For a majority, the contact occurred instantly.

- **For 76% instantly, for 16% gradually, and 7% were unsure**

We asked whether the participants were alone or with other people when they perceived the deceased. Most participants were alone.

- Alone: 62%
- With another person: 26%
- With several people: 11%
- Unsure: 2%

As already mentioned in the previous pages, ADCs can sometimes be perceived simultaneously by several people gathered in the same place. These contacts are called *shared ADCs*. The literature indicates that a majority of ADCs occur without being witnessed by others. Either the experient is alone at the time of contact or other people are present but do not perceive the deceased. Shared ADCs are believed to be rare, but they are particularly striking because the shared experience of a contact reinforces the sense of reality of the event.

Our data confirm previous research on this point. Shared ADCs seem to be rare indeed, as a majority of our participants were the only ones to perceive the deceased, although other people were present.

- **72% were the only ones to perceive the contact, 21% the other person(s) present also perceived the contact, and 7% were unsure**

We asked those surveyed: If the other person(s) present also perceived the contact, please describe what they perceived. The following are some of the answers:

"I think [he perceived] the same thing I did, because we both ran down the street looking for the apparition."

"When I heard the footsteps in the room, my husband heard them too."

"When the bedside lamp turned on by itself, my husband also saw the light."

"On two occasions, yes, I was with a friend and we both perceived him."

In a follow-up question, we asked whether another person or other persons they know claim to also have had contact with the same deceased person at some point.

- **35% had an acquaintance(s) who had contact with the same deceased, 15% were unsure, and 50% had no acquaintance(s) who had contact with the same deceased**

I leave the floor to our participants:

"I was out of town. My sister, whom I live with, says she got up in the middle of the night and saw my deceased boyfriend sitting on my bed. At first she thought it was her boyfriend, but he was in her bed. And she knew it was Anthony because of the way he was sitting with his long legs stretched out and crossed in front of him, the way he often sat, but also like he wanted her to see him."

"On New Year's Day they saw him sitting close to me, smiling. We all celebrated that day every year together when my husband was still alive."

"Three years after my husband's death, our son felt his presence in the operating room as he (our son) was being prepared for cancer surgery."

"My other brothers were in different parts of the house. One brother was in the living room, my other brother was accompanying the mortician to the door. They both had the same, exact sentiment about my mother's communication, and why she did it, what she was saying to us."

Apparently, Kenneth wanted to ensure that his wife would be well cared for after his passing:

"Numerous people claimed to also have had contact with Kenneth. Some of these individuals were not aware of his passing before the contact. The first individual, Bruce, was merely a casual, but friendly, contact, a retired military officer. After Kenneth's passing, Bruce and Lizbeth have been trying to help me and to take care of me... from a distance, much like a father (or mother) would with a daughter. But I did not know them that well before. While infinitely thankful, I was also puzzled. Bruce recently wrote to me and said that Kenneth had appeared to him in the months following his passing. However, Bruce will not share the details with me until we are face to face, with 'our feet under the same table', as he puts it. The experience transformed him, and he cannot talk about it via telephone or email. He insists he can only do so in person. That has not happened yet. However, this is the primary reason he has taken care of me. Another contact, Rosemary, did not know of Kenneth's passing. Then Kenneth appeared to her in a dream, instructing her to reach out to me at the soonest, which she did a year or so later. She did not have our current address because we had moved since our last communication/contact. Rosemary, within the past week, has also written to me that both Kenneth and I appeared together in a dream a few days ago, meeting with her to explain important things she needed to know about the future. She has no recall of the details. She was, nevertheless, joyful over the 'meeting' (contact). There were other individuals who contacted me in this same respect over the years."

This apparition was simultaneously perceived by two people gathered in the same place:

"In a library, the very real apparition of an uncle who died many years ago. He was also seen by a young man sitting next to me."

Sometimes, several people located in different places perceive the same deceased simultaneously or within a short period of time, for example at the time of death, as reported by our participant who had herself experienced an ADC with her grandfather when he passed away:

"My brother dreamed that my grandfather appeared to him and asked him if he thought he should leave or not (my grandfather was hospitalized with terminal cancer). In his dream, my brother was somehow giving our grandfather permission. He died the same night, at 2:20 a.m. [...]. When I called him on the phone the next morning to tell him that our grandfather had died, he immediately said, 'Yes, I know, he died last night, he asked me for permission to leave beforehand.'"

In the descriptions to follow, participants, who had themselves experienced an ADC with this deceased individual, report contacts that their family members or friends had had with this same deceased person, but at different times. Here are some responses to our question: Did another person(s) you know claim to also have had contact with the same deceased person at some point?

"My five-year-old nephew told my brother that he saw Grandma in a pretty dress, that she was talking to him, she was radiant and smiling... He couldn't remember what she said to him but just that she loved her children very dearly (these are my little nephew's exact words[46]) and that she would come back on Tuesday to see him..."

"My sister, in whose house my son committed suicide. During one night, she saw him in this room."

"My daughter's friend's mother saw him leaning against the dishwasher when we were drinking tea. I didn't see him. She told me he was sad."

"My partner perceived my mother's presence on the evening of her death, sitting on my side of the bed, next to me. Personally, that night, I did not perceive her presence at all."

For the following cases, the same deceased person had been perceived separately by two persons respectively, in addition to the participant, days or months apart:

"Two of our daughters perceived my husband's presence. One, a few minutes after his death, when I was talking to her on the phone, she felt a presence that said, 'I'm OK, don't cry, I'm still here.' She instantly knew it was her dad. A few months after his death, another of my daughters, one day when she was very loaded, with a heavy load in her arms, found herself stuck by a rather massive door. She thought, 'I need some magic help so I don't break everything in my boxes.' That's when she felt a cold draft and the door opened, she was able to pass through... She was quite shaken by this experience, and although very resistant to the idea of an afterlife, she admitted that she had felt her daddy!"

"My mother and my mother-in-law caught a glimpse of my son a few days apart, each one at her home. Both of them said the same thing to me: 'I saw François pass by, it was him'."

It is well known and often observed that pets have a remarkable sensitivity for what could be called extrasensory manifestations. The work of the English biologist and researcher in the field of parapsychology Rupert Sheldrake — who proposed the concept of morphic resonance — is a reference in this field.[47]
We asked if a pet (cat, dog, etc.) was in the same place at the time of the ADC.

- **20% were in the company of a pet, 7% were unsure, and 74% were not in the company of a pet**

For those who actually were in the company of a pet at the time of the ADC, a quarter noticed that it was behaving in an unusual way.

- **25% noted an unusual behavior of the animal, 16% were unsure, and 59% did not notice any unusual behavior of the animal**

Here are some examples of unusual pet behavior:

"My Dad died two days after my eighth birthday in 1967. It was now 1973. I was 14 years old and was alone in my home. My mom and her new husband had gone out for the evening. I had adopted a puppy, *Sugar*, who was on the bed with me as I spoke on the phone with my friend Caroline at 11 p.m. I saw a shadow on the door of my bedroom and *Sugar* jumped off the bed and ran down the hall. I had a long cord on the 'landline' and pulled it as long as I could to find him, keeping Caroline on the phone, but he was nowhere to be found! I pulled out the closets and the furniture and he came back at 1 a.m., wagging his tail, walking into my bedroom like he just had the happiest experience. I was overcome with emotion and held him, crying. I went to my dresser and being 'tough', I pushed it up against my bedroom door. I fell asleep and at 3:15 a.m. I heard someone calling my name, but I was unable to open my eyes because there was a BRIGHT light in the corner of my bedroom. *Sugar* jumped off my bed and sat in front of this Bright White light. When I looked closer I saw my father! He was smiling ear to ear, 'talking', but his mouth was not moving. He said, 'I want you to know Mommy loves you. I will always Love you, and THE most important thing to know and learn in life IS Love.' The light then faded. *Sugar* started whimpering and jumped in my arms. I was sobbing and crying hysterically. I stayed awake the rest of the night, touching any and everything to make sure I AM awake and this is NOT a dream whatsoever, and eventually fell asleep. I remember it like it just happened."

"I felt my dad physically present. My cat literally doubled in size with all her hair sticking up."

"I felt the warm arms of my deceased father-in-law; he had been at a distance in the corner of the room. My sister-in-law felt cold and suddenly asked me what was wrong. The cat, asleep on my lap, then sprang up, arched back and fur standing up, claws dug into my leg, staring at the corner of the room where Henry was. She would never go near that corner, even if she was not fed for two days and her food put down there, she was frightened to go near that area."

"[My cat was] Fluffed up. Transfixed in place, staring at my dad where he was standing. No confusion. Never seen her like that before."

"My cat was bristling when my grandfather suddenly burst into the room where he was staying before he died."

"Unbelievably, the dog looked obsessed and barked at the chair where my mom used to sit in the dining room. This happened about three or four times in the same month. About six months had passed since my mother's death."

"The dog barked and the peacock screamed like never before."

"When my husband visited me in our house, the dog was all weird. He was wagging his tail like when you get a visit from a loved one."

In the testimony to follow, the alleged presence of the grandmother was only perceived by the dog and not by its owners, who nevertheless immediately linked the unusual behavior of the dog to the deceased grandmother:

"Several years ago, not long after our nan died, my wife and I experienced some strange activity in our flat, our dog jumped off our lap, walked over to an empty seat, sat and then gave his paw to the empty seat as if commanded."

Respondents were asked about their emotional state of mind just prior to the ADC. The responses do not support the materialistic hypothesis stipulating that people experience ADCs when they are overwhelmed by the sorrow of grief and desperately need a sign of their loved one.

We put this question to our respondents: In your own words, please describe your emotional state immediately before the ADC.

I have made a selection of responses that I consider to be fairly representative, although of course each situation is unique, just as all participants in our survey are unique.

"I was on holiday so I was relaxed and happy."

"It was two weeks after my mum's death and I was struggling with grief. I was tearful and anxious about being in her house for the first time since her passing. I was weighed down by sadness and loss."

"I neither drink, smoke or take drugs... I was relaxed and rested. And there he was at the end of my bed."

"Having a laugh with family."

"Grieving as my Dad had only died three weeks before."

"Normal, it was about a year after I lost him. Normal sadness, but OK."

"Emotional state was excellent, because deceased's passing was in my view perfect for him."

"Relaxed and at peace with my mother's passing."

"Just a regular day, generally happy."

"Sound state of mind, did not expect this at all."

"Normal grieving process with resolving feelings of guilt."

"We had just found out about 12 hours prior [to the ADC] of our son's accident and that he had not survived. Naturally I was very upset as anyone would be, but I considered myself very calm and an emotional support for others, especially for my husband."

"I wasn't too distressed when my dad passed away. My mum had died seven years prior and he wasn't the same person after that. So, it was almost a relief to know that he wasn't suffering anymore. So, I wasn't heartbroken or very tearful. As the eldest I was probably worrying about the arrangements that needed to be made."

"Sad and bereaved but that evening, calm and a bit more cheerful after supper with my friends."

"I was obviously grieving at the time, but I was calm and in a good state of mind at the specific time that I had the experience."

"I was in a wonderful mood, very much enjoying a beautiful morning and a nice drive while listening to a very humorous discussion on the radio."

"Missing my son and feeling depressed and sad."

"I was in a calm and relaxed state. Neither happy nor sad. Definitely sober."

"Saddened by the death of my son."

"I felt good despite a little sadness. I did not have a burdened heart because my relationship with the deceased had been over for several years."

"No particular emotional state at that moment... I got up to give my son a baby bottle."

"Calm, though with the natural sadness due to Dad's death two days before."

"A lot of grief because I had just lost my grandfather... a huge sadness."

"I was calm, I wasn't depressed or in bad health. I wasn't cheerful either, just neutral."

"Normal, busy with activities, not thinking about dead people or anything like that."

Finally, we asked those surveyed if they were frightened by the contact allegedly initiated by the deceased. At the time it occurred, a large majority were not frightened by the experience, but a small minority were.

- **85% were not frightened, 3% were unsure, and 12% were frightened**

It is remarkable that 85% of our respondents were not frightened by the ADC, even though it occurred completely unexpectedly and was unsolicited, and that it was apparently in complete contradiction with the range of possibilities of reality, as defined by our Western societies.

Here is a testimony from a respondent who was frightened by her experience:

"After my grandfather died, I went home to rest. I left the light on because I felt him in the room. I didn't sleep all night and I was very scared because I knew he was there."

Those who had been frightened were asked at what point in the experience they had been frightened.

- **53% were frightened during the whole ADC, 32% only at the beginning, and 16% only at the end**

Did the ADC stop when they were frightened?

- **For 35% contact stopped immediately, 15% were unsure, and for 51% contact did not stop immediately**

To those who answered that the contact stopped immediately, we asked how they felt about the interrupted contact:

- I was relieved: 37%
- I regretted: 43%
- I didn't mind: 5%
- Unsure: 16%

ADCs, especially apparitions, can frighten some experients and cause them for example to run out of the room. However, like 43% of our participants who answered this question, they often regret their visceral reaction afterwards and some wish for a new contact.

This was the case for this participant:

"In the early morning of the first day of 2018. It was 7 a.m. and a presence woke me up. I was alone that morning because my husband was exceptionally absent on this holiday for his work. I saw a bright light with a very white centre, very pure, of human size. On the outer edges there was a less bright white, a bit like a cloud. Like the presence at the foot of my bed of a person, but I could not identify this person. It was a benevolent and very powerful presence. At first, I was not afraid, I felt good. It seemed to me that it was there to give me a message. After a few seconds I realized that this was not normal and I looked around to see where this light could be coming from. I tried to hold on to something rational, but to no avail. Clearly, nothing could explain the presence of this light, the shutters were closed and no lamps were lit. That's when I got scared and then it was over. Today I am certain that I saw this presence and did not dream, and I am so sorry I was afraid. I am certain that someone wanted to notify me of something. It was only two and a half months later that I understood the message. I have this certainty. My grandmother has passed away. I am sure today that that morning it was my grandfather (my grandmother's husband), who died more than twenty years ago, who was at the foot of my bed."

I mentioned in the previous pages that several teams associated with our project are analyzing/have analyzed specific aspects of the after-death communication on the basis of our data collection. Renaud Evrard, Assistant Professor of Psychology at the University of Lorraine, Nancy, France, and his colleague Marianne Dollander are one of the external teams collaborating with us. They have been looking into the issue of frightening ADCs and have published a paper in *Evolution Psychiatrique*.[48]

The paper presents the analysis of 108 accounts from the English and French datasets of our data collection, corresponding to a subset of the sample of respondents who described their ADC as frightening. The mixed-methods analysis of closed and open questions shed light on the content of the messages, the anxieties associated with these experiences, the ways in which the participants shared these experiences with others, as well as their after-effects. This analysis shows that even the ADCs labelled as frightening are in fact not really felt as such by the experients: "We can see that despite the fact that we analyze so-called frightening ADCs, the messages are very rarely seen as being of the order of malicious will imposed by the entities. The vast majority of messages turn out to be positive, some focusing specifically on relationship failures, others preparing for the announcement of a demise or a future negative life event."[49]

"It is interesting to note that announcing or forecasting messages, or those for which the person is only the medium or the channel of a message to be conveyed to others, re-enact an essential scene of psychic life. The fact of passing phantasmatically through another allows the subject to feel less his share of responsibility in his psychic life, in a process more respectful of his defense mechanisms.

Given the globally positive dimension of the messages extracted from these experiences, we can therefore legitimately ask ourselves what are the sources of the anxieties associated with these experiences."[50]

The content of these fears was analyzed by Evrard and Dollander. Why did 12% of the 1,004 participants in our survey report being frightened by the ADC, during all or part of the experience? Where does this fear come from, since the messages perceived during the contact were not felt as frightening? It appears that the surprise effect and the impression of experiencing an event that is supposed to be totally impossible, which results in doubting one's own mental sanity, play a large part in these fears: "The monstrous manifestations of dangerous spectres, whose cultural representations of the ghost deluge us with, are clearly absent. The fear comes mainly from the surprise effect: it is the shock of the unknown, a shock that is at once perceptual, emotional and rational. Questions can emerge very quickly about the intentions of the entity and the meaning of the encounter. Sometimes it is the phenomena that seem to occur in the physical world that cause misunderstanding. Other fears relate rather to emerging doubts about the mental health of the person and the possibility of sharing this incongruous experience.

"Often, this anxiety resolves when the person expresses their fear (verbally or by withdrawing from the situation), because they feel obeyed and not harassed, thus maintaining a sense of control. This is not always the case in the few seconds or minutes that episodes involving forms of sleep paralysis[51] may last, where the loss of physical control can generate anxiety (61.6% of all 1,004 respondents were not frightened during partial temporary paralysis, see Elsaesser et al., 2020, p. 14[52]). However, this fear is mostly transitory or even combined at the time with positive feelings. When we analyze the repercussions of the phenomenon, it will be confirmed that people maintain a positive or very positive perception of their experience."[53]

We further explored the issue of possible fears triggered by ADCs with an additional question. We asked the small minority (12%) of respondents who had been frightened by the ADC what in particular had triggered their fear:

- I was destabilized by the fact that the deceased was apparently able to establish a contact with me: 42%
- I feared to be losing my mind/hallucinating: 17%
- I thought the deceased's intention was to harm me: 16%
- Other: 25%

It seems that it was the very fact of experiencing an ADC that destabilized our respondents, rather than the contact itself:

"It was very surprising and unsettling; it scared me, even though I knew it was my father."

"I was frightened of the unknown, of the other side, of death, of what happened. I was not frightened that my mother established contact with me, I know that it is only love she wanted to transmit."

"I was a child so I didn't believe what I was really seeing at first. But after looking at that spot 100 times, he was still there. Not to hurt me but just there and, being a child, I was scared of the unknown."

The apparent incongruity of the event shocked our participant a little, but without frightening her:

"I wasn't frightened at all... it was just a new and strange experience and I felt a little shocked and alarmed, but then went back to sleep unbothered."

Although only 16% of the 12% who were frightened by the ADC feared that the deceased's intention was to harm them, this was the case for this participant:

"I got scared when he got too close to me and I felt threatened. Prior to that, I was surprised by the certainty that it was my father walking behind me."

Contacts involving unknown deceased persons are obviously more difficult to deal with:

"I wasn't prepared for it and woke up to a stranger sitting on my bed reaching to touch me!"

As the many testimonies presented in the previous pages attest, ADCs are usually immediately perceived by the experients as a deeply moving and consoling experience and they do not doubt for a second its authenticity. In a second phase and after reflection, they may wonder how such an event is possible, as it is so strongly in contradiction with the dominant conception of the nature of reality, and perhaps with their own convictions prior to the ADCs, and they may be surprised to have welcomed the experience with such naturalness and joy.

This is precisely what two of our respondents have experienced:

"I was scared after the ADC, but not during."

"An awareness of the abnormality of this experience."

These correspondents also attribute their fear to a lack of information:

"I was not aware at the time that this was an ADC."

"I don't really know why, but when I heard my name spoken in his voice, I felt a sense of fear because there was no way I could have heard that."

"Because I didn't understand what was going on."

"Fear, interest and lack of knowledge."

Another unfortunate consequence of the lack of knowledge about ADCs is the fear of experients for their mental health:

"I thought I was crazy and found it scary... I regret that, because I didn't get to 'commune' with my daughter before she passed away."

The lack of information also destabilized this respondent and made her doubt her sanity. If she had had the necessary tools to understand what she was experiencing, she could have savored this moment in all tranquility:

"I was awakened [by the ADC] and sat up hurriedly in my bed. I was wide-eyed by the vision and lay in the night which had become dark again, completely overwhelmed. I didn't know at the time that this could happen and I doubted my sanity. I was in so much pain. I had the deepest conviction that it really happened, but it seemed crazy. I would not experience it at all the same way if such an event happened now. I would be happy instead of thinking I was losing my mind."

Again, prior knowledge of the ADC phenomenon would have prevented our participant from worrying about her mental health, just as it would have allowed her psychiatrist to provide her with better advice:

"The week after my father died (I was 19). I couldn't sleep because I had the feeling that I was being watched, that my father was watching me in the corner of my room, and it scared me to death. My body was bristling all over, the shivers were freezing me. I went to a psychiatrist to ask what was happening to me because it was traumatic for me. I was young. The answer: the mourning has not been done, take sleeping pills. It was only years later that I realized I was not unbalanced."

What if ADCs were not an "anomalous", "exceptional", "unusual", or even "paranormal" phenomenon, but simply a common and healthy human experience, possibly experienced by half of the inhabitants of our planet?

Let's dream for a moment and imagine that all the people who would experience a spontaneous and direct contact with a deceased loved one were already fully informed about the phenomenon of ADCs. They would know the name, the phenomenology, the impact, the prevalence, the research undertaken and widely disseminated, and they would have had the opportunity to follow informed and diversified discussions on the subject in the media and other channels of communication. If they were to experience an ADC themselves, they would then have all the tools they need, not only to understand what is happening, but also to evaluate their experience, with full knowledge of the facts.

This would also make it much easier to *share* an ADC with others. One can imagine the relief of the experients if their entourage was already aware of the subject and listened to the account of their experience with full knowledge of ADCs. A shared knowledge of this phenomenon would give a common language, while obviously leaving each person the latitude to interpret it according to their own belief system.

What is our respondents' experience in this regard? We asked them if they had shared their ADC with family members or friends and how their account was received:

"My husband and my sister. It was a difficult experience to explain, but I felt that they both believed me as they could see that it had somehow changed me."

"My partner at the time who, whilst cynical, recognized the comfort and affirmation it gave me."

"All my family and friends. They still cannot take in the evidence presented to them."

"My husband. He thought I was nutty."

"Husband and daughter. They didn't believe it. Thought I was making it up."

"Family members. Some were welcoming of it, others thought I was crazy."

"Our two children. One seemed to be comforted by it (he had had some 'feelings' of his father's presence), but the other child was disappointed that she had had no similar experiences."

"Only a few close people. They were open to the possibility that it really happened."

"I shared the experience with my husband who believed me without question. Other people I thought maybe were slightly patronizing, thinking I was imagining things due to grief."

"I told my two sons and two other people in the family, but I didn't feel that I was really understood. It left me feeling frustrated and very lonely."

"I told my mother, who knew she was dying, about my ADC to reassure her. I don't think she believed me, or listened, too bad…"

"My children, my friends, to those I meet who are open-minded. It's too beautiful not to share it."

For those who decided not to share their experience, we asked them the reason for their choice:

"It's hard to explain to people, they don't understand, but will when they pass over."

"Where I live people wouldn't believe me."

"Too many people who have never experienced or wanted to learn about the afterlife. I still think those people would perceive me as being unbalanced."

"I didn't think anyone would believe me, that they would think it was just another sign of my grief."

"Because in our environment people will think I am mentally ill."

"Because I understood that not everyone wants to know... Or they are not prepared to hear it... There is always disbelief and my fear of judgement has sometimes been my best protection... although I would like to share it."

"They are not used to these kinds of things. The Catholic religious system in Spain is very strong and has created a powerful resistance to these phenomena which are often ridiculed."

A number of people prefer to keep their ADC to themselves because it is too personal and too intimate to be shared with others. Some are afraid of being ridiculed. Others may fear to expose this experience, which is so meaningful and important to them, to a reaction of skepticism or even dismissal from the listener and they prefer to keep it private.

"It was special to me and important to me and I wanted to keep it private because I felt it was significant only to me."

"Don't know how to explain... It feels as if this encounter was a thing between her and me, not meant for anybody else."

"It's something very intimate for me."

"I'm a person who doesn't like to talk about things that happen to me and even more so when it's something so personal, I prefer to keep it to myself."

"I preferred to keep it to myself, it's a moment that belongs only to us."

The main insight gained from this section on the circumstances of occurrence of the ADCs is that spontaneous after-death communications can take place in any situation, anywhere and at any time of the day or night. A vast majority of our respondents were in good health and more than half of them were awake at the time of contact.

It is surprising that only a small percentage (12%) of our participants was frightened during all or part of the contact (and almost half of them subsequently regretted the interruption of the ADC). Their potentially pre-existing belief that it is absolutely impossible for the deceased to make contact with the living may give them the impression that they are experiencing an impossible event. It is not easy to deal with an experience that, according to our belief system, cannot happen.

A broader and more inclusive conception of the nature of consciousness and consequently of the nature of reality would allow for a better understanding and integration of this type of experience. This is what is at stake in consciousness research which is in full expansion in various disciplines. It should be noted, however, that a large majority of our respondents welcomed the contact with delight, naturalness and gratitude, regardless of their pre-existing beliefs.

Partial temporary paralysis

Prior to our work, the phenomenon of partial temporary paralysis had never been described by researchers as an identified feature of ADCs.

For the writing of my book *Quand les défunts viennent à nous*,[54] I had analyzed 22 descriptions of ADCs that had been sent to me following a call for testimony inserted in an article I had published in the magazine *Inexploré*.[55] Three of the 22 experients reported that during the contact they were unable to move or speak, or both. One might suppose that this is a rare phenomenon as it had never been reported in the literature as an identified feature of ADCs, but 3 of the 22 persons who described their ADC to me had experienced it. This is not a negligible number and therefore this experience could not be considered as marginal in the very modest sample used for that book. To my knowledge, I was the first person to describe this element of spontaneous after-death communications. When designing the questionnaire for our survey, my colleagues and I obviously took the opportunity to ask a series of questions about this aspect of ADCs in order to determine whether the cases I had analyzed were an exception, or even an anomaly, or whether partial temporary paralysis was really a constituent element of ADCs.

The data collected indicate that this is indeed a recurring phenomenon as **120** of our participants reported partial temporary paralysis during their ADC.

- **12% reported partial temporary paralysis, 8% were unsure, and 80% haven't noticed anything like it**

How can one imagine this partial temporary paralysis? I give the floor to a participant:

"It happened a few weeks after the death of my wife, at the home of very close friends. It was about two o'clock in the morning and I was dozing, at most, but conscious. I suddenly felt a presence accompanied by a form of paralysis (my limbs could no longer execute the orders of the brain, I wanted to move a finger, a hand, but without succeeding). This did not trouble me because I immediately thought of my wife and of a particular event concerning us. Moreover, nothing was painful nor unpleasant. I then felt that something was resting on me, a very slight pressure was exerted on my body. Convinced that it was my wife, I got a glimpse of her (I sleep on my side). I immediately asked her if 'she felt well where she was' and she replied, 'Yes, I'm fine.' I then felt her move closer to me, but this was accompanied by a noise which increased in intensity as she approached. She uttered an extremely short sentence, but it was not very audible because of the noise. I asked her to repeat the sentence, which she did. I then understood that she was saying 'I love you'. She used to tell me that often. I then asked her if we were going to be reunited soon, to which she replied, 'No, that's not going to happen for a while.' Here too I recognized this particular way of formulating this sentence which was unique to her.[56] Suddenly I saw her detach herself from my body, pass in front of me, and there I clearly and unequivocally recognized her face (which had a slightly waxy tone) protruding from a sort of cape. She passed quite slowly in front of me, then her departure accelerated, and she ascended towards the sky. I saw her shrink until she appeared only as a dot and then disappear. I then instantly regained complete control of my movements. It took me some time to fall asleep again, troubled and happy about what had just happened. I was fully aware of what was happening to me (by which I mean that it was by no means a dream), and today, more than a year later, every detail is still very clear in my mind. This has been of immense comfort to me, and has contributed greatly to getting through this period as smoothly as possible."

Follow-up questions provided additional information.
Did you feel that you could not *move* during the contact with the deceased?

- **55% could not move, 20% were unsure, and 26% haven't noticed anything like it**

Did you feel that you could not *speak* during the contact with the deceased?

- **47% could not speak, 14% were unsure, and 39% haven't noticed anything like it**

Here are some extracts from the narratives of our participants:

"I couldn't move or shout."

"I felt paralyzed as soon as I saw her, but I immediately moved to cover my head because I was so scared."

"I immediately felt a form of paralysis, and I checked it out: my brain was telling my hand to move, but I couldn't carry out the command."

"I immediately thought that my father had come to give me a sign because this was not my first ADC and therefore my first sleep paralysis. Because each time it's the same: I'm semi-conscious, and I can't move my arms or legs and it's like my body is leaden and embedded in my mattress."

"My whole body was paralysed, when I tried to move I felt a huge weight! And the voice told me not to move."

"Simply unable to move and speak."

Did you notice some other sort of physical restriction or partial temporary paralysis?

- **25% noticed some other form of partial temporary paralysis, 25% were unsure, and 50% haven't noticed anything like it**

I present here some examples of other types of physical restrictions:

"I could hardly breathe and I had to find the courage to tell him in a firm voice not to scare me."

"My body was paralysed as well as my eyes, but I could speak."

"My eyes could not move."

"Thought paralysis: I could only listen at first."

"Impossible to breathe, heart clenched, as if crushed."

"I was locked up like in a cocoon."

Despite the sensation of partial temporary paralysis, this respondent nevertheless perceived the contact as a reassuring and beautiful experience:

"10 months after the death of my son Eric, it was All Saints' Day 1990 (a trying day). In the evening I was in my bedroom, not sleeping, when he appeared to me in a light of extraordinary whiteness and with his right arm he gestured to show me a place of intense luminosity, of a whiteness and clarity that I have never seen elsewhere! Even a city that is all lit up at night does not produce this light. It was magnificent. I was transfixed, as if paralysed, lying on my bed. Eric was smiling at me, beaming, and then he vanished. At that moment I felt his hand brush my cheek and a warmth invaded my body, whereas before I had felt like I was freezing. This apparition calmed me a lot because I saw him very happy. It made me even more sure that there is life after death."

Several accounts describe uncontrollable movements of the limbs, especially the legs, as illustrated by the following testimony:

"My grandmother came to me in my sleep or half-sleep, I don't know if I was dreaming. I had the impression that I was no longer in control of my legs, which seemed to lift up on their own."

The following respondents attribute this phenomenon to the effect of surprise rather than to physical paralysis:

"I think we are struck dumb by the eeriness and emotional charge of perceiving a deceased loved one."

"The surprise factor paralyses you for a fraction of a second."

"Was it really paralysis or the effect of surprise? I don't know."

And this is how one of our participants explains this phenomenon:

"The paralysis seems to be there so as not to interrupt the deceased in this moment which is always very short."

One might assume that this feeling of partial temporary paralysis should be particularly frightening, despite the brevity of the contacts, and yet a majority of our participants were not frightened:

- **62% were not frightened by the partial temporary paralysis, 12% were unsure, and 26% were frightened by the partial temporary paralysis**

I give the floor to our respondents:

"I was not afraid at any time."

"The first time you experience it, it's scary. But afterwards, when it happens again, you're not afraid anymore, you know it's a contact that's going to be made. My ears are ringing, and I can't move. I am 'alerted' that the contact is coming."

"I have the feeling that I have been guided in order not to be afraid."

"I was not afraid because I was in a state of love and comfort."

However, fear dominated this experience:

"I can't find an explanation for this event, which for me was a terrifying experience because I felt the deceased very present."

For those who had been frightened, we asked if the contact had stopped when they were afraid.

- **For 25% the contact has stopped, 18% were uncertain, and for 57% the contact has not stopped**

"Once when I was scared it stopped and when I realised it was him, I was never scared again."

Several hypotheses on the cause of this partial temporary paralysis could be put forward, including that of sleep paralysis, but for the time being we do not wish to comment on this. One of our teams will analyze this phenomenon and publish the results in a scientific journal.

Information on perceived deceased

The questions to follow concern the 'profile' of the perceived deceased. They raise a number of questions, such as whether the profile of causes of death, in particular so-called violent deaths (accident, murder and suicide), is different from that of the general population and whether sudden and therefore unpredictable deaths are over-represented in our sample. These questions are beyond the scope of this book, but a website such as *Eurostat*[57] might be useful for those who wish to explore the issue further.

The first question referred to the gender of the deceased. Do experients perceive mostly male or female deceased? Let us keep in mind that a much higher number of women than men participated in our survey, namely 85% of women, compared to only 14% of men (1% checked *other, e.g. transgender*).

Here are the answers to the question: Was the deceased a man, a woman, or a child (0–16 years)?

- **55% perceived a man, 33% perceived a woman, 4% perceived a child, and 9% other**

Gender of perceived deceased
The following graph shows the results for the data in the three project languages. It turned out that in the Spanish data collection — which is the smallest with 148 participants — none of the male participants perceived a male deceased. This can also be explained by the high female participation in our survey.

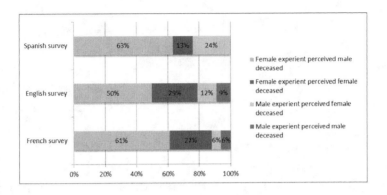

Who are the perceived deceased in relation to the experients? What was their relational bond before the demise? As one would expect, it is mainly family members and spouses/partners who are the object of ADCs.

The category of parents, in-laws and surrogate parents ranks first. The figures are very similar for the responses in all three languages. Couple relationships come in second place. The indication "Sweetheart" refers among others to a first love during adolescence. We have several cases in our data collection of people who had not seen their first love for years or even decades and yet perceived them after their passing. We observe a notable difference for the Spanish cases, which represent only 8% for this section. In addition to couple relationships, the bonds of blood are clearly an important factor in the occurrence of ADCs, as the category of friends, acquaintances and colleagues only occupies fourth place in our ranking.

Here is the graph reflecting the responses to the question: Who was the deceased in relation to you?

Relational bond – English, French and Spanish datasets

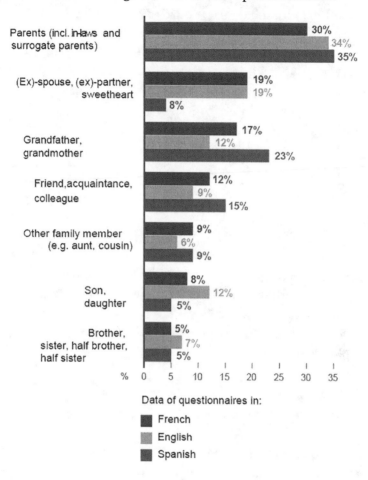

Data of questionnaires in:

- ■ French
- ▨ English
- ■ Spanish

Emotional bond

We asked about the emotional connection between the experients and the perceived deceased. The results are not surprising. It is clear from the answers of our respondents that the emotional relationship — the bond of love — is indeed an important factor in the occurrence of ADCs.

The answers to our question: What was your emotional connection with the deceased? are reflected in the three graphs below.

The graph of English cases presented first shows that *extremely close and loving* (60%), *very close* (13%) and *quite close* (11%) emotional relationships account for 84% of the responses collected.

Contacts with deceased with whom the experients were not particularly close are rather rare (*quite distant* 3% and *distant* 3%). These contacts quite often serve to transmit a message intended for someone close to the deceased (ADCs for a third person).

Confrontational (1%) and *extremely difficult* (2%) relationships were also reported by our English-speaking participants. An unresolved relationship issue at the time of death seems to be a driving force for contacts to occur since we have seen that some conflicts could be resolved after the demise. We have a number of cases in our data collection suggesting that reconciliation beyond death is possible and that it is never too late to mend a relationship.

As can be seen from the three graphs below, the results are on the whole very similar for the data in the three languages of the survey, with the exception of the *perception of unknown deceased*. Indeed, with 12% of participants having perceived a deceased person they did not know, the Spanish data collection represents the highest figure for this item.

Emotional bond, English dataset

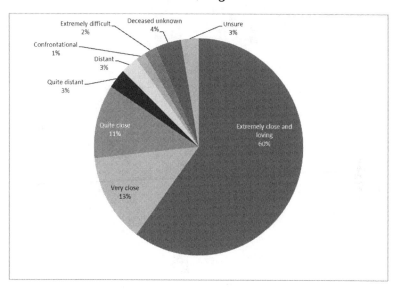

Emotional bond, French dataset

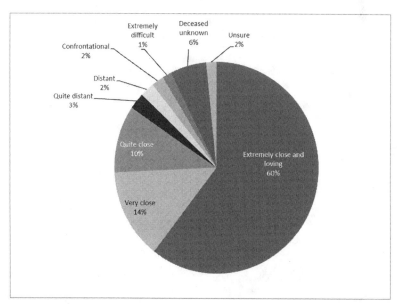

Emotional bond, Spanish dataset

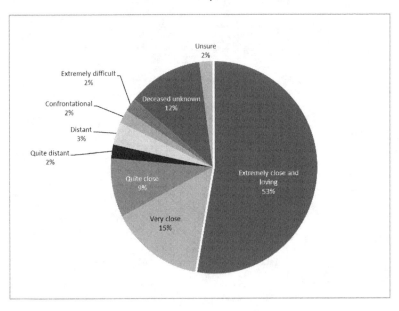

The next question allowed us to determine the cause of death. Further analysis will be required to determine whether violent deaths (accident, murder and suicide) are over-represented in our data collection compared to the general population.

- Disease: 42%
- Cardiac arrest: 14%
- Accident: 11%
- Old age: 7%
- Suicide: 7%
- Murder: 2%
- Unsure: 4%
- Other: 14%

The circumstances of the passing were the subject of our next questions.

If the persons were ill, how did they die?

- Suddenly: 23%
- After a short illness: 35%
- After a long illness: 35%
- Unsure: 7%

Where did the persons die?

- In hospital: 45%
- At home: 28%
- At the scene of the accident/heart failure, etc.: 12%
- Unsure: 4%
- Other: 11%

Oftentimes, mourners who subscribe to the hypothesis of the survival of consciousness after physical death ask themselves whether their deceased loved ones are well, if they are suffering or, on the contrary, if they are happy in their new form of existence.

We asked the participants in what emotional state/mood the deceased was. Several options could be ticked.

- Serene: 28%
- Radiant with bliss: 14%
- Eager to comfort me: 25%
- Compassionate: 14%
- Sad: 6%
- Agitated: 3%
- Frightened: 2%
- Threatening: 1%
- In another state of mind: 8%

Although a large majority (81%) of the perceived moods were of a positive nature (serenity, bliss, eagerness to comfort, compassion), 6% of the deceased were perceived as sad, 3% as agitated, 2% as frightened, and 1% as threatening. However, the testimonies of our participants to follow allow for a finer interpretation of that data.

I will illustrate the different items by excerpts of testimonies, some of which have already been presented in the previous pages.

Serene = 28%: "It was very pleasant, as if he radiated infinite peace"; "Son, being dead takes some getting used to, but you'll like it"; "He seemed to be at peace, at last, and wanted me to know it. That's how I sensed it."

Radiant with bliss = 14%: "I'm in total bliss!"

Eager to comfort me = 25%: "Everything is going to be OK, I'm watching over you, and I'm going to send you a loving person"; "I am by your side and will remain as long as you are suffering."

Compassionate = 14%: "I think she was trying to make sure I was okay. The level of compassion was incredible"; "On her visit she appeared younger in age, serene, composed, beautiful, happy, smiling, full of love and compassion"; "He was both compassionate and angry, telling me to take care of myself and to avoid crossing the street in such a thoughtless manner."

Sad = 6%: According to several accounts presented below, it seems that at least some of the deceased who appeared to be sad were saddened by the grief of their loved ones, and not necessarily sad in their alleged new form of existence: "He was peaceful in himself and sad for his parents [he died suddenly in an accident]"; "My mother's voice was recognizable, but she seemed to be making a great effort to speak, with deep pain, strength and sadness. Eager to learn about my condition, she asked if I was OK"; "He came up to me with a distressed face. I couldn't hear what he said, but I understood that he was very sad that I was so desperate"; "I felt that he was worried about his girlfriend who was having a hard time accepting his death. I felt he was 'demanding' ... not threatening, at no time did I feel him threatening, but I did recognize his way of doing things... and his way of saying things. He was a very persuasive and demanding person. He kept pushing me until I did what was needed for his girlfriend."

Agitated = 3% and **Frightened** = 2%: The messages perceived by our respondents suggest that some of the deceased were agitated or frightened at the time of realizing their change of state; they may not have realized immediately that they were dead: "On the evening of my partner's death, I was 'in touch' with him, feeling his fear as he began to understand that he had died"; "He needed help"; "He didn't know where he was." Some of the messages suggest that their fear or agitation may have only been a transient state: "In the first dream ADC he was very frightened (he had not understood that he was dead — sudden death), then during the second contact he was very serene"; "He made me understand that he wasn't well, then the second time that it was better"; "Just after his demise, my loved one was agitated, and then sad. I think at that time he didn't know he had died. Then everything I perceived was happy, full of love and compassion, with the strong determination to support me."

Threatening = 1%: A very small number of the deceased were perceived as threatening. A more detailed analysis will be necessary to determine whether these cases involve more specifically contacts with unknown deceased persons. ADCs with strangers are of a different nature, as they lack the bond of love and tenderness between the deceased and the experients that make them such consoling and beautiful experiences. Here is one of the rare cases of a contact with an ambiguously identified deceased person, felt as frightening/threatening: "I was 11 or 12 years old, I was staying with my grandmother in the south of France. I was alone in the room when I went to bed. I was tossing and turning in bed, I couldn't sleep, I felt that someone was watching me, someone was near me. A few minutes later I saw a transparent veil coming out of the wall and brushing my cheek, it was very cold, freezing even. I was very frightened at the time and then he left and I never saw him again. I think it was my grandfather but I'm not sure."

A number of the above testimonies show an evolution of the mood of the perceived deceased. It is possible that the mood of the deceased is not constant but evolving, and the figures presented would thus only be a snapshot of the state of mind of the deceased at a given moment.

Some of the testimonies presented in the preceding pages evoke a radical and improbable change of mood in the experients, surprising in view of the sad circumstance of the death of a loved one. Instead of being disheartened, even crushed by the grief of bereavement, they felt a sense of joy, peace, love and plenitude never before experienced in such intensity and purity. Were these really the feelings of the experients, or had the deceased found a way to make them feel *their own emotions* inherent in their alleged new condition? Could they have succeeded in making them feel their present emotional state of mind?

These extracts from testimonies already presented in the previous pages are consistent with this hypothesis: "Just after my father passed away in 2014, I felt an intense joy that lasted three and a half days, hence abnormal right after a death. It was an unusual joy because it was very intense and I also felt an inner serenity that I had never felt to such an extent before."

Another respondent describes her experience eloquently: "When I think of my deceased loved one (almost all day long, as was the case when he was incarnated...), it is about my inner feelings with my thoughts. Yet, my inner feeling is marked by the painful experience of his absence. When my deceased loved one is present, I first feel him outside of me, and it is his state of mind that I feel, and his state of mind is nothing but love and joy."

This participant concurs with this view: "When this happens, it is wonderful. I am no longer in the feeling of my grief but in the feeling transmitted by my loved one. When it happens, I don't suffer at all anymore. I am so happy."

The belief system of the deceased gave us additional information, for cases where it was known to the experients. The answers collected show that strong faith is by no means a precondition for an ADC to occur.

We asked the question whether the deceased was a:

- Strong believer (in religious terms): 13%
- Moderate believer (in religious terms): 25%
- Spiritual (outside any specific religious institution): 18%
- Agnostic: 7%
- Atheist: 14%
- Unsure: 23%

Did the deceased believe in an afterlife? Only about half of our participants had this information.

- The deceased believed in the survival of consciousness: 29%
- The deceased did not believe in the survival of consciousness: 16%
- Respondents did not have this information: 55%

In this section we have looked at the "profile" of the perceived deceased. Unsurprisingly, ADCs overwhelmingly involve the closest family members (parents, in-laws, surrogate parents, and grandparents) as well as spouses, partners, romantic relationships and friends who have preceded us in death. Fortunately, a limited number of parents have suffered the loss of a son or daughter, so this category only occupies the penultimate place in our ranking. The data collected show that the emotional relationship — the bond of love — that united the two parties in life is clearly a trigger for ADCs to occur. This very strong bond seems not to be extinguished with the death of the physical body. Relationship problems left unresolved at the time of death seem to have sometimes been sorted out after the demise, suggesting that it is never too late to solve relationship issues.

An important element of this set of questions concerns the perceived emotional state of the deceased. It is indicative of a sustained and dynamic relationship between the living and the dead, thus implying an interaction. The state of mind of the deceased seems to be influenced/affected by that of their significant others. However, the mood of the deceased as captured by our survey may not be permanent, but instead may be evolving, and therefore the figures presented above might be only a momentary snapshot of their state of mind.

Another fascinating insight is that some of our participants experienced states of mind completely out of sync with the sad occasion of the death of a loved one. They felt an elation and serenity never before experienced in such intensity, suggesting that it was the deceased who succeeded in making them feel their own emotions inherent in their alleged new form of existence. I am obviously proposing here a hypothesis that needs to be confirmed — or refuted — by further research.

Impact of ADCs on the belief system

ADCs suggest the existence of a bond between the living and the dead that seems to survive physical death. We can assume that this strong experience has an impact on the belief system of the experients and the conception of their own death. The next set of questions helps to determine the belief system of our group of participants.

Where did our respondents stand *prior* to their ADC in terms of their belief in the existence of an afterlife compared to the general population?

Here are the answers to our question: Did you believe in life after death before your ADC?

- **Before their ADC, 69% believed in an afterlife, 20% were unsure, and 11% did not believe in it**

It turns out that the percentage of our participants who believed in an afterlife *before* their own experience is quite similar to the results of several surveys on this topic, including one presented in 2014 by ARDA, Association of Religion Data Archives[58] indicating that 71% of respondents believed in the existence of an afterlife.[59] Another American survey reports that, also in 2014, 73% of Americans believed in the existence of an afterlife.[60] In a survey of more than 9,000 British people in their forties published in 2015, Professor David Voas states, however, that 60% of the women, but only 35% of the men, believed in life after death.[61]

Furthermore, a survey conducted by Icelandic professor Erlendur Haraldsson indicates that in 2006, 34% of Icelanders surveyed thought that an afterlife was *possible*, 28% *probable* and 22% *certain*.[62]

Adherence to this hypothesis increases with age and women are more likely than men to subscribe to it. Further research is needed, of course, but at first glance these figures imply that our respondents' beliefs on this subject are in the average range of populations and that they were not particularly inclined to believe in the existence of an afterlife prior to their ADC.

Has the ADC changed our respondents' beliefs about the existence of an afterlife? We put the question to our respondents.
Today, do you believe in life after death?
The strengthening of beliefs in the existence of an afterlife is very significant as only one percent of respondents do not believe in an afterlife as a result of the ADC.

- **Today, 93% believe in an afterlife, 6% are unsure, and 1% do not believe in it**

Our respondents expressed their convictions:

"I always believed in an afterlife, but not one where we remember our previous life or the connections we had developed with loved ones. Just thought good people went to heaven, never thought that memories of people in this life would remain with us."

"I thought I believed in life after death, now I know without a shadow of a doubt there is life after death... I've experienced it multiple times and always when I'm not expecting it, it knocks me off my feet and takes my breath away."

"I do not fear it. I was present when my mum passed and I saw how brave she was and how peaceful her passing was. The fact that she then was able to let me feel her presence and give comfort cemented my belief in the afterlife."

"Although I did believe in life after death, I had never had an experience myself. After this experience, I knew without a doubt."

"I think there might be something to it. Anyway, it comforts me to know that someone I loved deeply and who has passed loves me enough to still be here with me."

"This does sound odd considering I have always believed we survive bodily death, but losing someone so loved was a challenge. I began to doubt everything that I had read/researched over the last 40 years. But after my own experience it only solidified my beliefs."

"This contact has both shaken my beliefs about the afterlife and allowed me to accept a different relationship with the deceased."

"Even though I already believed in the afterlife, such strong signs and experiences caused a further shift and understanding of the afterlife."

"Having several experiences and seeing different deceased people has given me absolute evidence that there is a life after death."

In the questions to follow, the participants took a position on the authenticity of the ADC.

Did you believe that deceased persons can contact living persons *before* your ADC?

- **Before their ADC, 63% believed that the deceased could contact the living, 23% were unsure, and 14% did not believe it**

Today, do you believe that deceased persons can contact living persons?

Again, the reinforcement of beliefs in the authenticity of ADCs is very significant as only one percent of participants do not believe in the ability of the deceased to contact the living following their ADC.

- **Today, 95% believe that the deceased can contact the living, 5% are unsure, and 1% do not believe it**

Here is a selection of the views of some of our respondents:

"I knew that the deceased could get in contact with the living, but I did not imagine with what strength and energy they could access this desire. I felt a very strong desire in my deceased partner to see me and to stay."

"I am now convinced that our deceased are still here and that they can contact us."

"This ADC showed me that physical death is not the end of everything. The journey continues in another way — there is purpose. Physical death is also not the end of relationships as it seems some forms of communication are still possible."

"I have learned a lot through pain, but all the knowledge I have gained I can pass on to those who miss their deceased loved ones and I can share with them the peace and serenity that comes into our hearts after learning that death does not really exist and that the bonds of love are not severed. In addition, I can tell them that their loved ones continue to live in another dimension and that they can — and that we can — make contact naturally."

As expected, ADCs impact the conception of death of the experients.

Did you notice a change in your perception of death following the ADC?

- **59% noted a change in their conception of death, 8% were unsure, and 33% noted no change**

It should be noted that at least part of those respondents who indicated that their conception of death had not changed as a result of the ADC (33%) may already have been convinced of the survival of consciousness after physical death *prior* to their own experience. Considering this hypothesis, the ADC would not have changed — but strengthened — their conviction.

Some of the people we surveyed expressed the following views on the subject:

"It changed how I view death and that we don't really need to be sad for the dead, but are sad for ourselves not having them around anymore."

"I was more firmly assured that he was still alive, close and just not visible, but there, always there."

"After this experience and looking back on all of the others in my life which suddenly made sense, I now perceive death as moving from one room into the next."

"I didn't have an imagination of what could happen with the soul and energy after death. Now I believe I have a concept. It's something completely unphysical as I experience it."

"I feel consciousness continues for at least some time after death and must be primary rather than an artifact of brain activity."

"I understood the transcendence and permanence of consciousness, of the Soul, of the Spirit; the meaning of dying and leaving this plane of existence for another; that there can be reunions that do not necessarily occur only after our own death..."

"I experienced it as a source of hope as well as an additional incentive to accept the mystery, the existence of transcendence."

"I have never been afraid of death, at least not of my own. What I was afraid of was the death of the other, his loss. The two visions of my husband and other more symbolic signs now give me the quasi conviction that our bond endures. As a result, I am in a continuity of life with him ever since I realized that death is only about the physical aspect of the person."

"My view of death has changed radically: today I see death as the passage to a new state, another page of our existence, and I tend to think that the best is yet to come after our death."

"Death used to scare me because I didn't know what could happen afterwards. Now, after the various experiences I had, I feel more serene, I know that death is not really the end. I know that we have the right to be sad, that the separation is difficult and extremely hard, but that there is something waiting for us afterwards in a world where it seems that the deceased are happy and at peace."

The fear of death is inherent to the human condition. It underlies every moment of our existence and affects our daily lives much more than we want to admit. Not thinking about it, banishing it from our minds, only aggravates our anxieties. The idea of death is constantly present in our subconscious, since it limits all our activities and projects in time and, in absolute terms, makes all our efforts absurd. If, on the other hand, our actions, our joys and our sorrows were to find an extension in permanence, if the meaning of our existence were no longer measured solely in the time span of our earthly life, then the conception of our daily life would be profoundly transformed, since our existence would take on a fundamentally different meaning. How can we overcome our ancestral fear of death and place our lives in a broader perspective? It would seem that the strength of spontaneous after-death communications is such that the experients are indeed (partially) relieved of this fundamental fear. This was the case for over 60% of our respondents.

We asked our respondents if, following their ADC, their fear of death had:

- Decreased: 31%
- Disappeared: 30%
- Remained the same: 33%
- Increased: 1%
- Unsure: 5%

I have selected some thoughts on this of those surveyed:

"I no longer fear death — just maybe the process of dying. I don't use the word 'death' but 'passing'. I look at 'passing' as moving on to the next phase. The body per se which is forever changing becomes irrelevant."

"Made me sure of life after death and the survival of loved ones… though it has not taken away what I think is a natural fear of death and the dying process."

"My perception changed from one of fear and dread to one of fearless acceptance and joyful wonderment at the grand plan."

"It lessened my strong fear of death."

"I have no fear of death. I have had other encounters of family members who passed away. But the grandmother experience was very intense. She was solid and I was able to hold her like a living person/body."

"I had always had a fear of death, after the ADC that fear is gone."

"I am not afraid of death now and see it as a continuation of life, albeit in a different form."

"Before, I was afraid of death. Now I am glad to know that I will be together with my husband one day, after I die."

"The confirmation that life does not stop after the passage on earth, that there is a continuity. I no longer dread death except for the pain it brings to the people who care about us."

"I am no longer afraid of death because I know that there is something afterwards. Also, I feel less lonely because I now think that my deceased significant others are not as far away as we think."

Religious beliefs and spirituality

We examined whether experiencing an ADC modified the religious beliefs and spirituality of the experients.

Religious beliefs only increased very slightly after an ADC. The group was very moderately religious before the ADC, with only 94 people out of 1,004 who "strongly agreed" in considering themselves a religious person, compared with 123 after the ADC. 396 participants had a neutral position on the subject before the ADC, with a small variation of 370 participants who remained neutral on the religious issue after the ADC.

- **9% considered themselves religious before the ADC, compared to 12% after the ADC**
- **40% were neutral before the ADC, compared to 37% remaining neutral after the ADC**[63]

Literature indicates that being a believer, agnostic or atheist does not influence the nature of the experience or the probability of having one. The belief in the survival of consciousness or the firm negation of this hypothesis does not seem to have any impact on the probability of experiencing a spontaneous contact with a deceased person either. The *interpretation* of the experience, however, is linked to the belief system and the specific life experience of the experient.

Spirituality, on the other hand, is strongly reinforced by these experiences. While only 362 participants "strongly agreed" to consider themselves spiritual before the contact, this number increased to 635 after the ADC. This shift is very significant. 202 persons had a neutral attitude before the experience, while only 82 remained neutral after the ADC.

- 36% considered themselves spiritual before the ADC, compared to 64% after the ADC
- 20% were neutral before the ADC, compared to 8% after the ADC[64]

Impression of reality of the ADC

The aim of our research project was not to reflect on the authenticity of ADCs but to analyze in depth their phenomenology and their impact on the experients, including on the bereavement process. We nevertheless decided to question the participants about their *subjective impression* of reality of their experience.

Had they heard of ADCs before their own experience? A surprisingly high number did indeed have some pre-existing knowledge.

- **58% with pre-existing knowledge, 7% were unsure, and 35% without pre-existing knowledge**

Did their prior knowledge of ADCs influence their own experience? Only a few thought it did.

- **15% felt that their pre-existing knowledge had influenced their experience, 12% were unsure, and 73% did not think so**

Obviously, having knowledge of a phenomenon does not mean that one's own experience is in line with expectations. For those who responded in the affirmative to the previous question or who were unsure, we asked how their previous knowledge of ADCs had influenced their own experience, if at all:

"It just opened me up to the possibility. I could experience the ADC fully as I was not trying to convince myself that I was not hallucinating. I'm also convinced that that made me more accessible for my brother and that it increased the probability for me to even notice."

"I think I was more open to the possibility that what I was experiencing was an ADC rather than just a psychological occurrence. I was more curious of it as a result of this as it occurred — more aware of it."

"It allowed me to accept it. However, it was just so him I can't imagine I'd question it. I think it was really his determination to communicate and his love that created the experiences I've had. I certainly have no control of when he decided to communicate."

"The belief in them helps open the door for spirits to give them to you — so I feel knowledge helped, it happened with an open heart."

"I was open to believing my own experiences."

"It made me think that others have had similar experiences, so perhaps there was some legitimacy to them. Also, I was not afraid of the experience."

"They made me more comfortable when I experienced my own ADCs."

"Made me more understanding of what was happening."

"I was emotionally prepared and knew what was happening. I knew it wasn't my imagination."

The accounts of those who stated that some prior knowledge of ADCs had been useful in their own experience underline the importance of disclosing this phenomenon to the general public. Widespread dissemination of current knowledge on ADCs is useful and necessary for several reasons, and in particular to allow experients to live this experience in the best possible conditions, as illustrated by the following testimony:

"I was not afraid because I had read many testimonies."

However, some did not believe that their prior knowledge of ADCs had influenced their experience:

"No influence, because I never thought this could happen to me."

"Can we be influenced by other people's experiences when we consider them as a grief mechanism?"

We examined our respondents' belief in the ADC phenomenon through additional questions.

If you had heard of ADCs *before* your own experience, did you think that they:

- Were most certainly authentic: 41%
- I was open to the idea, but needed evidence: 41%
- It was unlikely that they would be authentic: 2%
- Were certainly not authentic (but rather a hallucination/ illusion created through grief): 4%
- I did not ask myself the question: 9%
- Unsure: 3%

We can suppose that their own experience has strengthened their belief in the authenticity of ADCs and this is indeed largely the case as the responses to the following question attest.

Shortly *after* your experience (a few hours/days after the contact), did you think that your ADC:

- Was authentic beyond doubt: 77%

- Could possibly really have happened: 14%
- It was unlikely that it was authentic: 1%
- Was certainly not authentic but rather a hallucination/illusion created by grief: 2%
- I did not ask myself the question: 5%
- Unsure: 1%

As the answers to the next question show, the belief in the authenticity of the contact has increased considerably *in retrospect*. ADCs often lead to a new or heightened interest in spiritual matters, which may bring experients to read up on the subject or to exchange with others who have had similar experiences. Over time, this information contributes to a better understanding and allows experients to attribute an even deeper meaning to their ADC, as explained by these participants:

"I needed to know that he was OK. After his kiss and caress I understood that energy is transformed. I started to look for testimonies and studies about experiences after the death of a loved one. I underwent a spiritual transformation."

"It put me on a completely different spiritual path that has grown beyond what I ever expected."

"I became far more interested in the subject, studied and investigated it, and now have a strong, calm belief in it."

"I realized I'd been short sighted thinking that once the body dies that is the end. It led me to study and research Psi, consciousness, quantum bio-physics."

"I have spent a lot of time reading about ADCs, digging deeper into that matter. I now have no doubt in my mind that death is not the end, but rather the beginning. That I will meet my brother again and that there will be more lives to come (reincarnation). I believe we die as soon as we have fulfilled our purpose/have learned all there was to learn in that specific life. And I do believe that death just means returning home and to a state of peace and love we cannot even imagine and should therefore be celebrated."

The answers to our next question do indeed show an evolution since, with the passage of time, the number of respondents who were convinced beyond doubt of the authenticity of their experience increased to 90%.

Today, with hindsight, do you think that your ADC:

- Was authentic beyond doubt: 90%
- Could possibly really have happened: 8%
- It is unlikely that it was authentic: 0%
- Was certainly not authentic but rather a hallucination/ illusion created by grief: 0%
- I did not ask myself the question: 0%
- Unsure: 1%

The question of expectation and need

Do ADCs originate from an expectation or a need following the loss of a loved one? The data collected clearly show that ADCs are not necessarily linked to bereavement, since 27% of our respondents were no longer in mourning or had never been in mourning for the perceived deceased,[65] and 23% thought about the perceived deceased only *sometimes, rarely, very rarely* or *never*, or did not even know them.[66]

ADCs do indeed respond to the needs of the bereaved because of their inherently therapeutic nature, but this does not mean that they originate from them. The responses to the following set of questions illustrate this assumption.

Were some respondents particularly in need of a contact with the deceased loved one? In order to identify their level of grief, we asked whether our participants had thought about the deceased since their death:

- Almost constantly: 23%
- Several times per day: 22%
- Often: 31%
- Sometimes: 13%
- Rarely: 3%
- Very rarely: 2%
- Never: 2%
- Unsure: 0%
- Deceased was unknown to me: 3%

We inquired whether the participants had thought about the deceased in the minutes preceding the ADC. The data collected show that contacts do not necessarily occur when the bereaved are thinking about the deceased loved one, perhaps in a moment of deep despair, but rather when their minds are occupied with everyday activities.

- **55% did not think about the deceased, 15% were unsure, and 30% thought about the deceased**

How did our participants feel in the days/weeks prior to the ADC in terms of the grieving process? The results show that more than a quarter of the participants were not sad and were no longer grieving, or had never grieved the perceived deceased. As a consequence, and as mentioned above, bereavement cannot be the trigger for ADCs in all cases.

Here are the answers to our question: During the days/weeks previous to the ADC, and in terms of the bereavement process, were you:

- Extremely sad and in deep mourning: 36%
- Moderately sad and moderately mourning: 14%
- A little sad but having partially overcome the pain of mourning: 17%
- Not sad and not mourning anymore: 13%
- I have never been in mourning (of the perceived deceased): 14%
- Unsure: 6%

It is obvious that the death of a relative or friend is not necessarily a tragedy or a source of pain for those close to them, especially when the person was very elderly or very ill and the death is seen as liberation. The following case describes this type of situation when the experient does not consider the contact as a reassurance because he was not grieving. Could it be that the aunt needed to stay connected to the physical world a little longer?

"A week after my father's sister died, I went to work one rainy morning. When I arrived at the station, I took refuge on the station platform, waiting for my train, which was about to arrive. This is when another train arrived in the opposite direction and stopped in front of me. It was raining heavily and the cars had their windows open. When I looked up... my aunt was watching me! I ran a short distance to see who it was... but the car was empty. I was not distressed by my aunt's death, as she had fought a hard battle with cancer and her death was a liberation. I told my cousin (her daughter) about it and she said that a man had seen her sitting at the door of her house dressed very well (this man did not know she had died). We assume that the passage to the afterlife must undergo a certain process."

We asked our respondents how they felt *during* the ADC. The answers are obviously as diverse as the experients themselves are, even if the essence of the feelings is relatively homogeneous. In selecting the responses to be reproduced here, I have tried to present a range as wide and representative as possible:

"So happy, little frightened to move... in case he disappeared."

"Calm yet elated to see my Dad again, in deep awe and wonder at what I was experiencing, but I also had a deep understanding of what was happening and a sense of 'coming home'."

"I felt inner peace, I felt whole. I felt that everything would be OK."

"Happiness and joy at seeing him again and knowing he was OK."

"I felt: wow... how can this be happening? He is alive and he is here!"

"Surprised, unafraid, happy to receive the experience and the caring from him on the other side."

"Frightened at first as I didn't know what it was and felt I couldn't move or open my eyes. I then smelled my mum's presence and was then able to open my eyes... I could not see her though."

"A surprise, a shock even... My legs gave out and I had to sit down."

"A deep compassion for his immense distress."

"The surprise of discovering this energy of joy that I didn't know he had when he was alive."

"A questioning: How is this possible?"

"At first, surprise. My heart was racing. I walked out of the room, took a deep breath to calm myself down, and then went back into that room and talked to him."

Finally, we asked what the participants thought of their ADC *today*, with hindsight. Here are some representative extracts from their answers:

"It remains a mystery but I've spent the last several years researching these types of experiences so I'm comfortable with it now, but my materialistic view of life has totally changed."

"Exactly the same... certain still that it was real, comforted, deeply sure."

"Sad because I'd like it to happen again."

"Hugely privileged to have experienced it. Also reassured that there will hopefully be more communications to come."

"Such joy that death is not the end. Such happiness that she still exists and that we may see each other again."

"The more I think about it, the more I understand what happened."

"It is burned into my memory, and solidified for me that we do indeed continue to exist. It also made it easier for me to continue to connect with her, and to sense her energy. And I feel so incredibly grateful to her for making it happen."

"It's 54 years later and I remember exactly what occurred, what he looked like, etc."

"Happy, sometimes wonder and awe that this experience happened."

"A personal satisfaction to have been able to share this experience with many parents who have lost their children, through interviews, conferences, Chilean radio and television."

"Very comforted and still somewhat amazed."

"After many years, I still see it as something important, both the contact and the message."

"With peace of mind, I took it as something natural."

"It was a beautiful and rare moment."

The self-generated phenomenon hypothesis

The question of the ontological status of ADCs inevitably arises. However, as already mentioned several times, the aim of our research project was not to examine the *authenticity* of ADCs. In investigating the phenomenology of spontaneous after-death communications and their impact on experients, we were interested exclusively in people's *experiences*. The series of questions presented in the previous pages allowed us to analyze the *subjective impression of reality* that experients have of their ADC, but in our investigation, we did not go into this subject in depth, nor did we examine whether these phenomena are indicative of the survival of consciousness after physical death.

In analyzing the data collected, however, some obvious facts have nevertheless imposed themselves on us which I would like to briefly outline, to some extent on the fringe of the theme of this book.

If ADCs are not authentic, then they are mental constructs, in other words, intrapsychic experiences. What are the assumptions usually made by people who subscribe to a materialist view of reality? They postulate that ADCs are illusions, or even hallucinations, self-generated by people deeply affected by the loss of a loved one. In other words, these experiences would be unconscious compensations due to the grief of mourning. Our survey shows, however, that **13%** of our respondents were not sad and no longer grieving, and **14%** never grieved for the perceived deceased.[67] The number of experients who perceived an unknown deceased varies according to the questions asked. The graph showing the emotional bond between the experients and the deceased for the Spanish data indicates the highest figure with **12%** of unknown perceived deceased.[68] One is obviously not in mourning for a stranger.

Therefore, bereavement could not be the trigger for the ADC for all these cases.

The following types of ADCs illustrate this point:

- During an **ADC at the time of death**, the experient is informed of the death of a family member or friend by the deceased themselves (the demise is a previously unknown information). These experiences precede the announcement of the passing (by the hospital, the family, etc.). The experient is not (yet) in mourning and therefore the factor of psychological need, conscious or unconscious, cannot be the trigger of the ADC.

- During an **ADC for a third person**, the experient, who is not grieving for the perceived deceased or doesn't even know him or her, perceives a communication intended for a bereaved person. The messages to be transmitted usually serve to inform the recipient that the deceased is alive and well. This type of ADC cannot be triggered by grief.

- **ADCs for protection** occur in situations of crisis or imminent danger and result in the avoidance of a tragic event such as an accident, a fire, an assault, a drowning, etc. These contacts have the particularity of occurring sometimes years or even decades after the death when the experient is no longer grieving or has never been in mourning (e.g. the experient was a young child when his grandfather, perceived during the ADC, died). These experiences provide previously unknown information — that of a potential danger of which the experient was unaware — and thus belong to the category of evidential ADCs. The fact that the experient is not in mourning reinforces its evidential nature.

- During an **ADC with an unknown person**, the experient is obviously not mourning the perceived deceased. Unlike contacts involving known, and often loved, deceased persons, there is no emotional bond between the deceased and the experient for this type of ADC. They are thus experiences of a fundamentally different nature and the question of the meaning of their occurrence arises. These ADCs suggest that it is the deceased who need contact with a living person, for whatever reason, and seem to manifest themselves wherever possible, wherever they can be perceived, even by strangers. Therefore, its evidential value is high, since the grief of bereavement cannot be the trigger for their occurrence.

Impact of ADCs on the bereavement process

The testimonies presented in the previous pages illustrate this perfectly: ADCs can console the bereaved. According to experients, the contact brought them comfort, joy, support and strength to continue their life path without the beloved family member or friend. Beyond the brief but striking perception of the deceased, which is in itself quite remarkable, it is the **information** transmitted and the **emotions** perceived and felt by the experients that are an essential element, if not the essence, of these experiences.

However, it is important to emphasize that these contacts do not (always/entirely) remove the sadness. In spite of the powerful message of hope of the ADC, the grief over the physical absence of the deceased loved one remains, of course, for a long time, and sometimes for a lifetime.

The *absence* of ADCs can also be a source of sorrow for those who wholeheartedly wish for a last sign of the deceased loved one that has not (yet) occurred. However, I would like to strongly emphasize that, in my view, the absence of ADCs should in no way be understood as an abandonment on the part of the deceased nor as an indicator of the quality and intensity of the love that united the two persons before death. Research to date cannot determine why some people experience ADCs and others do not.

ADCs do not exempt the bereaved from working through their grief, which is indispensable and must be done, with or without an after-death communication. They must accept the definitive physical absence of the deceased loved one and learn to live without him or her.

Are our deceased loved ones constantly by our side? We don't know. We do know, however, that they don't manifest themselves to us on a daily basis but only in rare and privileged moments — in moments of grace.

How important are ADCs to the experients? What place do they give them in the events that have marked their lives? The data collected show that these experiences are clearly very significant. For more than a third of our respondents, the ADC is "life-changing" and for almost half of them it is "important".

Here are the responses to the question: Do you consider the ADC to be:

- Life-changing: 36%
- Important: 49%
- Moderately important: 9%
- Not very important: 2%
- Not important: 2%
- Unsure: 2%

Following the ADC, the experients feel that they continue to be loved, the deceased seems to be watching over them from another dimension, love seems to have survived death. These elements are a great source of solace and are beneficial to the grieving process.

A series of questions helped us to better understand the impact of ADCs on the grieving process.

We asked the participants if the ADC had brought them comfort and emotional healing. This was indeed the case for a large majority.

- Emotional healing is noted: 73%
- No emotional healing noted: 10%
- Unsure: 8%
- I never mourned the perceived deceased: 8%

Let's have the respondents elaborate on their thoughts:

"How fortunate am I... In the pain of losing a child, with the surrounding pain and grief having broken my heart... this death broke all of my family's hearts... there came Light. The light and goodness came from our love that crosses over after death. I found complete peace and healing."

"I was really struggling to cope and couldn't see any way through the fog of grief. I missed my mum so much and wanted to know she was OK and near... this did that."

"Knowing my Son came to me... in a calm and loving way to comfort me... has made me carry on to help others that have lost their children... understanding the deepest loss imaginable, and truly believing we will see them again and they have just gone on ahead before us."

"Hearing from my son after a horrific accident and seeing him appear to be whole and talk to me was a blessing!"

"I get great comfort from knowing my husband is alive in spirit and know he will be waiting for me when it is my turn to cross. I am devastated by the loss of my beautiful husband, but his contact is helping me with my healing."

"The experience comforted me very much, the grief was greatly alleviated."

"When someone dies it's really hard to believe that person is really gone. To be able to speak to them again, see them again, and feel their presence was enormously comforting."

"It is way easier to deal with death if you believe it not to be final. And to have the certainty and the comfort of knowing the person near and well."

"I did not grieve to the same extent as the rest of my family because I had the comfort of knowing my grandfather was not really 'dead'."

"It is obvious that the phenomenon is emotionally consoling. On the rational and materialistic level, it has a powerful force of its own that always fights doubt and skepticism, and this remains a mystery that reason is forced to accept."

Guilt is part of the grieving process, and indeed one of its most painful components. Guilt over words spoken that can no longer be withdrawn, or explained and softened. Guilt for having missed a last encounter, in the hospital or elsewhere — the immense sorrow of having to face the fact that now it is too late. ADCs apparently have the power to remove these regrets and remorses by liberating the experients through a final farewell.

"I was feeling guilty for not visiting him in hospital, and his appearance to me while smiling at me took that guilt away."

"I believe she came to me at her death, to set me free of guilt from avoiding her because of religious disputes."

"Because I did not live near my family home, I did not see my mother often, and I carried great guilt because of that. I'm sure I would have gone into a depression had she not come to me (in spirit) on the plane."

"My grieving process is not over, but this experience has freed me from the heavy burden of not having the opportunity to say goodbye."

One might imagine that having perceived the loved one, even if only for a few seconds, would point out even more cruelly his or her physical absence. When the contact stops, the feeling of loneliness should be devastating. However, this was not the feeling of the vast majority of our participants.

- **For 80% the contact did not make the physical absence more painful, 8% were unsure, and for 12% made it more painful**

At first sight, this result may be surprising. I would stipulate that the reason may lie in the impression of the continuity of the inner bond that persists beyond the brief perception of the deceased. Apparently, the conviction of the existence and continuity of this bond no longer needs to rely on a brief perception of the deceased as it occurred during the ADC in order to endure.

As we have seen, ADCs are indicative of the presence of a strong and enduring inner bond between the living and the dead. How does this concept fit into the clinic of grief counselling? In earlier times, mourning patients were encouraged by bereavement counsellors to disinvest from their relationship with the deceased in order to make room for new objects of attachment. This model of rupture, supported by the Freudian contribution, advocated the acceptance of the loss, whereas the modern clinic encourages the maintenance of continued bonds. It no longer advises mourners to go through the grieving process and then detach from this past relationship, but instead invites them to nurture and cherish this inner bond with the deceased. ADCs fit perfectly into this modern view of bereavement.

Evrard and Dollander's paper on frightening ADCs, cited above, addresses this issue: "Messages communicating knowledge about the afterlife could also correspond to another form of consolation, intellectual rather than directly emotional. The purpose of such messages seems to be to facilitate detachment; the conviction that the deceased is well where he is allows the bereaved to feel at peace. In the process of accepting the loss, this type of message decreases psychic tension and in particular the unconscious alliance that is source of guilt. The idea of an extended life elsewhere facilitates a transition: if the loved one is 'still alive,' and even happy, in a comfortable space, then the worry is no longer necessary. In spirit, the person can now conceive of a psychic space which welcomes the reality of death.

The multisensory experience of the after-death communication updates in the present the relationship with the object, by making it possible to repair it where the bond was potentially damaged due to death. If the physical body exists no longer, the psychic object is not dead! It must therefore henceforth occupy another position in the psychic space. The ADC seems to manifest this work of subjectivation and repositioning of the psychic object. It allows residual tensions to find a way out. De facto, the subject is no longer deprived of the object relation with the deceased; it is now authorized not to terminate this relation: it must evolve post-mortem. The other is, in the best cases, situated in the position of an omnipresent and omnipotent object of love, which watches over the happiness of the living. This representation of survival offers a beneficial compensation for the obstacles to relational continuity in a culture that makes death a radical discontinuity."[69]

Evrard and Dollander conclude: "These data on so-called frightening spontaneous experiences rather suggest that these experiences may be catalysts for non-pathological grief. In contradiction with the rupture model, these results reinforce the model of continued bonds by suggesting paradoxical mourning: grief is accomplished at the cost of always keeping the relationship with the deceased open and alive."[70]

Acceptance of the irrevocability of the physical absence of the loved one is the essential element — and the most difficult to achieve — of the grieving process. ADCs facilitate the acceptance of this loss. In this respect, these contacts are therapeutic in nature as they respond to the needs of the bereaved.

- **For 61% the ADC facilitated the acceptance of the loss, 13% were unsure, and for 26% the ADC did not facilitate it**

We asked the participants if the ADC was important to their grieving process.

- **For 68% the ADC is important for the grieving process, 11% were unsure, and for 20% it is not important**

Some respondents explain their point of view:

"I think it is highly important to the grief process to know that love energy never dies and we will be reunited with our loved ones one day, when it is our time to pass over."

"It was a turning point in my grieving process."

"Because of the circumstances of his death (overdose), people were not talking about it publicly and this made it even harder to come to terms with what had happened. I was trying to mourn privately but his death felt like a hole that could never be filled. After his visits all that was erased."

"It's a solace because I know that my dad is still out there somewhere, but I haven't finished grieving despite that. What is difficult for me, even though I'm relieved because he's not suffering anymore and it's better for him, is not seeing him, hearing him, hugging him — that is hard."

"I would still be in emotional turmoil if I had not gotten the message."

"It's like learning a whole new language and way of being, an acceptance and appreciation for what continues after the worst thing occurred."

"I believe I would still be in my frozen moment of deep grief without having had this experience."

"Without the absolute certainty that his spirit lives on, I would not be able to be strong on this side of life."

"It added hope, made me realize the person is not gone, just not readily perceived."

"The ADC questions the very idea of 'mourning' ... There is no mourning to be done, except for the mourning of physical presence. But the presence of loved ones by our side is absolutely certain, in my opinion."

"The grief was so violent that the ADC was a lifesaver because even the thought of our children did not stop me from imagining a way to join him. The ADC was a kind of shock that allowed me to lift my head and accept the continuation of my life without him."

This respondent, however, did not see any obvious benefit of the ADC for her grieving process:

"I'm just not sure. I loved my sister, my dad and my friend who killed himself. But I am not the type that gets immobilized with grief, at least so far. As much as I know life after death is a fact, like every other normal person, I want my kids to outlive me and I want to stay on this side of the grave as long as possible, assuming my life is tolerable and worth living still. I absolutely believe in the fact of life after death, but I don't feel qualified to state emphatically or categorically that having experienced more than one ADC was an aid in the bereavement process for me."

What about the sadness caused by the death of a loved one? ADCs provide reassurance about the fate of our loved ones who have passed away. According to the experients, they have found a way to manifest themselves to them and let them know that they are alive and well. Sadness is something else, it is inevitable because it is caused by the loss of the physical presence of the loved one.

What is the opinion of our respondents on this subject? We asked them.

Did the ADC affect the sadness triggered by the loss of the person or did the sadness remain the same?

- Sadness is reduced: 44%
- Sadness is removed: 10%
- Sadness remains the same: 31%
- Sadness is increased: 2%
- Unsure: 5%
- Other: 8%

These responses are not clear-cut. For just over half of our respondents, sadness was reduced or even eliminated by the ADC, but for 31% it remained the same, and for 2% it even increased.

Clearly, these experiences are not miraculous. Sadness is not erased by a magic switch. There is something else at stake.

I would hypothesize that spontaneous after-death communications trigger an awareness that allows the experients to understand *the true nature of death*. They initiate a new way of looking at the loss of the loved one and allow the bereaved to see the physical absence in a new light. These contacts open up the prospect of an afterlife and the possibility of a future reunion. It is obvious that, seen in this light, these experiences can impact on the sadness of the bereaved. Why did these contacts not free all our respondents from sadness? We don't know, but we do know that bereavement is an extremely complex, multifaceted process, determined by many factors, and different for everyone.

I quote some of our participants who described how their sadness had been modified by the ADC:

"Not immediately, because of my learning curve, but the sadness of grief is definitely reduced now because of this new awareness to what can be, both now and in the future."

"The sadness triggered by the loss is completely gone. There is still a sadness (or perhaps impatience) at the separation that continues."

"The sadness over the loss of my son was better for a short time afterwards, but still continues to be great."

"A different and much reduced sadness."

"The sadness is somehow superseded. The memory of what has been shared is strengthened, and so is the inner presence."

"The emotion of the separation remains, but it is not despair. More like you can get the blues from time to time when you're in a long-distance relationship."

"It doesn't heal the grief but it makes it meaningful to continue our life here, without the physical presence of the deceased. However, in the days following the contacts, I didn't suffer anymore or much less, because I felt like he did when I perceived him."

"The sadness remains, deep and ingrained, but a hope has emerged."

I come back once again to the necessity of accepting the irrevocability of the definitive physical absence of the deceased loved one. Once this evidence is understood and accepted, the bereaved can cultivate the renewed inner bond with him or her — a continued relationship that will endure and that nothing can ever break. ADCs open the perspective of this continued relational bond which would manifest itself, very exceptionally and very briefly, during these powerful experiences.

What do our respondents think? We asked them how they would describe their relationship with the deceased.

- My relationship ended when he/she died: 4%
- I thought that the relationship ended with death but my ADC revealed that the bond continues: 34%
- I believed that my bond with the deceased continued after death and my ADC deepened the connection: 49%
- Unsure: 6%
- Other: 7%

Here is how some of our respondents describe their continued inner relationship with the deceased:

"I have closure — no longer in the limbo state of having a missing brother. I've been able to grieve his physical loss, but I've gained an on-going, real relationship with him… it's like we're just in different rooms, but his influence on others, and myself, in this physical world is proof to me that he's alive still, just in another form."

"You're back in touch with your loved one and ready for a new, better, but different relationship."

"My relationship is intact afterwards just as before; I just have to cope with the physical absence."

"The emotional pain dissolved. I have a new relationship with my dad. Different, but closer now. He understands me and his love for me is complete."

"The process of mourning involves the evolution of the relationship, in its internalization and metamorphosis. And in the acceptance of what is lost and what remains."

"I have always known that the bond continues, but that we must accept the change in the nature of that bond."

"I have fewer doubts about the inner relationship that goes on. I think it is not one way from me to him, but that he hears me and listens to me and sends me signs to say, 'I am here'."

"It made me feel closer and more connected to my dad after his loss."

"My relationship exists today in another form between the visible and invisible worlds, but it is neither heavy nor omnipresent. It is simply expressed when needed."

Mourning is a time of great sadness and fragility. The death of a loved one turns our lives upside down and plunges us into a suffering that seems to have no end, as described so eloquently by one of our respondents:

"When a spouse dies, we have the impression of losing everything: our companion in life, our balance, a part of ourselves, our protection, our common projects, sometimes our shared possessions... everything collapses, we sink into an endless abyss. When this bond is established, we have the feeling that we have recovered something, that we have a lifeline to hold on to, that all is not lost, and the hope that arises allows us to move forward a little."

Experiencing an ADC in this dark period is indeed highly beneficial, even therapeutic, provided that the bereaved are able to make a clear distinction between the definitive physical departure of the loved one — which forces them to reorganize their lives accordingly — and this renewed inner relationship that can now be strengthened and in which these contacts fit perfectly. If, on the other hand, ADCs trigger the illusion that their loved one is still there and that nothing has changed in their lives, if they wait impatiently for the next contact, then this is problematic because the bereavement process can be blocked by the denial of the loved one's definitive physical departure.

How did our participants deal with this delicate aspect of spontaneous after-death communications? We put this question to them:

Do you really wish for more contact(s) with the deceased or is/are the contact(s) perceived already sufficient for you?

- I really wish for a new contact: 47%
- The perceived contact(s) is/are sufficient for me: 33%
- Unsure: 8%
- Other: 12%

Our respondents took a stand on this issue:

"I would love more contact but feel that he has to continue with his journey as have I. We were soul mates and had a special relationship, so whatever contact I have is wonderful and I am full of gratitude for it."

"I definitely want to see my sister, my father and all those who have passed away that I was close to, again. But, I kind of believe in 'One world at a time'. It might sound weird, or kind of cold or aloof, but because I know my loved ones are as alive as I am, and I will see them again without doubt, I don't really feel the need to be in frequent contact with them. I really believe that they are busy too, wherever they are, and that we will get together and enjoy each other again when I relocate to where they are now."

"I am trying to get used to the idea of not having any more contacts, and I am trying not to ask for any. I have received much more than I could have imagined. If it ends, I will endeavour to accept it. But deep down, I can't tell you that I don't wish for more, that would be dishonest. The bond was very, very strong when my loved one was alive. It is still strong. And I think I can honestly say that it is still strong on both sides."

"I am deeply convinced that there will be other contacts. But I don't expect anything. Everything is right."

"On the one hand, yes, I still wish to have contacts, and on the other, I want my mother to be able to continue her journey after death in complete freedom."

"I would love a new contact, but the ones I have had are valuable and sufficient for me."

"I have no expectations... I take with delight what manifests itself. I do not want to hold him back..."

"I think these contacts happen when they need to happen."

"I am certain that waiting for a new contact is like tying him to that plane of existence from which he has already left."

"I desire the contact, but I understand that it must happen when it is appropriate and necessary."

We inquired if our respondents were in the habit of consulting a spirit medium with the intention of making contact with a deceased person before their ADC. This was not the case for a large majority.

- **20% consulted a spirit medium before their ADC, 1% were unsure, and 79% sought no consultation**

However, there was a change after the ADC as 352 people out of 1,004 felt the need to make further contact with the deceased through a spirit medium.

- **36% consulted a spirit medium after their ADC, 1% were unsure, and 63% sought no consultation**

When you are lucky enough to be able to consult a good spirit medium, you still have to know how to manage these privileged moments and in particular not to overuse it. The repeated, even frantic, consultation of mediums can become addictive and lull the bereaved with illusions that nothing has changed in their lives and that there is no need to begin the work of mourning. Facing reality is the first decisive step of this process.

How did our respondents deal with the issue of consulting a medium? From their testimonies, it appears that the ADC did not trigger a frenzy of mediumistic consultations, since the majority consulted only a few times:

"He has been dead for ten months and I have seen three of them."

"Only once in a public session but it did not work."

"Twice in three and a half years. That was enough to be at peace. I don't need to contact him anymore, because I know that everything is fine with him, that he is guiding me, and that I will be reunited with him when the time comes."

"Once in seven years."

"Once to help my niece in her mourning process for her husband."

"Once per year."

One of our respondents clearly understood the necessity of not blocking the grieving process by consulting a spirit medium too often:

"I consulted this medium about ten times and then I wanted to let my husband go. It also seemed to me that these sessions were preventing me from moving on without him."

When the grieving process is well underway or in the process of being resolved, the need to seek contact with the deceased through a spirit medium naturally diminishes or even disappears.

"I wanted to dialogue with him but now I don't feel the need to exchange via a medium anymore, even if it is tempting."

"Because [the ADC] was liberating for both of us and then we each went our own way."

Apart from consulting a spirit medium, what else can people do if they want to make contact with a deceased family member or friend? ADCs are clearly not the solution since they are *spontaneous*, allegedly initiated by the deceased, and cannot in any way be generated intentionally. Nonetheless, there exist many traditions, practices and techniques, including meditation, which supposedly may induce or facilitate connection with the deceased.

One of these techniques is the psychomanteum work, a reminiscence of the ancient Greek tradition of consulting the dead via a "psychomanteum", which typically involved gazing into a darkened pool of liquid under low illumination conditions so as to encourage meaningful visual imagery. In their paper "Mirror- and Eye-Gazing: An Integrative Review of Induced Altered and

Anomalous Experiences", Caputo, Lynn, and Houran state, "[...] over the last few decades clinical and experimental studies across the social, biomedical, and parapsychological sciences have investigated the role of mirrors in producing a range of unusual or anomalous sensory or perceptual phenomena. These can sometimes be regarded more broadly as variants of 'encounter experiences' (Evans, 2001; Houran, 2000; Pekala et al., 1995), and specifically those that manifest under more controlled (or structured) versus spontaneous (or unstructured) conditions (see Houran, 2000; Houran et al., 2019)."[71]

The psychomanteum was popularized by Raymond A. Moody in his book *Reunions: Visionary Encounters with Departed Loved Ones*.[72] Moody believes that the psychomanteum is a useful tool to resolve grief. The procedure is simple: subjects sit in a room that is kept in darkness, with a mirror on one wall, and lit only by a candle or dim bulb. They gaze into the reflected darkness in the hope of seeing and making contact with deceased significant others.

Some years later, Dianne Arcangel has also made this technique popular with her book *Afterlife Encounters: Ordinary People, Extraordinary Experiences*.[73]

It would be beyond the scope of this book to present all identified techniques for allegedly making contact with the deceased, but I would like to present a second technique that has gained momentum in recent years, namely the *Induced After-Death Communications (IADC®)* therapy. In 1995, the American psychologist Allan Botkin developed this therapeutic method, originally designed to help war veterans overcome post-traumatic stress. "[The IADC® Therapy] focuses on reducing the sadness associated with grief by using a modified protocol of the mind-body psychotherapy EMDR (Eye Movement Desensitization and Reprocessing[74]). Once a greater degree of resolution is achieved, a state of receptivity is then cultivated. In this state, many clients perceive a deep and loving connection with the deceased loved one. This is typically experienced through one or more of the five senses or through some other 'sense of presence' perception. Clients who undergo IADC® Therapy report significant reduction of the sadness associated with the death of a loved one. They frequently report resolution of any unsettled issues in the relationship with the deceased, and they report receiving answers to their questions and reassurances of their loved one's wellbeing. Perhaps most meaningfully, however, clients report experiencing a deep sense of connection with their loved one and a transformation in feelings of separation. Although most clients believe in the authenticity of the experience, beliefs play no role in the efficacy of the treatment."[75]

Can parallels be drawn between spontaneous and induced ADCs?

Spontaneous ADCs and induced ADCs (IADC) have some similarities but also important differences. ADCs occur spontaneously, without intention or solicitation from part of the experients. IADCs, on the other hand, are more akin to consulting a spirit medium in the hope of contacting a deceased significant other, with a clearly identified *intention*.

ADCs are very short (a few seconds, a few minutes at most), whereas IADCs last much longer (90-minute sessions, including the time for the conditioning process and debriefing). A much greater amount of information is thus delivered during IADC sessions, although ADC experients often claim that, despite the brevity of their experience, they had obtained a lot of information from the deceased, as if the contact had occurred outside of time, or in a different type of time.

Another notable difference relates to the circumstances of the contact. Clients who consult an IADC therapist are in mourning, sometimes in a situation of complicated grief, and expect the session to make them feel better, to ease their grief, and, ideally, to offer them the blessing of a last word of love from the deceased significant other. ADC experients, on the other hand, expect nothing, hope for nothing, and are often overwhelmed by the beauty and power of the experience they receive as an unexpected gift. Furthermore, as we have seen in the previous pages, ADC experients are not always in mourning.

There are, however, similarities between spontaneous ADCs and induced ADCs (IADC), in particular with regard to the impact of these experiences on the grieving process. The messages perceived during both types of contact are similar in the comfort they provide, the love they convey and the conviction of the experients that their deceased loved one has indeed survived physical death.

The issue of sadness is essential in the grieving process, and it is also central to the method developed by Dr. Botkin. During an IADC session, and with the use of the EMDR technique, clients are invited to talk about their grief and to fully feel their sadness, the intensity of which increases until it reaches its peak before gradually subsiding. It is in this particular state of consciousness that the alleged contact with the deceased occurs. For spontaneous ADCs, on the contrary, the impact on sadness is the *consequence* of the contact, with 44% of our respondents indicating that sadness was reduced as a result of their experience, and 10% for whom it was even eliminated. For 31%, however, the sadness remained the same, and for 2% it was increased.

I close here the parenthesis of contacts with the deceased allegedly induced by different techniques.

A majority of respondents felt that the grieving process would have been different if they had not experienced the ADC.

- **For 57% the grieving process would have been different, 21% are unsure, and for 22% it would have been the same**

I have made a selection of comments from those who feel that the grieving process would have been different without the ADC:

"The process would have been different, and perhaps extended and more severe without the hope that comes from ADC."

"It would have been longer, more painful and damaging."

"I think the death would have been much harder if she hadn't showed us or told us how beautiful it was."

"Without being able to talk to her and having her contact me the way she did and giving me the proof, I would be severely depressed to this day. Now I'm sad that she's gone but I know I'll see her again and being able to talk to her still, that helps a lot."

"Until I received his messages I was almost suicidal. He has lifted me up and sent me on a new direction in life."

"I feel that feeling him and being able to make contact brought me tremendous comfort. I truly believe he was trying to make sure I was OK. The level of compassion was amazing, so I definitely think it made a huge difference."

"When a loved one dies you have the feeling of loss, but in addition, you feel abandoned by the person. When the loved one contacts you, the sense of abandonment diminishes because you feel that they still care about you, even though they left the physical world."

"I know from contact with my deceased brother that he is no longer the mentally tortured person he was when he took his life. It is overwhelmingly reassuring to know that, and to know that others can overcome the difficulties their physical brains and bodies caused them in life."

"It was the first time I felt joy after my husband's death — I wouldn't have had that brief relief from grief that early on without the ADC."

"I can't imagine having lost him completely. It was wretched even with the ADC. Without it, I'm not sure if I would've chosen to continue living."

"As he committed suicide in a state of advanced despair, I would have been very sad for him, and I would not have known how to console myself about this terrible act. Thanks to my 'vision', I knew that he had been right to leave, and that now he was happy. So, I was really not sad at all."

Finally, we asked how the participants felt about having experienced the ADC. The results show that it is a highly valued experience since more than 90% "treasure" it or are "very glad" to have had it.

- I treasure it: 71%
- Very glad: 20%
- I don't mind: 3%
- Very unhappy: 0%
- I wish it had never happened: 1%
- Unsure: 4%

In this section on bereavement, we have gained a wealth of information about the role of ADCs in this very difficult period of bereavement, which we have all faced or will face one day. The deceased loved ones are no longer with us, and they will never be physically present again, but to know that they seem to be alive and comfortable in their alleged new existence of which we know (close to) nothing is undoubtedly an immense source of relief and consolation. The feeling that the deceased are watching over us and are at our side, perhaps at any time or when circumstances so require, is a source of solace to the bereaved.

ADCs greatly facilitate the awareness of the existence of a renewed and lasting inner bond with the deceased, which is one of the main objectives of the grieving process. A large proportion of our participants (73%) experienced emotional healing as a result of the ADC and most of them reported a beneficial impact on their grieving process.

A few words in conclusion

Our research project could not have been carried out — and this book would not exist — if our 1,004 participants had not taken the time and trouble to complete a very long questionnaire. On behalf of our team, I would like to thank them all wholeheartedly. Thanks to the wealth of their contributions, our understanding of the phenomenon of spontaneous after-death communications has deepened and the beneficial and transformative impact of these experiences has become evident.

Several lessons can be drawn from our survey. Firstly, the data collected allow a better understanding of the modalities and circumstances of the occurrence of ADCs. One of the questions asked showed that these contacts occur mainly in the family and couple context, with some variations for the different language groups. The research findings show that a very close and loving relationship between the experient and the deceased during their lifetime is clearly an important element for the occurrence of ADCs. Contacts with deceased persons with whom the experients were not particularly close are rarer and often serve to convey a message to family members or friends of the deceased.

Furthermore, the data collected highlights an aspect that has not often been mentioned or studied in previous research: the perception of deceased persons unknown to the experients. The meaning of these ADCs is not immediately apparent. Clearly, they do not serve to comfort the experients, but seem to focus on the needs of the deceased, who apparently manifest themselves wherever possible, wherever they can be perceived, even by strangers. ADCs with unknown deceased persons are more frequent than we had assumed and seem to be of a completely different nature than contacts with a deceased loved one.

Experients are often puzzled or ill at ease, even frightened by these contacts, as they lack the emotional connection that makes them such beautiful and consoling experiences. Although some hypotheses can be put forward, the mystery as to the function and the very meaning of these contacts with unknown deceased persons remains.

Another important finding of the survey is that bereavement is not a prerequisite for experiencing an ADC. More than a quarter of our respondents were no longer grieving or had never grieved for the deceased person they perceived during the ADC, and one of the questions asked revealed that 12% of the respondents perceived a deceased person they did not know. The data collected challenge the often put forward materialistic hypothesis that ADCs are merely illusions, or unconscious compensations due to the grief of bereavement.

The survey also revealed that ADCs have a significant impact on the belief system of the experients. Experiencing a spontaneous contact with a deceased has consequences on the conception of death, and therefore of life. These experiences often initiate a reflection and even a questioning of the beliefs held prior to the ADC. A new or renewed interest in existential questions can be the consequence. Our data show that spirituality is strongly reinforced by ADCs, as the number of our respondents who consider themselves spiritual has almost doubled following their experience.

A series of questions gave us information about the experients' impression of reality of the ADC. Whether or not they had subscribed to the hypothesis of the existence of an afterlife prior to their experience, they were almost unanimously convinced of the authenticity of their ADC, and this conviction became even stronger with the passage of time.

The shift in the belief system in favor of the hypothesis of survival of consciousness after physical death is very significant, with only one percent of our respondents not endorsing it after their ADC. Furthermore, the impact of ADCs on the ancestral fear of death is striking — with more than 60% of our respondents attesting that their fear of death has diminished or disappeared following the ADC — and testifies to the power of these experiences. The impact of ADCs on beliefs is undeniable.

Another key finding of the survey is the powerful effect of ADCs on the grieving process. The vast majority of respondents claim that their experience had brought them comfort and emotional healing. ADCs are much more than a mere perception of the deceased. It is the emotions felt and perceived during the contact and the information received that give them their full meaning. The essential information inherent in the very occurrence of the ADC provides the subjective conviction to the experients that their loved one has survived the death of the body. A large majority of our participants perceived a message that was tailored to them personally. The perceived messages are relatively homogeneous. Overall, the deceased communicate that they are alive and well and assure the bereaved of their support and love.

The essential challenge of the mourning process is to accept the definitive physical absence of the loved one and to become aware of the existence of a renewed and lasting inner bond with him or her. ADCs fit perfectly into this process because they open up the prospect of a continued and dynamic relational bond between the living and the dead that allegedly can materialize in rare and precious moments. This bond does not only seem to be reflective of the relationship as it was at the time of death, but it seems to evolve in a dynamic way after the demise. Several testimonies reproduced in the preceding pages suggest that reconciliation beyond death is possible and that it is never too late to understand, to make amends, to forgive and be forgiven, and to express love.

One might have assumed that the brief perception of the deceased might have made his or her physical absence even more painful and increased the sense of loneliness of the bereaved. However, this was not the feeling of 80% of our respondents. The data collected show that a vast majority of our participants are convinced of the existence and permanence of this inner bond with their deceased loved one, and their conviction is so strong that it no longer needs to be supported by a brief perception of the deceased such as it occurs during the ADCs in order to endure.

The survey results show that ADCs are beneficial, even therapeutic in nature, as they meet the needs of the bereaved. However, it should be emphasized that these experiences do not (always/entirely) remove the sadness due to the definitive physical absence of the loved one, nor do they allow the work of mourning to be dispensed with.

The last lesson to be highlighted is that our participants give an important place to the ADC in the events that have marked their lives. They remember their experience in great detail years or even decades after it happened. The testimonies on the previous pages bear witness to this: the vast majority of participants consider their ADC to be a profoundly moving, impactful, comforting and intrinsically positive experience. The data collected indicate that having experienced a spontaneous contact with a deceased loved one is an event that is highly valued and cherished by nearly all of our participants.

This is not the end of the story but the beginning, as we start to build an understanding of this potentially transformative and often deeply consoling phenomenon. Much is still to be done. We are confident that consciousness research in general, and the continuation of our research project — as well as the conduct of similar projects by others — in particular, will yield further insights and an even deeper understanding of spontaneous after-death communications.

Call for testimonies

If you think you have experienced an ADC and would like to share it, please send me your concise testimony to the following e-mail address:

evelyn@evelyn-elsaesser.com

Your experiences will be very valuable for our ongoing research.

Thank you in advance!

Endnotes

1. Burton, J. (1982). Contact with the dead: A common experience? *Fate,* 35(4), 65-73.

    Castelnovo, A.; Cavallotti, S.; Gambini, O.; D'Agostino, A. (2015). Post-bereavement hallucinatory experiences: A critical overview of population and clinical studies. *Journal of Affective Disorders.* 186:266–74. http://doi.org/10.1016/j. jad.2015.07.032. Epub 2015, July 31.

    Keen, C.; Murray, C.; Payne, S. (2013). Sensing the presence of the deceased: A narrative review. *Mental Health, Religion & Culture,* 16(4), 384–402. http://doi.org/10. 1080/13674676.2012.678987.

    Rees, W.D. (1971). The hallucinations of widowhood. *British Medical Journal,* 4 (5778), 37–41. http://doi. org/10.1136/bmj.4.5778.37.

    Rees, W.D. (1975). The bereaved and their hallucinations. In: B. Schoenberg; I. Gerber; A. Wiener; A. Kutscher; A.C. Carr (Eds.) *Bereavement: Its psychosocial aspects.* New York: Columbia University, 66–71.

2. For ease of reading, I chose to use the masculine form to collectively refer to the two genders.

3. A device consisting of a small board, or planchette, on legs that rest on a larger board marked with words, letters of the alphabet, etc., and that by moving over the larger board and touching the words, letters, etc., while the fingers of spiritualists, mediums, or others rest lightly upon it, is employed to answer questions, give messages, etc.

4. Instrumental TransCommunication is the name that has been given by Professor Ernst Senkowski, a German physicist, for the technique of contacting spirits, using any electronic means to capture the images of spirits (ITC), and to record their voices (EVP: Electronic Voice Phenomenon).

5. Burton, J. (1982). Contact with the dead: A common experience? *Fate*, 35(4), 65–73.

Castelnovo, A.; Cavallotti, S.; Gambini, O.; D'Agostino, A. (2015). Post-bereavement hallucinatory experiences: A critical overview of population and clinical studies. *Journal of Affective Disorders.* 186:266–74. http://doi.org/10.1016/j.jad.2015.07.032. Epub 2015, July 31.

Keen, C.; Murray, C.; Payne, S. (2013). Sensing the presence of the deceased: A narrative review. *Mental Health, Religion & Culture,* 16(4), 384–402. http://doi.org/10.1080/13674676.2012.678987.

Rees, W.D. (1971). The hallucinations of widowhood. *British Medical Journal,* 4 (5778), 37–41. http://doi.org/10.1136/bmj.4.5778.37.

Rees, W.D. (1975). The bereaved and their hallucinations. In: B. Schoenberg; I. Gerber; A. Wiener; A. Kutscher; A.C. Carr (Eds.) *Bereavement: Its psychosocial aspects.* New York: Columbia University, 66–71.

6. Ref: FHSRECSS00084.

7. https://koestlerunit.wordpress.com/study-registry/registered-studies/– ref: KPU Registry 1046.

8. Elsaesser, E.; Roe, C.A.; Cooper, C.E.; Lorimer, D. (2021). The phenomenology and impact of hallucinations concerning the deceased. *BJPsychOpen*, Volume 7, Issue 5, September 2021, e148, DOI: https://doi.org/10.1192/bjo.2021.960

9. Castro, M.; Burrows, R.; Wooffitt, R. (2014). The paranormal is (Still) normal: The sociological implications of a survey of paranormal experiences in Great Britain. *Sociological Research Online*, 19(3), 1–15. https://doi.org/10.5153/sro.3355

10. For all statistics presented, percentages have been rounded for ease of reading and may add up to 99 or 101 rather than

100.

11. This figure refers to all the data collected, i.e. the 1,004 questionnaires completed in the three languages.

12. The total average indicated above does not correspond exactly to the average of the language groups because these groups are of different sizes.

13. As noted above, all proper names and place names mentioned in the testimonies have been changed to protect the identity of the participants.

14. Private correspondence, 22 July 2020.

15. These two figures exceed 100% because some participants had described more than one ADC.

16. The hypnagogic state is a particular state of consciousness intermediate between that of wakefulness and that of sleep which takes place during the first phase of sleep: falling asleep.

17. The hypnopompic state is a particular state of consciousness that occurs at the moment of awakening. Although often confused, the hypnagogic and hypnopompic states are not identical.

18. See table page 126.

19. This graph reflects all the data collected, i.e. the results of the 1,004 questionnaires completed in the three languages of the project (English, French and Spanish).

20. Fenwick, Peter; Lovelace, Hilary; Brayne, Sue (2010). Comfort for the dying: Five year retrospective and one year prospective studies of end of life experiences. *Geriatrics*, Volume 51, Issue 2, September-October 2010, pp. 173–179.

21. Mazzarino-Willett, A. (2010). Deathbed Phenomena: Its role in peaceful death and terminal restlessness. *Am J Hospice Palliat Care*, 2010;27(2):127–133.

22. Callanan, Maggie and Kelley, Patricia (2012). *Final*

Gifts: Understanding the Special Awareness, Needs, and Communications of the Dying. New York; London: Simon & Schuster Paperbacks.

23. Kübler-Ross, E. (1974). The languages of the dying patients. Humanitas, 10(1), 5–8.

24. Kübler-Ross, Elisabeth (1974). The languages of dying. Journal of Clinical Child Psychology, Vol 3, 1974, Issue 2: Death and Children, pp. 22–24.

25. Marks, Adam; Marchand, Lucille (2015). Near Death Awareness. Facts and Concepts, #118, Palliative Care Network of Wisconsin.

26. Barrett, William (1926). Death-Bed Visions. Methuen & Company Limited. ISBN 978-0850305203.

27. Barrett, William F. (repr. 2011). Death-Bed Visions: How the Dead Talk to the Dying. Guildford: White Crow Books, pp. 37–38. Original edition: London: Methuen, 1926.

28. Osis, K. and Haraldsson, E. (1977). At the Hour of Death. Avon. ISBN 978-0380018024.

29. Brayne, Sue; Farnham, Chris; Fenwick, Peter (2006). An understanding of the occurrence of deathbed phenomena and its effect on palliative care clinicians. American Journal of Hospice and Palliative Care, January-February 23(1), pp. 17–24.

30. Fenwick, Peter; Brayne, Sue (2010). End-of-life Experiences: Reaching Out for Compassion, Communication, and Connection-Meaning of Deathbed Visions and Coincidences. American Journal of Hospice and Palliative Medicine (PubMed https://doi.org/10.1177/1049909110374301).

31. Fenwick, Peter; Fenwick, Elizabeth (2008). The Art of Dying: A Journey to Elsewhere. London: Continuum.

32. Op. cit. p. 225.

33. Op. cit. p. 6.

34. Op. cit. p. 27.

35. Shared Crossing Research Initiative (SCRI) (2021). Shared

Death Experiences: A Little-Known Type of End-of-Life Phenomena Reported by Caregivers and Loved Ones. *American Journal of Hospice and Palliative Medicine*, April 5, 2021. http://doi.org/10.1177/10499091211000045.

36. There exists abundant literature of excellent scientific level on NDEs, such as: Greyson, Bruce (2021). *After: A Doctor Explores What Near-Death Experiences Reveal about Life and Beyond*. New York, NY: St. Martin's Essentials.
     Van Lommel, Pim (2010). *Consciousness Beyond Life: The Science of the Near-Death Experience*. New York: HarperOne.

37. Moody, Raymond (2001). *Life After Life: The Investigation of a Phenomenon – Survival of Bodily Death*. San Francisco, CA: HarperSanFrancisco. ISBN 0-06-251739-2.

38. Moody, Raymond and Perry, Paul (2010). *Glimpses of Eternity: Sharing a Loved One's Passage From This Life to the Next*. New York, NY: Guideposts. ISBN 0-8249-4813-0.

39. http://www.after-death.com/

40. Holt, Henry (1914). *On the Cosmic Relations* (PDF). Cambridge, MA, USA: Houghton Mifflin Company/ Riverside Press. Retrieved December 13, 2007.

41. https://www.merriam-webster.com/dictionary/ psychokinesis

42. https://noetic.org/profile/dean-radin/

43. Radin, Dean (2009). *The Conscious Universe: The Scientific Truth of Psychic Phenomena*. New York, NY: HarperEdge.

44. Private correspondence, August 2019.

45. Private correspondence, 2009.

46. In the original French account, the wording used does indeed in no way correspond to the language level of a child.

47. www.sheldrake.org

48. Evrard, R.; Dollander, M.; Elsaesser, E.; Roe, C.A.; Cooper, C.E.; Lorimer, D. (2021). Exceptional necrophanic experiences and paradoxical mourning: Studies of the

phenomenology and the repercussions of frightening experiences of contact with the deceased. *Evolution Psychiatrique*. Volume 86, Issue 4, November 2021, pp. e1–e24, https://doi.org/10.1016/j.evopsy.2021.09.001

49. *Op. cit.* p. e12.

50. *Op. cit.* p. e13.

51. See section Partial temporary paralysis, page 240.

52. Elsaesser, E.; Roe, C.A.; Cooper, C.E.; Lorimer, D. (2020). Investigation of the phenomenology and impact of spontaneous and direct After-Death Communications (ADCs): Research findings. https://www.evelyn-elsaesser. com/wp-content/uploads/2020/02/Booklet_Web_English_Research.pdf

53. Evrard, R.; Dollander, M.; Elsaesser, E.; Roe, C.A.; Cooper, C.E.; Lorimer, D. (2021). Exceptional necrophanic experiences and paradoxical mourning: Studies of the phenomenology and the repercussions of frightening experiences of contact with the deceased. *Evolution Psychiatrique*. Volume 86, Issue 4, November 2021, p. e14. https://doi.org/10.1016/j.evopsy.2021.09.001

54. Elsaesser, Evelyn (2018). *Quand les défunts viennent à nous: Histoires vécues et entretiens avec des scientifiques*. 3rd edition. Paris: Éditions Exergue.

55. Elsaesser-Valarino, Evelyn (2013). VSCD, Hallucination ou dernière communication? *Inexploré – le Magazine de l'INREES*, N° 19, pp. 84–88.

56. In the original French testimony, the wording used is indeed unusual.

57. https://ec.europa.eu/eurostat/statistics-explained/index. php/Causes_of_death_statistics

58. ARDA is a free online database of information on American and international religion.

59. General Social Survey 2014 Cross-Section and Panel Combined: http://www.thearda.com/quickstats/qs_106.asp

60. https://ropercenter.cornell.edu/paradise-polled-americans-and-afterlife

61. https://www.iser.essex.ac.uk/2015/01/19/life-after-death-60-per-cent-of-uk-women-in-their-forties-believe-in-an-after-life

62. Haraldsson, Erlendur (2011). Psychic experiences a third of a century apart: Two representative surveys in Iceland with an international comparison. *Journal of the Society for Psychical Research*, Vol. 75, 2, No 903, pp. 76–90.

63. Other responses not reproduced here.

64. Other responses not reproduced here.

65. See page 275.

66. See page 274.

67. See page 275.

68. See page 252.

69. Evrard, R.; Dollander, M.; Elsaesser, E.; Roe, C.A.; Cooper, C.E.; Lorimer, D. (2021). Exceptional necrophanic experiences and paradoxical mourning: Studies of the phenomenology and the repercussions of frightening experiences of contact with the deceased. *Evolution Psychiatrique.* Volume 86, Issue 4, November 2021, pp. e12–e13. https://doi.org/10.1016/j.evopsy.2021.09.001

70. *Op. cit.* p. e1.

71. Caputo, Giovanni B.; Lynn, Steven Jay; Houran, James (2021). Mirror- and Eye-Gazing: An Integrative Review of Induced Altered and Anomalous Experiences. In: *Imagination, Cognition and Personality: Consciousness in Theory, Research, and Clinical Practice*, 2021, Vol. 40(4), p. 420.

72. Moody, Raymond (1993). *Reunions: Visionary Encounters with Departed Loved Ones.* New York, NY: Ivy Books.

73. Arcangel, Dianne (2005). *Afterlife Encounters: Ordinary People, Extraordinary Experiences*. Charlottesville, VA: Hampton Roads Publishing Co.

74. Eye movement desensitization and reprocessing (EMDR) is a form of psychotherapy developed by Francine Shapiro starting in 1988 in which the person being treated is asked to recall distressing images; the therapist then directs the patient in one type of bilateral stimulation, such as side-to-side eye movements or hand tapping.

75. https://iadctherapy.com/about/

76. Guggenheim, B., Guggenheim, J. (1996). *Hello From Heaven! A new field of research: After-Death Communication confirms that life and love are eternal*. New York: Bantam Books.

77. Guggenheim, B., Guggenheim, J. (2011). *Des nouvelles de l'au-delà: De nouveaux champs de recherche sur l'après-vie confirment que la vie et l'amour sont éternels*; avec une introduction d'Evelyn Elsaesser-Valarino; traduit par Evelyn Elsaesser-Valarino. Paris: Éditions Exergue.

78. Elsaesser, Evelyn (2018). *Quand les défunts viennent à nous: Histoires vécues et entretiens avec des scientifiques*. 3rd edition. Paris: Éditions Exergue.

Books by the author

In English/translated into English
Elsaesser, E. (1997). *On the Other Side of Life: Exploring the Phenomenon of the Near-Death Experience.* New York; London: Insight Books Plenum Press/Perseus. ISBN 0-306-45561-7.

Elsaesser, E. (2023). *Talking with Angel about Illness, Death and Survival: A novel.* Alresford, UK: John Hunt Publishing — Roundfire Books. ISBN 978-1-80341-330-3.

Ring, K.; Elsaesser, E. (2000, Reprint 2006). *Lessons from the Light: What we can learn from the near-death experience.* Portsmouth, New Hampshire, USA: Moment Point Press. ISBN 1-930491-11-5.

The author's other books, book chapters and papers in several languages are available on her website: www.evelyn-elsaesser. com/books

Publications resulting from the research project on After-Death Communications (ADCs)

Elsaesser, E. (2022). *Contactos espontáneos con un fallecido: La realidad de las VSCD*. Madrid: Ediciones Urano/Kepler. ISBN 978-84-16-34474-1.

Elsaesser, E. (2021). *Contacts spontanés avec un défunt: Une enquête scientifique atteste la réalité des VSCD*. Paris: Éditions Exergue. ISBN 978-2-36188-397-3.

Elsaesser, E.; Roe, C.A.; Cooper, C.E.; Lorimer, D. (2022). Phänomenologie und Auswirkungen von spontanen Nachtod-Kontakten (NTK) – Forschungsergebnisse und Fallstudien. *Journal of Anomalistics / Zeitschrift für Anomalistik*, Band 22, S. 36–71, http://dx.doi.org/10.23793/zfa.2022.36.

Elsaesser, E. (2021). *Spontane Kontakte mit Verstorbenen: Eine wissenschaftliche Untersuchung bestätigt die Realität von Nachtod-Kontakten*. Amerang Germany: Crotona Verlag. ISBN 978-3-86191-224-8.

Elsaesser, E.; Roe, C.A.; Cooper, C.E.; Lorimer, D. (2021). The phenomenology and impact of hallucinations concerning the deceased. *BJPsychOpen*. Volume 7, Issue 5, September 2021, e148, DOI: https://doi.org/10.1192/bjo.2021.960

Evrard, R.; Dollander, M.; Elsaesser, E.; Roe, C.A.; Cooper, C.E.; Lorimer, D. (2021). Exceptional necrophanic experiences and paradoxical mourning: Studies of the phenomenology and the repercussions of frightening experiences of contact with the deceased. *Evolution Psychiatrique*. Volume 86, Issue 4, November 2021, pp. e1–e24, https://doi.org/10.1016/j.evopsy.2021.09.001

Evrard, R.; Dollander, M.; Elsaesser, E.; Roe, C.A.; Cooper, C.E.; Lorimer, D. (2021). Expériences exceptionnelles nécrophaniques et deuil paradoxal: études de la phénoménologie et des répercussions des vécus effrayants de contact avec les défunts. *Evolution Psychiatrique.* 86(4), pp. 799–824, https://doi.org/10.1016/j.evopsy.2021.05.002

Penberthy, J.K.; Pehlivanova, M.; Kalelioglu, T.; Roe, C.A.; Cooper, C.E.; Lorimer, D.; Elsaesser, E. (2021). Factors Moderating the Impact of After Death Communications on Beliefs and Spirituality. *OMEGA: Journal of Death & Dying,* July 9, 2021, https://doi.org/10.1177/00302228211029160.

Woollacott, M.; Roe, C.A.; Cooper, C.E.; Lorimer, D.; Elsaesser, E. (2021). Perceptual Phenomena Associated with Spontaneous After-Death Communications: Analysis of visual, tactile, auditory and olfactory sensations. *Explore: The Journal of Science and Healing,* 17/3, https://doi.org/10.1016/j.explore.2021.02.006.

All publications of the ADC research project are accessible on the project website: www.adcrp.org

About the author

Evelyn Elsaesser, who lives in Switzerland, is an expert on death-related experiences, notably spontaneous and direct After-Death Communications (ADCs), Near-Death Experiences (NDEs), and End-of-Life Experiences (ELE). Over the last thirty-five years, she has dedicated a large part of her time to the research and dissemination of information on these specific but related phenomena. She is the author of numerous books, book chapters and articles on these subjects. Her books have been translated into many languages.

Over the last decade, she has focused her work specifically on spontaneous and direct After-Death Communications. As a first step, she translated into French the book *Hello from Heaven*[76] dealing with ADCs by the American authors Bill and Judy Guggenheim. This translation was published in 2011 under the title *Des nouvelles de l'au-delà*.[77] In 2017, she published her own book on ADCs entitled *Quand les défunts viennent à nous: Histoires vécues et entretiens avec des scientifiques*.[78]

Following the publication of this book, she received hundreds of e-mails and letters from people who had had spontaneous contacts with a deceased family member or friend. It was clear from this correspondence that the persons who had the ADC (called experients) were infinitely grateful, and relieved, to finally be able to put a name to the experience. Even though contacts may have occurred decades ago and had deeply impacted and delighted them, they could neither easily share them with their entourage nor fit them into their own conception of reality.

It became evident that the time had come to undertake a major research project devoted to these experiences, which are very common and yet little investigated. She developed a concept for a research project with a view to obtaining a grant, which was generously given to her by a foundation. Once the project team had been set up, the research project entitled *Investigation of the phenomenology and impact of spontaneous and direct After-Death Communications (ADCs)* could be conducted.

The widest possible dissemination of current knowledge on ADCs is of paramount importance to the author, both for the experients and for everyone else, because we can all experience an ADC one day. An expert and diversified communication and documentation will give a common language and a shared knowledge of this phenomenon, which is so frequent and yet nonexistent in the media and public discourse.

Evelyn Elsaesser is the project leader of "Investigation of the phenomenology and impact of spontaneous and direct After-Death Communications (ADCs)".
She is co-founder and member of the Executive Board of Swiss IANDS (International Association for Near-Death Studies).
She served for many years as coordinator of the Swiss branch of the Scientific and Medical Network (SMN).
Project website: www.adcrp.org
Personal website: www.evelyn-elsaesser.com

ACADEMIC AND SPECIALIST

Iff Books publishes non-fiction. It aims to work with authors and titles that augment our understanding of the human condition, society and civilisation, and the world or universe in which we live. If you have enjoyed this book, why not tell other readers by posting a review on your preferred book site. Recent bestsellers from Iff Books are:

Why Materialism Is Baloney
How true skeptics know there is no death and fathom answers to life, the universe, and everything
Bernardo Kastrup
A hard-nosed, logical, and skeptic non-materialist metaphysics, according to which the body is in mind, not mind in the body.
Paperback: 978-1-78279-362-5 ebook: 978-1-78279-361-8

The Fall
Steve Taylor
The Fall discusses human achievement versus the issues of war, patriarchy and social inequality.
Paperback: 978-1-78535-804-3 ebook: 978-1-78535-805-0

Brief Peeks Beyond
Critical essays on metaphysics, neuroscience, free will, skepticism and culture
Bernardo Kastrup
An incisive, original, compelling alternative to current mainstream cultural views and assumptions.
Paperback: 978-1-78535-018-4 ebook: 978-1-78535-019-1

Framespotting
Changing how you look at things changes how you see them
Laurence & Alison Matthews
A punchy, upbeat guide to framespotting. Spot deceptions
and hidden assumptions; swap growth for growing up. See
and be free.
Paperback: 978-1-78279-689-3 ebook: 978-1-78279-822-4

Is There an Afterlife?
David Fontana
Is there an Afterlife? If so what is it like? How do Western
ideas of the afterlife compare with Eastern? David Fontana
presents the historical and contemporary evidence for
survival of physical death.
Paperback: 978-1-90381-690-5

Nothing Matters
a book about nothing
Ronald Green
Thinking about Nothing opens the world to everything by
illuminating new angles to old problems and stimulating new
ways of thinking.
Paperback: 978-1-84694-707-0 ebook: 978-1-78099-016-3

Panpsychism
The Philosophy of the Sensuous Cosmos
Peter Ells
Are free will and mind chimeras? This book, anti-materialistic
but respecting science, answers: No! Mind is foundational to
all existence.
Paperback: 978-1-84694-505-2 ebook: 978-1-78099-018-7

Punk Science
Inside the Mind of God
Manjir Samanta-Laughton
Many have experienced unexplainable phenomena; God,
psychic abilities, extraordinary healing and angelic encounters.
Can cutting-edge science actually explain phenomena
previously thought of as 'paranormal'?
Paperback: 978-1-90504-793-2

The Vagabond Spirit of Poetry
Edward Clarke
Spend time with the wisest poets of the modern age and of the
past, and let Edward Clarke remind you of the importance of
poetry in our industrialized world.
Paperback: 978-1-78279-370-0 ebook: 978-1-78279-369-4

Readers of ebooks can buy or view any of these bestsellers by
clicking on the live link in the title. Most titles are published
in paperback and as an ebook. Paperbacks are available in
traditional bookshops. Both print and ebook formats are
available online. Find more titles and sign up to our readers'
newsletter at http://www.johnhuntpublishing.com/non-fiction
Follow us on Facebook at
https://www.facebook.com/JHPNonFiction
and Twitter at https://twitter.com/JHPNonFiction